Crosslinguistic Influence in Second Language Acquisition

SECOND LANGUAGE ACQUISITION

Series Editors: **Professor David Singleton**, *University of Pannonia, Hungary* and Fellow Emeritus, *Trinity College, Dublin, Ireland* and **Dr Simone E. Pfenninger**, *University of Zurich, Switzerland*

This series brings together titles dealing with a variety of aspects of language acquisition and processing in situations where a language or languages other than the native language is involved. Second language is thus interpreted in its broadest possible sense. The volumes included in the series all offer in their different ways, on the one hand, exposition and discussion of empirical findings and, on the other, some degree of theoretical reflection. In this latter connection, no particular theoretical stance is privileged in the series; nor is any relevant perspective – sociolinguistic, psycholinguistic, neurolinguistic, etc. – deemed out of place. The intended readership of the series includes final-year undergraduates working on second language acquisition projects, postgraduate students involved in second language acquisition research, and researchers and teachers in general whose interests include a second language acquisition component.

Full details of all the books in this series and of all our other publications can be found on http://www.multilingual-matters.com, or by writing to Multilingual Matters, St Nicholas House, 31-34 High Street, Bristol BS1 2AW, UK.

SECOND LANGUAGE ACQUISITION: 95

Crosslinguistic Influence in Second Language Acquisition

Edited by
Rosa Alonso Alonso

MULTILINGUAL MATTERS
Bristol • Buffalo • Toronto

Library of Congress Cataloging in Publication Data
A catalog record for this book is available from the Library of Congress.
Names: Alonso Alonso, Rosa, editor.
Title: Crosslinguistic Influence in Second Language Acquisition/Edited by Rosa Alonso Alonso.
Description: Bristol; Buffalo: Multilingual Matters, [2016] |
Series: Second Language Acquisition: 95|Includes bibliographical references and index.
Identifiers: LCCN 2015029080| ISBN 9781783094820 (hbk : alk. paper) | ISBN 9781783094813 (pbk : alk. paper) | ISBN 9781783094837 (ebook)
Subjects: LCSH: Language and languages—Study and teaching. | Second language acquisition—Study and teaching. | Multicultural education. | Languages in contact. | Interaction analysis in education.
Classification: LCC P53.447 .C76 2016 | DDC 418.0071–dc23 LC record available at http://lccn.loc.gov/2015029080

British Library Cataloguing in Publication Data
A catalogue entry for this book is available from the British Library.

ISBN-13: 978-1-78309-482-0 (hbk)
ISBN-13: 978-1-78309-481-3 (pbk)

Multilingual Matters
UK: St Nicholas House, 31-34 High Street, Bristol BS1 2AW, UK.
USA: UTP, 2250 Military Road, Tonawanda, NY 14150, USA.
Canada: UTP, 5201 Dufferin Street, North York, Ontario M3H 5T8, Canada.

Website: www.multilingual-matters.com
Twitter: Multi_Ling_Mat
Facebook: https://www.facebook.com/multilingualmatters
Blog: www.channelviewpublications.wordpress.com

Copyright © 2016 Rosa Alonso Alonso and the authors of individual chapters.

All rights reserved. No part of this work may be reproduced in any form or by any means without permission in writing from the publisher.

The policy of Multilingual Matters/Channel View Publications is to use papers that are natural, renewable and recyclable products, made from wood grown in sustainable forests. In the manufacturing process of our books, and to further support our policy, preference is given to printers that have FSC and PEFC Chain of Custody certification. The FSC and/or PEFC logos will appear on those books where full certification has been granted to the printer concerned.

Typeset by Deanta Global Publishing Services Limited.
Printed and bound in Great Britain by Short Run Press Ltd.

Contents

	Contributors	vii
	Preface	xiii
1	Was there Really Ever a Contrastive Analysis Hypothesis? *Terence Odlin*	1
2	Transfer and the Relationships Between the Languages of Multi-Competence *Vivian Cook*	24
3	Comprehension, Learning and Production of Foreign Languages: The Role of Transfer *Håkan Ringbom*	38
4	The Implications of Linguistic Relativity for Language Learning *John A. Lucy*	53
5	Crosslinguistic Lexical Influence: Cognate Facilitation *Rena Helms-Park and Vedran Dronjic*	71
6	Crosslinguistic Influence in the Acquisition of Spatial Prepositions in English as a Foreign Language *Rosa Alonso Alonso, Teresa Cadierno and Scott Jarvis*	93
7	Can Classroom Learners Use Statistical Learning? A New Perspective on Motion Event Construal in a Second Language *Jeanine Treffers-Daller and Xu Ziyan*	121

8   L1-Fraught Difficulty: The Case of L2 Acquisition of English
    Articles by Slavic Speakers   147
    Monika Ekiert and ZhaoHong Han

9   Learning Grammatical Gender in a Second Language Changes
    Categorization of Inanimate Objects: Replications and New
    Evidence from English Learners of L2 French   173
    Panos Athanosopoulos and Bastien Boutonnet

10 Crosslinguistic Influence in Third Language Acquisition   193
    Ulrike Jessner, Manon Megens and Stefanie Graus

11 Contemporary Perspectives in Crosslinguistic Influence   215
    Janusz Arabski and Adam Wojtaszek

    Index   225

Contributors

Rosa Alonso Alonso holds a PhD in Linguistics at the University of Santiago de Compostela and works as an Assistant Professor at the University of Vigo, Spain. Her research interests include crosslinguistic influence, motion events and academic writing. Since 2000 she has been the editor-in-chief of *Vigo International Journal of Applied Linguistics*

Janusz Arabski graduated from UCLA. He took his PhD at Adam Mickiewicz University in Poznan. He was one of the founders of English Studies at the University of Silesia in Katowice, Poland, the former Institute Director for over 20 years and held the position of Emeritus Professor of English Linguistics. He published a number of books and articles in the areas of applied linguistics, psycholinguistics, contrastive studies and lexicography. Foreign language learning has been his main field of research. He was on the editorial board of several national and international academic journals. Over the years he organised many international conferences on foreign language acquisition and learning. Professor Arabski lectured and taught at many universities in Europe, Asia and the Americas. He was Vice-President of the International Society of Applied Psycholinguistics (ISAPL).

Panos Athanasopoulos is Professor of Applied Linguistics at Lancaster University. His research interests include bilingual cognition, experimental cognitive linguistics, and linguistic and cultural relativity. His recent research programmes have examined the influence of grammatical categories like number, gender and aspect on object classification and event perception, as well as the influence of language on perceptual categories such as colour. His work has appeared in a range of specialist and widely read journals such as *Applied Psycholinguistics, Bilingualism: Language and Cognition, Cognition, Cognitive Science, Language and Cognitive Processes, Linguistics, Proceedings of the National Academy of Sciences of the USA* and *Psychological Science*.

Bastien Boutonnet is a Postdoctoral Research Associate at the University of Wisconsin, Madison. His research interests range over the following areas: interactions between high-level and low-level cognition, neuroscientific methods: EEG, brain dynamics, oscillations, bilingual language processing and philosophy of language. His recent contributions have examined how words cue our visual systems and how words affect how objects are perceived. Future research plans will involve looking more specifically at the brain dynamics subserving interactions between language and vision.

Teresa Cadierno is Professor at the Institute of Language and Communication at the University of Southern Denmark. Her research interests include instructed second language acquisition, with a special focus on the acquisition of grammar by L2 learners; L2 input processing and the role of formal instruction in L2 acquisition; applied cognitive linguistics, especially the acquisition and teaching of L2 constructions for the expression of motion events; and the investigation of re-thinking for speaking processes in a foreign language.

Vivian Cook is an Emeritus Professor of Applied Linguistics at Newcastle University and previously taught applied linguistics at Essex University and EFL and linguistics in London. His main current interests are how people learn second languages, in particular from the multi-competence perspective, and how writing works in different languages, particularly in street signs. He is a founder of the European Second Language Association, and co-founder and co-editor of the journal *Writing System Research*. He has written books on the learning and teaching of English, on Chomsky and on writing systems, including popular books on English spelling and on vocabulary, and is currently editing handbooks on multi-competence and on the English Writing System. He has given talks in countries ranging from Chile to Japan, Canada to Iran and Cuba to Norway.

Vedran Dronjic currently holds the position of A.W. Mellon Postdoctoral Fellow in the Department of Modern Languages at Carnegie Mellon University. His research centres on the cognitive underpinnings of language knowledge, with a focus on morphological processing, the mental lexicon, speech production, reading ability and the development of language awareness.

Monika Ekiert is an Associate Professor in the Department of Education and Language Acquisition at LaGuardia CC, City University of New York. Her research interests lie at the interface of L2 acquisition and L2 instruction. Currently, she is involved in research projects focusing on communicative adequacy in L2 oral performance and crosslinguistic influence in L2 acquisition.

Stefanie Graus obtained her BA from the University of Innsbruck and she is working on the LAILA (Linguistic Awareness in Language Attriters) project. She is interested in crosslinguistic influence and awareness in multilingual learners.

ZhaoHong Han is Professor of Language and Education at Teachers College, Columbia University, USA. Her research interests straddle both second language learnability and teachability. Her most recent book (co-authored with Teresa Cadierno) is *Linguistic Relativity in SLA: Thinking for Speaking* (2010, Multilingual Matters).

Rena Helms-Park is an Associate Professor of Linguistics at the University of Toronto Scarborough. Her research interests include L1 and L2 lexical acquisition, crosslinguistic transfer and the psycholinguistics of reading. Her most recent book (co-edited with Xi Chen Bumgardner and Vedran Dronjic) is *Second Language Reading: Psycholinguistic and Cognitive Perspectives* (2015, Routledge).

Scott Jarvis is an Associate Professor in the Department of Linguistics at Ohio University. His work focuses on crosslinguistic influence and lexical diversity, with a special emphasis on methodological problems and solutions. Among his better-known works is the book *Crosslinguistic Influence in Language and Cognition,* co-authored with Aneta Pavlenko.

Ulrike Jessner is a Professor at the University of Innsbruck and the University of Veszprem. She has published widely in the field of bilingualism and multilingualism with a special focus on the acquisition of English in multilingual contexts. She is the co-author of *A Dynamic Model of Multilingualism* (with Philip Herdina in 2002) and *Linguistic Awareness of Multilinguals: English as a Third Language* (2006). She is also founding editor of the *International Journal of Multilingualism* and the book series *Trends in Applied Linguistics* (with Claire Kramsch from Berkeley University) Furthermore she has been engaged in the development of the research area of third language acquisition/multilingualism both as organiser of the biennial international L3-conferences and as founding member and President of the International Association of Multilingualism.

John A. Lucy received his PhD from the University of Chicago. He has taught in the Department of Anthropology at the University of Pennsylvania, and is currently the William Benton Professor of Comparative Human Development and of Psychology at the University of Chicago. His research focuses on the relation between language and thought, especially on the role language differences play in shaping thought and the ways languages come to influence thought during childhood. His publications include *Language Diversity and Thought* (Cambridge, 1992) reviewing the history of research in this field; *Grammatical Categories and Cognition* (Cambridge, 1992), outing a new empirical approach; and an edited volume *Reflexive Language: Reported Speech and Metapragmatics* (Cambridge, 1993) concerning the ways language affects how we think about language itself.

Manon Megens is a PhD student in applied linguistics and English studies at Innsbruck University. She is interested in crosslinguistic awareness in processes of multilingual attrition. Manon Megens is also a founding member of the DYME research group (Dynamics of Multilingualism with English), an external lecturer at the department for architectural theory of Innsbruck University and a curator of communication and art education/mediation

Terence Odlin is the author of *Language Transfer: Cross-Linguistic Influence in Language Learning* as well as of several book chapters and articles on the same subject. He is an Emeritus faculty member at Ohio State University in Columbus, Ohio.

Håkan Ringbom was Emeritus Professor of English at Åbo Akademi University, Turku/Åbo, Finland. His published monographs include a study of the narrative technique of Beowulf and Lawman's Brut, a stylistic study of George Orwell's essays and his 1987 study of the role of the first language in foreign language learning. He also published some 50 articles in the fields of second language acquisition, multilingualism, corpus linguistics, contrastive analysis and stylistics

Jeanine Treffers-Daller is Professor of Second Language Education at the University of Reading. She is the Director of the Centre for Literacy and Multilingualism and Convenor of the Second Language Acquisition Research Group. Her current research projects involve bilingualism and language contact, in particular code switching, borrowing and contact-induced language change. More recently she has worked on conceptual transfer and the relationship between language and thought in bilinguals and L2 learners, in particular in relation to motion event construal (manner and path of motion). Recently she obtained funding from the European Science Foundation for an Exploratory Workshop on Thinking, Speaking and Gesturing in Two Languages (12–15 September 2012), together with Panos Athanasopoulos from Lancaster University.

Adam Wojtaszek is Associate Professor and the Deputy Director at the Institute of English, University of Silesia, Katowice, Poland. His major field of interest is linguistic pragmatics, psycholinguistics and language of persuasion. He has published two books on advertising language, *Deciphering Radio Commercials – A Pragmatic Perspective* (2002) and *Theoretical Frameworks in the Study of Press Advertisements – Polish, British and Chinese Perspective* (2011), as well as a number of articles on the topic. Within the area of psycholinguistics and second language acquisition studies, he has co-edited a number of volumes reporting on recent studies and developments, such as *Neurolinguistic and Psycholinguistic Perspectives on SLA* (2010), *The Acquisition of L2 Phonology* (2011a), *Individual Learner Differences in SLA* (2011b), *Aspects of Culture in Second Language Acquisition and Foreign Language Learning* (2011c) and recently *Studying Second Language Acquisition from a Qualitative Perspective* (2014). He is also the author of a chapter on morphosyntactic development in the volume edited by Danuta Gabryś-Barker, *Readings in Second Language Acquisition* (2012). He is also one of the organisers of the annual international SLA conference held in Szczyrk, Poland, a major event of international recognition, initiated in the mid-1980s by Janusz Arabski.

Ziyan Xu works as a lecturer in the School of Foreign Languages in Beijing Institute of Technology, teaching English as a foreign language to university students. She obtained her PhD from the University of the West of England in 2010. Her main study interests include second language acquisition, transfer, language teaching methodology and motion event conceptualisation.

*To the memory of Håkan Ringbom (1936–2015) and
Janusz Arabski (1939–2015)*

Preface

Rosa Alonso Alonso and Terence Odlin

Interest in the influence of one language on another goes back a long time, with a variety of motives – historical, psychological, social and pedagogical – figuring in diverse research traditions. For teachers curious about such research, the pedagogical concern with errors has naturally loomed large, especially because many second language missteps do indeed involve forms and meanings related to the learner's native language or some other language known to the learner. Nevertheless, while interest in interference is still a major part of transfer research, a wider range of topics, including positive transfer and multilingualism (together with the many cognitive factors underlying crosslinguistic influence) have garnered increasing attention. *Languages in Contact* by Uriel Weinreich (1953) proved to be a harbinger of the expansion of modern transfer research, yet, as the first chapter of the present volume shows, the history of such research goes back long before Weinreich. After *Languages in Contact,* a trickle of volumes on transfer appeared for about three decades, but since the 1980s, the stream has swelled, as evidenced, for instance, by the edited volumes of Gass and Selinker (1983), Kellerman and Sharwood-Smith (1986) and Dechert and Raupach (1989), as well as monographs by Ringbom (1987), Thomason and Kaufmann (1988) and Odlin (1989). Since the 1980s, the field has expanded further still with new topics coming into focus such as multingualism (e.g. Cenoz *et al.*, 2001; De Angelis & Dewaele, 2011; Gabryś-Barker, 2012; Hammarberg, 2009). Books looking at other dimensions of transfer have likewise continued to appear (e.g. Alonso, 2002; Arabski, 2006; Jarvis & Pavlenko, 2008; Ringbom, 2007). Yet despite the expansion of research, there is still no dearth of unexplored territory in the domain of language transfer.

The 11 chapters of this volume offer, it is hoped, an unprecedented look at the phenomenon of crosslinguistic influence from a cognitivist perspective. Having such a perspective implies that the volume shares some traits with other recent collections both in the field of cognitive linguistics more generally (Geeraerts & Guyckens, 2007) and in the specialized field of second language acquisition (Robinson & Ellis, 2008). For readers wondering just what cognitive linguistics is, one readable introduction to the subject defines the field thus:

> Cognitive linguistics is described as a 'movement' or an 'enterprise' because it is not a specific theory. Instead, it is a common set of guiding principles, assumptions, and perspectives which have led to a diverse range of complementary, overlapping (and sometimes competing) theories. (Evans & Green, 2006: 3)

Although the metaphor of the kaleidoscope is liable to overuse, it seems appropriate not only for the characterisation offered by Evans and Green, but also for characterising this volume on crosslinguistic influence since the collection of chapters offers viewpoints that, although distinct, overlap and complement each other, with occasional points of possible disagreement. Readers will find some perennial themes of cognitive linguistics in the volume, such as the notion of construal (e.g. Chapters 6, 7 and 8) and the notion of activation (Chapters 1, 2 and 5). Another issue of concern, linguistic relativity, has grown more prominent in cognitive linguistics in general and is likewise the focus for a number of studies here (Chapters 4, 6 and 9). Other cognitivist topics appear in other chapters, including the possible contributions of neurolinguistics (Chapters 3 and 5), the problem of cognitive development (Chapter 10) and the role of structure frequency in acquisition (Chapter 7).

The kaleidoscope also shows the relevance of different structural areas to different viewpoints. Crosslinguistic influence involving vocabulary is addressed in some analyses (e.g. Chapters 2, 3, 5 and 10), while other studies consider morphosyntactic categories (Chapters 4 and 9), semantic structures (Chapters 6, 7 and 8), and phonetic and phonological structures (Chapters 1 and 2). Of course, some boundaries between morphosyntactic and semantic transfer can be elusive, as in the discussion of crosslinguistic influence involving prepositions (Chapter 6) and articles (Chapter 8), and, not surprisingly, these analyses have possible implications for the study of cognitivist problems such as linguistic relativity. While every chapter discusses some empirical work, Chapters 6–10 present new empirical investigations. The vantage points from which crosslinguistic influence can be viewed also vary in the volume because of the many languages that figure in the theoretical discussions or in the empirical work, including Chinese, Czech, Danish, Dutch, English, Estonian, Finnish, French, German, Hindi, Japanese, Malay, Polish, Portuguese, Romanian, Russian, Slovenian, Spanish, Swedish, Tagalog, Thai, Turkish and Ukrainian.

With their different constellations of issues, structures and languages, the chapters provide new insights on longstanding concerns in the study of crosslinguistic influence including the consequences of great similarity in structures between languages (e.g. Chapter 3), and, conversely, the consequences of little or no similarity between the structures (e.g. Chapter 8). The relevance of crosslinguistic influence research for teaching comes under discussion in a number of chapters (e.g. 1 and 5), as does the phenomenon of multingualism. While transfer might be considered most typically a phenomenon in second language acquisition, Chapter 10 details the growth of work on multilingual transfer. Yet another issue crucial to the understanding of transfer is its intellectual history, and Chapter 1 offers an in-depth look at that history, thereby calling into question some widespread assumptions about when and why transfer studies arose.

However they use the kaleidoscope, readers may wish to read summaries of the studies, which they can find in the chapters themselves or in the thoughtful critique in the final chapter of the volume. Our dear friends and colleagues, Janusz Arabski and Håkan Ringbom passed away before this book was published. We are deeply grateful for the contributions they made to the book, and also for the outstanding contributions they made to this area of research. They were exceptional linguists and great men. We will miss them dearly.

References

Alonso, R. (2002) *The Role of Transfer in Second Language Acquisition*. Vigo: University of Vigo Press.
Arabski, J. (ed.) (2006) *Cross-Linguistic Influences in the Second Language Lexicon*. Clevedon: Multilingual Matters.
Cenoz, U., Hufeisen, B. and Jessner, U. (eds) (2001) *Cross-Linguistic Influence in Third Language Acquisition: Psycholinguistic Perspectives*. Clevedon: Multilingual Matters.
De Angelis, G. and Dewaele, J.M. (eds) (2011) *New Trends in Cross-Linguistic Influence and Multilingualism Research*. Bristol: Multilingual Matters.
Dechert, H. and Raupach, M. (eds) (1989) *Transfer in Language Production*. Norwood, NJ: Ablex.
Evans, V. and Green, M. (2006) *Cognitive Linguistics: An introduction*. Edinburgh: Edinburgh University Press.
Gabryś-Barker, D. (ed.) (2012) *Cross-Linguistic Influences in Multilingual Language Acquisition, Second Language Learning and Teaching*. Berlin: Springer.
Gass, S. and Selinker, L. (eds) (1983) *Language Transfer in Language Learning*. Rowley, MA: Newbury House.
Geeraerts, D. and Guyckens, H. (eds) (2007) *The Oxford Handbook of Cognitive Linguistics*. Oxford: Oxford University Press.
Hammarberg, B. (2009) *Processes in Third Language Acquisition*. Edinburgh: Edinburgh University Press.
Kellerman, E. and Sharwood-Smith, M. (eds) (1986) *Cross-Linguistic Influence in Second Language Acquisition*. Oxford: Pergamon.
Jarvis, S. and Pavlenko, A. (2008) *Crosslinguistic Influence in Language and Cognition*. New York and London: Routledge.
Odlin, T. (1989) *Language Transfer: Cross-Linguistic Influence in Language Learning*. Cambridge: Cambridge University Press.
Ringbom, H. (1987) *The Role of the First Language in Foreign Language Learning*. Clevedon: Multilingual Matters.

Ringbom, H. (2007) *The Importance of Cross-Linguistic Similarity in Foreign Language Learning: Comprehension, Learning and Production*. Clevedon: Multilingual Matters.
Robinson, P. and Ellis, N.C. (eds) (2008) *Handbook of Cognitive Linguistics and Second Language Acquisition*. London: Routledge.
Thomason, S.G. and Kaufmann, T. (1988) *Language Contact, Creolization and Genetic Linguistics*. Berkeley: University of Berkeley Press
Weinreich, U. (1953) *Languages in Contact*. The Hague: Mouton

1 Was There Really Ever a Contrastive Analysis Hypothesis?

Terence Odlin

Introduction[1]

The terms *Contrastive Analysis* (CA) and *language transfer* abound in discussions of crosslinguistic influence, but even a cursory reading of these discussions shows a wide range of definitions, characterisations and historical claims about the origins of these notions and terms. Discussions of the so-called Contrastive Analysis Hypothesis (CAH) likewise show considerable variation, as in the examples below.

> The CA hypothesis held that where structures in the L1 differed from those in the L2, errors that reflected the structure of the L1 would be produced. (Dulay *et al.*, 1982: 97)

> With the eclipse of descriptive linguistics and its concept of language learning, Robert Lado is now best remembered as the author of *Linguistics across Cultures*. In particular, he is represented as the architect of the Contrastive Analysis Hypothesis – essentially, the claim that whenever a learner's native and target languages differ, the learner will face difficulty and delay in acquiring the target language. (Thomas, 2006: 302)

> Lado (1957) developed the Contrastive Analysis (CA) approach to L2 acquisition. Under the Contrastive Analysis Hypothesis, learning a new language involves identifying and learning differences between the L1 and the L2. Similarities between the L1 and L2 are predicted to facilitate acquisition. L2s with more differences are predicted to take longer to learn. (Foley & Flynn, 2013: 98)

Still another characterisation of the CAH equated it with the following conditions:

> Where two languages were similar, positive transfer would occur; where they were different, negative transfer, or interference, would result. (Larsen-Freeman & Long, 1991: 53)

Along with Robert Lado (1915–1995), some other names are also invoked in discussions of the history of transfer research, such as Uriel

Weinreich (1926–1967), whose 1953 book *Languages in Contact* is referred to in the following passage:

> Adopting a general view of transfer as the use of knowledge or skills from one context in a different linguistic context, Weinreich (1953) introduced the concept of *transfer* in L2 acquisition: use of the L1 that leads to 'correct' usage in the L2. Interference, in contrast, involves use of the L1 that leads to 'incorrect' language use. (Foley & Flynn, 2013: 98)

Although Foley and Flynn do not give any source as an example of the 'general view' that they ascribe to mid-20th-century notions of psychology and language, Nick Ellis (2008) does offer a very specific source: the behaviourist construct of proactive inhibition (PI):

> Much of this [behaviorist] work was succinctly summarized in Osgood's 'transfer surface' that draws together the effects of time of learning, similarity of material, and retention interval on negative (and positive) transfer (Osgood, 1949).... PI underpins a variety of fundamental phenomena of language learning and language transfer, as Robert Lado proposed in his CAH... The CAH held that one could predict learner difficulty by reference to utterance-by-utterance comparison of a learner's L1 and L2. (2008: 384)

The six quotations given above vary considerably in what they address, including the issues of errors, of prediction, of positive and negative transfer, and of proactive inhibition. Even so, it would be a mistake to conclude that the characterisations of transfer and CA are completely different. There is arguably a gestalt interpretation of the history of transfer research that many readers might construct from these or other sources. For those completely new to second language acquisition (SLA), the gestalt history might consist in part of the following statements:

- It was Lado who formulated the Contrastive Analysis Hypothesis.
- The notion of language transfer has its origins in behaviourist psychology.
- Weinreich introduced the term *transfer* into L2 research.

Moreover, it seems likely that not only neophytes but indeed a wide segment of the SLA community, professors and students alike, would agree with at least one of the three statements. However, *none* of the three is true.

Intellectual interest in crosslinguistic influence goes back many decades before Lado, and probing that earlier history is necessary in order to understand transfer research in the mid-20th century and to scrutinise the historiography of transfer in research and in textbooks on SLA. As in other domains of intellectual history, complications arise in trying to untangle the strands of the story. This chapter will untangle some of the strands involving the so-called Contrastive Analysis Hypothesis. Doing so will require not only much attention to transfer research long before Lado and Weinreich but also much attention to those two figures. The results of the investigation suggest that the phrase Contrastive Analysis Hypothesis is nebulous and contributes little to understanding the intellectual history of transfer. Beyond the critique of a questionable term, the chapter can provide, albeit in a very limited space, encouragement to members of the SLA community who care to reflect on when SLA research actually began and also to reflect on where the field might be going.

The chapter proceeds from definitions of two key terms, *language transfer* and *contrastive analysis*, to looking at the origins of the term *transfer* independent of any work in psychology. It then considers the term *contrastive analysis* and proceeds from there to a critique of the so-called Contrastive Analysis Hypothesis. The word *habit* is also relevant to the intellectual history of transfer, and there will be considerable attention to uses of the term in linguistics and psychology and to recent notions such as automaticity that involve similar concerns. The concluding section of the chapter summarises the main points and discusses implications of the findings.

Preliminary Definitions

Throughout the chapter, the following definitions will serve as a reference point for the diverse ideas considered:

> Transfer is the influence resulting from the similarities and differences between the target language and any other language that has been previously (and perhaps imperfectly) acquired. (Odlin, 1989: 27)

> Contrastive analysis: Systematic comparison of two or more languages. (Odlin, 1989: 165)

These definitions seem accurate enough, but they certainly do not tell all that may interest SLA specialists. The definition of CA does depart from uses of the term as a historical designator and certainly from uses of the phrase Contrastive Analysis Hypothesis. Moreover, the definition of transfer characterises it as influence (and it is often called *crosslinguistic influence*), but what *influence* might actually mean remains a major research question. Even so, the notion of influence has a long history. In 1884, the German linguist Hugo Schuchardt (1842–1927) used *Einfluss* (influence) in his classic study of German and Italian in contact regions inhabited by speakers of various Slavic languages (especially Slovenian, Czech and Polish). Schuchardt had already considered language contact in pidgin and creole settings, and many linguists today remember him as a founder of the field of creolistics. In his work on contact in Central Europe, Schuchardt focused on what he considered to be examples of L1 influence, but he also occasionally commented on the psychology of SLA. Work on language contact in the decades after Schuchardt also reported crosslinguistic influence, but as the discussion in Weinreich's *Languages in Contact* will show, the psychology of bilingualism remained an under-explored area. As interest in transfer grew among contemporaries of Weinreich, such as Lado, so did the controversies over the general psychology of language and the specific psychology of L2 acquisition. Before the discussion of controversies, however, the origins of the term *transfer* require attention.

Transfer and its Independent Origins in Linguistics

In English, the use of *transfer* to denote crosslinguistic influence goes back at least to the 19th century, well before the behaviourist research cited by Ellis in the quotation in the introduction. The term appears in the writing of two American linguists, William Dwight Whitney (1827–1894) and Aaron Marshall Elliott (1844–1910). Both had studied in German universities, the former in Berlin and Tübingen and the latter in Munich, and both were probably influenced by German terms to be considered in the next paragraph. In a discussion of language contact in historical linguistics, Whitney declared, 'By universal consent, what is most easily transferred from one language to another is a noun' ([1881] 1971: 184). This assertion might suggest that Whitney considered crosslinguistic influence to be widespread, but in fact he shared the scepticism of many linguists of his time about the extent of such influence. Elliott used a variant of the term (*transference*) in an 1885 review of Schuchardt's book in the *American Journal of Philology* (and the review is reprinted in the 1971 edition of Schuchardt's work). Elliott employed *influence* as well as *transference* in the review, and he also used *transfer* in an 1886 article on language contact in Canada.

Since Whitney and Elliott had studied linguistics (aka philology) in Germany, they probably adopted *transfer* and *transference* as translations for two words used by German linguists: *hinübertragen* and *übertragen*, both of which can also translate as 'carry over'. *Hinübertragen* goes back at least to 1836, appearing in a famous study of mind and language by Wilhelm von Humboldt (1767–1835), and the metaphoric notion of carrying over is the same as in the Latin word *transferre* (Odlin, 2008; Odlin & Yu, 2016). With regard to *übertragen*, it goes back at least to 1875, appearing in an analysis of loanwords by a Finnish linguist, August Ahlqvist (1826–1889); although some uses of *übertragen* in his book involve simple cases of semantic extensions not related to language contact, other uses clearly refer to crosslinguistic influence (e.g. Ahlqvist, 1875: 51) in the language contact setting of Finland.[2] Schuchardt used *übertragen* at least a year before his book on language contact in Central Europe, as the term denotes crosslinguistic influence in one of his creolist studies (Schuchardt, 1883), and it also appears a number of times in his 1884 book as well as in an 1885 review of the book, the historical linguist Hermann Paul being the reviewer (also reprinted in the 1971 edition of the Schuchardt work). That the use of *transfer* comes from German linguistics rather than from any work in psychology seems all the more likely because neither Whitney nor Elliott discusses any psychological research, behaviourist or otherwise. Indeed, behaviourism was in its infancy in the late 19th century (Graham, 2010; Levelt, 2013; Singley & Anderson, 1989). Weinreich, it should be added, cites both the Whitney article and the Schuchardt book, and he calls the latter 'unexcelled' (1953a: 111).

In the several decades between Whitney and Weinreich, the term *transfer* did not disappear. Both Edward Sapir (1884–1939) and Otto Jespersen (1860–1943) used the term in their introductions to linguistics:

> We may suppose that individual variations arising at linguistic borderlands – whether by unconscious suggestive influence of foreign speech habits or by the transfer of foreign sounds in the speech of bilingual individuals – have gradually been incorporated into the phonetic drift of a language. (Sapir, 1921: 200)

> …it is, of course, a natural supposition that the aboriginal inhabitants of Europe and Asia were just as liable to transfer their speech habits to new languages as their descendants are nowadays. (Jespersen, 1922: 192)

While Jespersen's use of 'transfer' clearly involves the influence of a language already known on learning or speaking a new one, Sapir's use is a little ambiguous. One may wonder, for example, whether those susceptible to the 'suggestive influence of foreign speech habits' are monolingual speakers of a target language that foreigners are attempting to speak (e.g. monolingual speakers of Cockney English in a modern London neighbourhood having many Pakistani or Polish immigrants) or native speakers of a language (e.g. Middle English) attempting to learn the language of a conquering class (e.g. Norman French). In any case, there is no doubt that *transfer* in this passage refers to some kind of crosslinguistic influence. As with Whitney and Schuchardt, Sapir had a clear effect on Weinreich, who cites this passage (1953: 24). Also noteworthy is the use by both Sapir and Jespersen of the word *habits*. While the word might suggest that both men were behaviourists, in fact neither one was. The differing stances on behaviourism that linguists have taken will be discussed in various parts of this chapter.

Weinreich's *Languages in Contact* frequently uses *transfer*, which the author deems to be 'one form of interference' (1953: 7), and the notion of transfer as a type of interference is likewise evident on page 50. These instances squarely contradict the claim of Foley and Flynn (quoted in the introduction) that Weinreich viewed transfer as 'use of the L1 that leads to "correct" usage in the L2'. Although the adoption of *transfer* by Whitney, Elliott, Sapir and Jespersen shows that the term appeared long before *Languages in Contact*, Weinreich may well be the originator of a related term, *transferability*, which appears occasionally in the book (e.g. 1953: 31 & 34).

While *transfer* means some kind of crosslinguistic influence in all the sources discussed in this section, the role of actual bilingual individuals in the phenomenon is frequently more implicit than explicit. For instance, Elliott wrote, as linguists often do even now, of the transfer of forms across linguistic boundaries as if they have a life of their own independent of actual bilinguals:

> ...these alien forms, when taken up into one dialect, sometimes pass to others, and at each transfer undergo certain phonetic or morphological changes necessary to adapt them to easy use in the dialects, respectively, where they find a new home. (1886: 154)

Here the use of *transfer* is not in the more restricted sense found in SLA research and does not explicitly refer to any bilinguals at all. Even so, the psychology of bilingualism and multilingualism was a topic that some 19th-century linguists at least touched on; moreover, Schuchardt was very specific about the 'Einfluss der Muttersprache' (influence of the mother language) as the source of the many examples of Slavic influence he found, and he made occasional remarks about the psychological dimensions of transfer and language learning, including the need of the learner to risk making errors ([1884] 1971: 150). In fact, Schuchardt used as the epigraph of his book a Slovenian proverb to the effect that blunders are necessary in learning a language. This awareness of the relation between the psychological and structural dimensions of language contact is even more evident in Weinreich and in much work on language contact in recent decades (e.g. Thomason & Kaufmann, 1988; Winford, 2002).

The word *transfer* as a psycholinguistic term in SLA thus has its origins more in 19th-century ideas in linguistics than in the use of *transfer* in psychology either in the behaviourist period or beyond. On the other hand, the distinction between positive and negative transfer does suggest an eventual effect of behaviourist psychology, but only long after the initial appearance of the term *transfer* itself.

Contrastive Analysis and its Varied Meanings

Nick Ellis (2008: 384) reports a database search for the keyword entry 'contrastive analysis' which produced 1268 results. As this finding suggests, the term *contrastive analysis* remains widely used, especially since the search that Ellis reports was limited to the occurrences of the term in the research literature of the previous 30 years (hence, back to the 1970s, when there was a growing scepticism about the usefulness of CA). Nevertheless, some caution is necessary. *Contrastive analysis* is not just a term in SLA: it is sometimes used by specialists in fields such as translation theory (e.g. Chesterman, 1991) and anthropological linguistics (e.g. Lucy, 1992) for concerns other than those of acquisition and pedagogy, yet concerns compatible with the definition of CA given in the second section of this chapter.

When the term is used for the problems of SLA, it often takes on a very special cast, where Selinker (1992, 2006), for instance, uses it mainly as a historical label, e.g. '…though it predicted a lot of language transfer, CA generated a lot of "residue" and, as we know, CA is not a good acquisition theory' (2006: 202). This point will be considered further in the next section, which discusses the so-called Contrastive Analysis Hypothesis.[3] References such as Selinker's to a CA period should not obscure two historical facts. First, the term *contrastive* predates Lado's *Linguistics across Cultures*: it appeared at least as early as 1941 in an article by Benjamin Lee Whorf (1897–1941), who wrote of 'contrastive linguistics' ([1941] 1956: 240), by which he meant the comparative study of languages and cultures. Moreover, passages from Weinreich and Lado quoted in the next section show that they regarded contrastive analysis very much in the same way.

The Contrastive Analysis Hypothesis

Ever since a 1970 article by Ronald Wardhaugh was published in *TESOL Quarterly* entitled 'The Contrastive Analysis Hypothesis', the term has remained in use. The CAH, as Wardhaugh characterised it, is 'the claim that the best language teaching materials are based on a contrast of the two competing linguistic systems' (1970: 123). Wardhaugh, it should be emphasised, distinguished between what he termed the 'strong' and 'weak' form of the hypothesis, with the author using the two adjectives in an explicit analogy to what has often been called the Sapir-Whorf Hypothesis of linguistic relativity (Hoijer, 1954). The strong and the weak versions of the CAH are not defined explicitly by Wardhaugh, but he does suggest two ways in which they differ: (1) predictions of difficulty in learning a second language are essential in the strong version but are merely possible in the weak version (1970: 127); (2) nothing beyond a thorough comparison of two languages is needed to make predictions in the strong version, while the weak version 'starts with the evidence provided of linguistic interference and uses such evidence to explain the similarities and differences between systems' (1970: 126). It is worth noting that Wardhaugh's characterisation of the weak version seems odd; analysing similarities and differences between systems to explain the evidence would be more plausible than using the 'evidence to explain the similarities and differences'.

For Wardhaugh, the strong version was 'unrealistic and impracticable' (1970: 124); however, he judged the weak version potentially useful (even though he did express reservations about this version also). The putative untenability of the strong version arises, in Wardhaugh's estimation, from the problems of deciding how to describe and compare languages in cases where real differences are evident: for instance, the phoneme /p/ in French is not phonetically identical to English /p/. The question of what the best comparisons might be is *not* resolved, Wardhaugh judged, just by changing theoretical approaches; for him, the difficulties persist regardless of whether the analysis adopted is structuralist or generative. Uncertainties about the linguistic theories themselves remain and could thus affect estimations of difficulties. Wardhaugh also saw a need for ranking degrees of difficulty, noting that although instructors often take seriously the possible influence of, for instance, Spanish phonology on how a learner tries to pronounce English sounds, many teachers also have a sense that some parts of a language can be more easily acquired than others. Nevertheless, how one might best construct a pedagogical sequence remains problematic, Wardhaugh believed, due to the theoretical uncertainties.

The general characterisation of the CAH offered by Wardhaugh is in fact a paraphrase of an assertion made in 1945 by Lado's mentor Charles Fries (1887–1967) that 'the most efficient materials are those that are based upon a scientific description of the language to be learned, carefully compared with a parallel description of the native language of the learner' (1945: 9). Something close to the 'strong' version of the CAH inferred by Wardhaugh appears in a statement by Lado himself in his preface to *Linguistics across Cultures*: 'The plan of the book rests on the assumption that we can predict and describe the patterns that will cause difficulty in learning, and those that will not cause difficulty, by comparing systematically the language to be learned with the native language and culture of the student' (1957: vii).

Discussions of the CAH often invoke this quotation from Lado, but far less frequently cited is an earlier and similar assertion of Weinreich: 'The contrastive analysis of the phonemes of two languages and the way they are used yields a list of the forms of expected interference in a particular contact situation' (1953a: 22). The main difference from Lado in Weinreich's use of *contrastive analysis* is not the absence of the word *predict* – the use of 'expected' is obviously similar. Instead, Weinreich's concerns are those of language contact specialists, who typically focus on linguistic change and cases of 'interference' rather than on those cases which, as Lado put it, 'will not cause difficulty'. Throughout *Languages in Contact*, Weinreich seems to have regarded historical linguists and dialectologists as his primary audience. In *Linguistics across Cultures*, Lado's focus on an audience of teachers is certainly clear.

Some of the historical accounts in SLA textbooks (e.g. Rod Ellis, 1985) do cite Wardhaugh's article, though others do not (e.g. Dulay *et al.*, 1982), and in the latter case, the distinction proposed by Wardhaugh between a strong and a weak CAH is ignored. In fact, the quotation from Dulay *et al.* in the introduction suggests a focus on what Wardhaugh deemed the weak – and for him the more credible – version of the putative hypothesis. Foley and Flynn do not cite Warhaugh or the strong/weak distinction either, yet in contrast to Dulay *et al.*, their definition of the CAH (also quoted in the introduction) clearly focuses on what Wardhaugh saw as essential to the strong version, i.e. predictions. What the supposed CAH says about difficulties also differs in the two characterisations: for Dulay *et al.*, difficulty means errors, while for Foley and Flynn it means the length of time needed for acquisition. Although error rates and acquisition times would no doubt strongly correlate in many studies, they are distinct variables, and so the two characterisations of the CAH disagree in yet another way.

Such inconsistency in the way the CAH is defined no doubt contributes to the gestalt impression of the history of transfer discussed in the introduction. Another contributing factor is the neglect in noting the anachronism of Wardhaugh's term: that is, neither Fries nor Weinreich nor Lado actually used the term Contrastive Analysis Hypothesis. The relation of Weinreich to some supposed CAH is also inconsistently covered in accounts such as those cited in the introduction. Even so, some historical accounts do note important similarities between Lado and Weinreich; for example, Larsen-Freeman and Long (1990: 53) cite both of the following passages:

> The greater the differences between systems [languages or dialects], i.e. the more numerous the mutually exclusive forms and patterns in each, the greater is the learning problem and the potential area of interference. (Weinreich, 1953a: 1)

> Those elements that are similar [to the] native language will be simple... and those elements that are different will be difficult. The teacher who has made a comparison of the foreign language with the native language of the students will know better what the real learning problems are and can better provide for teaching them. (Lado, 1957: 2)

What led researchers to link Lado yet not Weinreich to some supposed CAH is probably the difference in focus between the two noted above, with Lado concentrating on educational concerns and with Weinreich on change and variation; even so, the psycholinguistic assumptions of both linguists are essentially the same. Another reason for the relative inattention to Weinreich may be the efforts of Dulay *et al.* to deny the relevance of *Languages in Contact* to SLA research. Before those efforts are discussed, however, it will help to consider the historical relation between linguistics and psychology.

Habits and Behaviourism

The scepticism in textbooks about contrastive analysis arose not only from empirical problems about what CA might actually predict (as in Wardhaugh's critique) but also from the impression that CA inevitably relied on behaviourist assumptions about the psychology of learning, as suggested in the quotation from Nick Ellis in the introduction. Authors of textbooks such as those of Dulay *et al.*, Rod Ellis, and Larsen-Freeman and Long have associated behaviourism with CA and the supposed CAH (although Wardhaugh did not address behaviourism in his article). As seen already, confusion over the origins of the term *transfer* in SLA contributed to the association, but another problematic term has been *habits*. In the foreword to Lado's book, Fries claimed that adult SLA is quite different from child language acquisition because of the 'special "set" created by the first language habits' (1957: v). The word *habit* was certainly prominent in behaviourist psychology; even so, the notion of habits proves more complicated, largely because linguists who distanced themselves from behaviourism nevertheless saw fit to use the word *habits* – and among them was Fries (whose beliefs will be contrasted with those of Lado on behaviourism).

However much or little linguists might agree about the psychology of language, it is necessary to consider just what behaviourism is. One might reasonably use the plural form *behaviourisms* instead, since not all behaviourists have thought alike, and since the history of behaviourist ideas involves notions from earlier intellectual movements such as the British empiricism of David Hume and John Locke as well as the logical positivism of the 19th century (Blumenthal, 1985; Graham, 2010). Still, three recurring traits seem to be most significant, especially for the kind of behaviourism that influenced some linguists, including Leonard Bloomfield and Robert Lado: (1) belief in the applicability of a stimulus-response (S-R) model to the study of language; (2) rejection of 'mentalist' terms and assumptions in such study; (3) advocacy of empirical methods that made experimental results the standard for evaluating theories.

For American behaviourists of the early 20th century (though not for Ivan Pavlov (1849–1936), who is often seen as the first behaviourist), the stimulus-response paradigm seemed applicable to the human species as well as to other mammals. The influence of behaviourism (aka verbal learning) on some linguists seems quite evident in an introductory textbook by Bloomfield (1933), who foregrounds S-R relations. The notion of habits proved easy to incorporate into behaviourism, as seen in a definition of *habit* in one behaviourist textbook of psychology which equates it with a 'learned response' (Morgan & King, 1971: 740).

In the verbal learning tradition, a crucial distinction was made between mentalist and mechanist theories, with the former being condemned as unscientific and the latter held up as the proper framework for attempting to understand the psychology of language. An article by Albert P. Weiss (1925) shows quite clearly the behaviourist commitment to an anti-mentalist philosophy, heralding the progress of verbal learning research and seeing the burden of proof to be not on those who look at language as simply another behaviour but rather on those who hypothesise 'the existence of a special mental force' (1925: 56). At that time, Weiss and Bloomfield were colleagues at Ohio State University, and Bloomfield was a founder of the Linguistic Society of America, the sponsor of *Language*, the (then) fledgling journal in which the Weiss article was published. Like his colleague in psychology, Bloomfield eschewed terms such as *thought*, *belief*, *concept* and *idea* as inaccessible to scientific observation and therefore as unacceptable as terms in developing a theory of meaning.

Partly because of Bloomfield, who is often seen as the most influential American linguist of the first half of the 20th century, and partly because of the growth of behaviourist psychology in that period, there arose a strong emphasis on experimental methods in the hybrid field of psycholinguistics (as it came to be known), especially after 1950. A volume expressly designed to foster greater collaboration between linguists and psychologists (Osgood & Sebeok, 1965), shows a growing awareness in the 1950s and 1960s of the need for experimental or quasi-experimental research in several fields including language acquisition and bilingualism. Moreover, many of the discussions (e.g. a chapter of Susan Ervin on language acquisition) formulate the theoretical issues in terms of S-R relations.

The third characteristic of behaviourism discussed here, the emphasis on experimental frameworks, has endured more robustly than the other two in the psychology of language in the post-behaviourist era. A critique by Noam Chomsky (1959) of a key book in the verbal learning tradition (Skinner, 1957) proved very influential among linguists in rejecting the S-R framework, and this rejection affected the perception of transfer in books such as that of Dulay *et al.* Chomsky also proved influential in restoring confidence in mentalism, although many of the cognitive linguists and psychologists who nowadays accept mentalist constructs part company with Chomsky on key issues in the study of meaning (e.g. Lakoff & Johnson, 1999; Langacker, 2008; Slobin, 1996).

Habits and Structural Linguistics

The movement in linguistics known as structuralism included a wide variety of linguists, some of whom, such as Bloomfield, took behaviourist stances, while others such as Sapir and Whorf did not reject mentalism. Whether behaviourist or not, many structuralists used the word *habit* to describe certain dispositions in language. Sapir (1929), for instance, made clear his sympathies for Gestalt psychology, not behaviourism (212) yet asserted too that 'the language habits of our [speech] community predispose certain choices of interpretation' (210). As noted already, Sapir also used *habits* in a passage in his introduction to language. Quite similarly, Whorf used *habitual* in the title of one of his most detailed discussions of relativity: 'The Relation of Habitual Thought and Behavior to Language' ([1941] 1956), with the title showing a remarkable mix of terms accepted by behaviourists (*habitual* and *behaviour*) with a mentalist one (*thought*). Still, in another (undated) essay, Whorf said, 'behaviorism does not show us which lines to work upon in order to be fully in accord with human intangibles, except by way of announcing in behavioristic terms things already obvious to common sense' (1956: 41).

Reservations about behaviourism are also evident in the views of Weinreich, who nevertheless did not shy away from the word *habit*, as seen in his phrase 'separate subphonemic habits' (1953a: 24). Weinreich also showed some interest in the contributions of behaviourism to the developing field of psycholinguistics, but *Languages in Contact* contains a mix of behaviourist terms (e.g. 'stimuli', 64) and mentalist ones (e.g. 'aware', 8). Most crucially, his analysis of crosslinguistic influence remained agnostic as to what the best psychological account might be. His book cites as evidence both mentalist and non-mentalist research, and in other writings, Weinreich states his conviction that the anti-mentalist stance of some structural linguists was impeding progress in linguistics, especially in regard to the study of meaning (Weinreich, 1953b, 1963).

However much (or little) credence structural linguists gave to behaviourism, there was a great deal in human language that seemed to call for words such as *habit* or *habitual*. Although behaviourists might claim that by invoking habits, Whorf and others were tacitly accepting the relevance of stimulus-response relations, one could just as easily argue that the word *thought* in Whorf's phrase 'habitual thought' shows a mentalist agenda. Yet what matters most in assessing the positions of Sapir, Whorf, Weinreich and others is the reality that they were linguists looking at psychology from the outside. Just as psychologists who explore language can hardly avoid making some assumptions about linguistic structure when they use terms such as *sound, form* or *word*, linguists can hardly avoid psychological assumptions if they delve into topics such as language acquisition. In the structuralist era, many linguists strove for precision in how they used grammatical terms such as *morpheme* and *constituent*, but they tolerated more ambiguity in using *habit* and other terms on the borders of their field.

Fries, Lado and Weinreich

More often than not, both Fries and Lado are represented as behaviourists in historical accounts of transfer (e.g. Odlin, 1989), although one analysis (Thomas, 2006) argues that neither Fries nor Lado was a behaviourist. The reality turns out to be more complicated, however, in light of recent observations from Larry Selinker, who studied with Lado at Georgetown University and with Fries, who did some guest teaching there:

> Lado was a behaviorist in that he openly believed (and told us in class) in the habit-formation theory, strength of stimulus-response, dominant in the behavioristic linguistics of the time... Fries, on the other hand, believed deeply in semantics and never seemed to be a believer in the dominant theory of stimulus-response learning. (Selinker, 2006: 209)

Despite the differences between Fries and Lado over the general psychology of language, both used the word *habit* in their discussions of language learning and as suggested above, such ambiguity does not seem to have troubled anybody. By the same token, the non-committal stance of Weinreich toward behaviourism did not keep Lado from citing *Languages in Contact* as support for his assertion that linguists 'report that many linguistic distortions heard among bilinguals correspond to describable differences in the languages involved' (1957: 1). In this regard, Lado cites two books, *Languages in Contact* and Einar Haugen's (1953) *Norwegian Language in America*.

Lado thus considered his approach to transfer to have considerable empirical support. His assumption was challenged, though, by Dulay *et al.* (1982), who claimed that the contact research of Haugen and Weinreich was not relevant to the discussion of second language acquisition. The strategy of Dulay *et al.* for contesting Lado's interpretation was to compare the definitions of *interference* by Weinreich and *borrowing* by Haugen with the 'CA hypothesis' which they ascribe to Lado (1982: 99). The point made by Dulay *et al.* proves valid with regard to Haugen, who was in fact more concerned about the L2 English influence on American Norwegian than about L1 Norwegian influence on English in immigrant communities. Even so, Dulay *et al.* fail to offer a convincing analysis with regard to Weinreich, whose position on interference differs from their characterisation; most crucially, several of the studies that Weinreich discusses are ones that focus on L1 influence on L2 (along with studies less relevant to such transfer, including some of Haugen's earlier research on L2 → L1 influence). Interestingly, among the L1 → L2 studies that Weinreich cites (1953: 20) is one of phonetic transfer that has Lado as a co-author (Reed *et al.*, 1948). Moreover, Weinreich frequently cites Schuchardt's study of how native speakers of Slavic languages use German and Italian. While Schuchardt considered different kinds of bilingualism, he focused on the mother tongue or 'Muttersprache' (noted above) as a key factor in what he termed imperfect bilingualism, 'unvollkommene Zweitsprachigkeit' ([1884] 1971: 150). Along with his interest in L1 → L2 transfer, Schuchardt was also aware of possible multilingual influences (e.g. L2 → L3), as he mentions the possible influence of a language which stands in place of the mother tongue ('einer anderen welche an ihre Stelle getreten ist', ([1884] 1971: 150).

Other examples of studies cited by Weinreich which involve L1 → L2 transfer have been noted elsewhere (Odlin, 1989: 24), and there are others as well in *Languages in Contact*. By the mid-20th century, a wealth of relevant contact research existed, yet as Selinker (1992: 26) suggests, many SLA researchers from the 1960s to the 1980s tended to ignore Weinreich's insights. If they had read *Languages in Contact* with more care, several would have probably rejected the extreme and rather widespread scepticism about transfer that was fashionable at the time.

The Notion of Habits in a Post-Behaviourist Era

As noted above, Chomsky had a considerable impact on SLA researchers such as Dulay *et al.*, who linked their scepticism about transfer to wider theoretical changes, especially the shift from theories of learning as habit formation to theories of rule-governed behaviour (1982: 140). However, the reality of the change seems somewhat problematic in view of an assertion by John Carroll, an early psycholinguist with an interest in SLA. Carroll recognised the ostensible challenge of Chomskyan linguistics, yet he voiced doubts about how much of a theoretical shift had really occurred: 'I am not convinced... that there is any real difference between a "habit" and a "rule" or between a "response" and a "rule-governed performance"' (1968: 114). He used his training as a psychologist to review a wide range of studies in psychology involving many kinds of transfer, but he remained pessimistic about their relevance to transfer insofar as the materials and learning conditions in those studies usually differed from the circumstances of learning a second language. Carroll did suggest, however, that the behaviourist construct of proactive inhibition (PI) was 'the kind of interference... we are probably dealing with in connection with contrastive linguistics' (119). He viewed PI as especially relevant to the question of how particular forms of guidance might overcome negative transfer. Some research in subsequent decades (e.g. Kupferberg & Olshtain, 1996; Otwinowska-Kasztelnic, 2010) supports his optimism.

As seen in the introduction to this chapter, Ellis (2008) has also affirmed the usefulness of PI, which he defines as the 'effect of prior learning inhibiting new learning' (p. 384). It is not the only learning factor that Ellis deems relevant to SLA or, indeed, to transfer. Even so, he cites examples of work on transfer that he views as support for PI, but his attempt at rehabilitating PI is especially noteworthy since he looks to the behaviourist tradition, yet does not – in contrast to Bloomfield and Weiss – reject mentalism, as is evident in the use of mentalist terms such as *conceptual schema*, *language knowledge* and *awareness* by Ellis and Robinson (2008). The relevance of some PI research for cognitive linguistics thus suggests that structuralist intuitions about habits warrant further reflection. It seems appropriate to consider how post-behaviourist research might help unpack the notion of habits in relation to transfer.

Recent work on transfer does suggest that much in the notion of habits can be analysed in terms of three widely used constructs: activation, automaticity and entrenchment. Activation patterns that differ crosslinguistically occur in a wide range of cases, as when a target-language word evokes more than one meaning in the native language lexicon yet not for monolingual speakers of the target. For instance, Elston-Güttler and Williams (2008) found that the English noun *bag* evokes the joint meanings of pouch and container among bilingual Germans whose L1 has a word (*tasche*) which can denote either a pocket or a bag. Automaticity is certainly a goal to strive for in acquiring a new language, serving as it does the needs for speed and economy in language processing; even so, what is automatic in the native language can contribute to a foreign accent. Hammarberg and Hammarberg (2009) determined that a learner of L3 Swedish relied more on L2 German similarities with Swedish in earlier stages of acquisition yet experienced greater difficulty in avoiding L1 English phonetic interference as she grew more proficient in the L3. Hammarberg and Hammarberg attribute this problem to the automaticity of L1 articulatory patterns. Entrenchment may arise from an L1 influence which persists and impedes – or perhaps even makes impossible – successful acquisition of structures such as English articles, which despite their formal simplicity involve great semantic and pragmatic complexity (Han, 2010; Odlin, 2012). The constructs of activation, automaticity and entrenchment are no doubt interrelated, but a precise understanding of the relationships seems possible only with much more research.

Conclusion

This chapter has raised several points about the history of the idea of language transfer in relation to the so-called Contrastive Analysis Hypothesis:

- The earliest known uses of *transfer* to denote crosslinguistic influence did not come from behaviourist psychology but rather from two American linguists in the 1880s, William Dwight Whitney and Aaron Marshall Elliott, both of whom had studied in Germany.
- The use of *transfer* by Edward Sapir and Otto Jespersen in the 1920s indicates continuity between the 1880s and the 1950s, the decade that saw the publication of Uriel Weinreich's *Languages in Contact* and Robert Lado's *Linguistics across Cultures*.
- The use of *transfer* probably arose as translations of German terms, *hinübertragen* and *übertragen*, the former going back at least to the 1830s and the latter to the 1870s.
- The term *contrastive* goes back at least to 1941, appearing in the work of Benjamin Lee Whorf.
- The term Contrastive Analysis Hypothesis came into widespread use only after the publication of an article by Ronald Wardhaugh in 1970. In that sense the term is anachronistic when it is ascribed to Robert Lado or his mentor Charles Fries.
- Inconsistencies abound in how Contrastive Analysis Hypothesis is characterised. The original characterisation by Wardhaugh is often ignored, and some discussions of the CAH focus on Wardhaugh's strong version whereas others focus on his weak version. Inconsistencies as to what indicates learning difficulty are also evident.
- Structural linguists varied in how much or little they espoused behaviourist ideas in psychology. Some (e.g. Bloomfield and Lado) did indeed subscribe to behaviourism, yet others (e.g. Sapir, Whorf and Fries) did not. Regardless of their views on psychology, many structural linguists freely employed the words *habit* and *habitual*.
- While Lado was a behaviourist, Fries was not, according to Larry Selinker.
- Despite attempts to disassociate the concerns of Lado's *Linguistics across Cultures* from those of Weinreich's *Languages in Contact*, the latter work did in fact consider many cases of L1 → L2 transfer. Moreover, Weinreich and Lado did not differ substantively in their analysis of what underlies transfer: crosslinguistic similarities and differences.
- Post-behaviourist research offers useful constructs to help unpack the notion of habits: activation, automaticity and entrenchment can all aid in understanding specific patterns of transfer.

Taken together, these points call into question much of the conventional wisdom about the intellectual history of language transfer. As such, the findings may encourage readers to reflect on a pair of questions:

(1) Was there really ever a Contrastive Analysis Hypothesis?
(2) When did the study of second language acquisition begin?

The two questions are interrelated since conventional answers to the second question often invoke some version or other of an assumed CAH. If, however, the answer to the first question is negative, the second question needs to be reconsidered.

An easy but not totally satisfying way to answer the first question would be to say that there was indeed a CAH: namely, the assertion by Fries in 1945 that 'the most efficient materials are those that are based upon a scientific description of the language to be learned, carefully compared with a parallel description of the native language of the learner' (which was quoted above and repeated for convenience here). It was this assertion that Wardhaugh paraphrased in his own overall characterisation of the CAH. However, none of the quotations of SLA specialists given in the introduction mentions materials in their characterisations of the CAH (and their inconsistency with regard to Wardhaugh's strong/weak distinction has already been noted).

Those who would hold that the CAH did indeed exist might argue that what it really involved was the psychology implicit in Fries' 1945 assertion: i.e. an assumption about the importance of crosslinguistic similarities and differences in guiding L2 acquisition. This assumption was in fact explicitly stated in 1957 by Lado in the first chapter of *Linguistics across Cultures* and by Fries himself in the foreword. Even so, any defence invoking implicit psychology has a clear weakness. One can just as easily find the same psychological assumption in Weinreich's position on crosslinguistic similarity quoted above and indeed much earlier in, for example, Hugo Schuchardt's use of *Einfluss der Muttersprache* in his 1884 book, which is full of comparisons of the two target languages, German and Italian, with various Slavic languages, especially Slovenian, Czech and Polish, being the native languages. If implicit psychological assumptions about crosslinguistic differences are taken as the criterion, one can just as logically give the date 1884 as the genesis of the CAH, thus long before 1945, 1953 or 1957.

If the transfer metaphor were to be invoked instead of crosslinguistic correspondences as the basis for the CAH, one can argue that the putative hypothesis arose in the 1830s with Wilhelm von Humboldt's use of *hinuübertragen* (carrying over). There is, of course, another possibility still: namely, that Humboldt was not the first to use the transfer metaphor and that it goes back to linguistic thinking in French or Latin, the latter having the word *transferre*. Unless defenders of some historically real CAH ever manage to agree on just what it was and exactly when it was formulated – and by whom – the notion will continue to be as nebulous as it has been.

The nebulousness of the term CAH argues for reconsidering the second question, i.e. when the study of SLA began. The problem of historical beginnings is not unique to SLA. Even though many beginnings are clear (e.g. the day that Abraham Lincoln became President of the United States – March 4, 1861), there is ample room for debate about when the Middle Ages began, or the Romantic era of literature. Textbooks introducing the field of SLA have often recounted discussions from the 1950s to the 1970s as the starting point, but authors of future texts would do well to heed the warning in a recent history of psycholinguistics:

> It is a widely shared opinion that the new discipline of psycholinguistics emerged during the 1950s. Nothing could be further from the truth. The purpose of this book is to sketch a history of psycholinguistics, the psychology of language, going back to the end of the eighteenth century, when empirical research began in earnest. (Levelt, 2013: 3)

Despite this warning, however, Chapter 1 of Levelt's history is titled '1951'. In effect, he recognises a major milestone in the field in that year: namely, the interdisciplinary activities of John Carroll and others. In the preface, moreover, Levelt characterises his book-length examination of developments before 1951 as a 'prehistory'.

Some discussions of SLA and/or language teaching offer glimpses of an intellectual history of SLA before 1957 (e.g. Kelly, 1969; Jarvis & Pavlenko, 2008; Thomas, 2004) but there are relatively few discussions of, for example, Humboldt, and very few indeed of Schuchardt, even though his work strongly influenced Weinreich's. At the very least, future textbooks should acknowledge the 19th-century uses of the term *transfer* (and also the corresponding German terms) in linguistics independent from any ideas in psychology.

However one construes the prehistory and history of SLA, it is no coincidence that the field rapidly grew at virtually the same time that the broader field of psycholinguistics did. The increasing interest in language acquisition among figures as different as Susan Ervin, Roger Brown and Noam Chomsky attracted the attention of SLA researchers committed to using empirical methods that would contribute to understanding the special problems of L2 and multilingual acquisition. Moreover, it was in this same period that the field of language contact showed a stronger sense of the relevance of psychology. In various parts of Weinreich's book, one can detect the author's awareness of the limits of linguistics in isolation from psychology, e.g. 'How firmly the patterns of linguistic interference become habitualized is already a matter beyond strictly linguistic causation' (1953a: 105). In the third chapter of *Languages in Contact*, 'The Bilingual Individual', Weinreich surveys what he could find in psychological research, but even though the number of studies is small, it shows a growth of interest since the discussion of Schuchardt about psychological factors ([1884] 1971: 150–152).

This earlier independence (or isolation) from psychology should not obscure the long-standing need for linguists to invoke psychological constructs, however vaguely conceived. Schuchardt, for example, used *Einfluss*, Whorf *habitual thought*, and Weinreich *habitualised*. As empirical psychology thrived ever more, there grew a tendency – and hardly a surprising one – for linguists such as Bloomfield or Lado to adopt some behaviourist notions. The adoption of the terms *positive* and *negative transfer* in SLA seems to follow the same pattern. Although the linguistic term *transfer* predates behaviourism, the positive/negative distinction seems to have resulted from linguists such as Stockwell *et al.* (1965) paying at least some attention to the verbal learning enterprise. Yet in the same contrastive analysis of Spanish and English grammatical patterns, Stockwell *et al.* devoted considerable attention to generative analyses of the then-new Chomskyan approach. Such eclecticism shows that linguists have not always felt constrained to ally themselves exclusively with just one psychological theory.

In SLA as in other areas of linguistics it is often easy to find objections to the use of some term or another, as in the disapproval of Corder (1983) of the term *transfer*. However, neither his objections nor those of other critics seem to impede the use of *transfer* among many specialists, and likewise quite a few other terms seem to maintain a life of their own. Despite the critique of the phrase Contrastive Analysis Hypothesis in this chapter, the term may survive for quite a while to come. Like the use by Selinker of *contrastive analysis* cited above, invoking the supposed CAH at least offers a convenient label to direct attention back in time to the mid-20th century. Nevertheless, anyone who employs CAH should be aware of its deficiencies.

Despite the nebulousness of the term CAH, SLA specialists using it probably have the impression of there being a common and consistent understanding of the term. Such impressions are not unique to SLA; Lehrer (1983) has found that referential illusions arise in conversations about wine among non-specialists and has noted more serious problems of referential consistency among psychiatrists and phoneticians (though, in the latter case, instrumental studies have helped reduce the ambiguities). The nebulousness of CAH is reason enough to make it suspect, but there are other liabilities as well.

In the phrase Contrastive Analysis Hypothesis, the words *contrastive analysis* seem to suggest a questionable notion to many specialists, quite possibly as a result of using CA in historical references to earlier controversies. Yet no alternative term has been widely adopted when discussing language transfer. Crosslinguistic comparisons are indispensable in doing transfer research, whatever the theoretical orientation of the researcher. In Universal Grammar studies, for instance, analysts frequently invoke *parameters* (e.g. Verb-Object versus Object-Verb word order), but parameters obviously imply a contrastive analysis in the sense of the definition used in this chapter, i.e. a crosslinguistic comparison. The phrase *crosslinguistic comparison* could, of course, work as a synonym for *contrastive analysis*, but the latter is a bit more economical. Furthermore, the idea that languages can and should be compared in second language research and second language teaching is *not* one of the problems in the assumptions of Fries and Lado. Whatever else may be questionable in their positions, their advocacy of comparisons has always made sense.

The word *hypothesis* in Contrastive Analysis Hypothesis seems, if anything, even more problematic than the first two words. Thesis and dissertation students are often required to state hypotheses in their research and to state them as precisely as possible. Any student guided to think of hypothesis formulation as a precise enterprise might well expect the Contrastive Analysis Hypothesis to be just as unambiguous as their own hypotheses and just as unambiguous in terms of any empirical testing used to evaluate it. Yet the nebulousness of the term CAH as actually used can occasion misunderstandings, including a mistaken belief that some imagined hypothesis about the importance of transfer was tested and found to be false. Reading surveys of recent and earlier transfer research (e.g. Jarvis & Pavlenko, 2008; Ringbom, 2007) can forestall such misunderstandings, of course, but the word *hypothesis* does invite misconceptions.

The progress of transfer research in recent decades as well as in earlier ones shows that Fries and Lado did not err either in ascribing great importance to crosslinguistic influence or even in believing that contrastive predictions are possible, although there remains the challenge of identifying the kinds of predication most likely to succeed (Odlin, 2014). That said, some assumptions of Fries or Lado (or both) will not be shared by many SLA researchers at all nowadays, including Lado's belief in behaviourism or Fries' scepticism about parallels between child language learning and L2 acquisition. It is fair to say, moreover, that the great attention to crosslinguistic comparisons in the mid-20th century has given way, quite rightly, to an interest in conceptions of SLA such as interlanguage which take transfer into account yet also recognise complex processes like overgeneralisation that are sometimes independent of crosslinguistic influence (Selinker, 1972, 1992, 2014). Nevertheless, anyone interested in SLA should be aware that the study of transfer in L2 and multilingual acquisition has (like psycholinguistics more generally) a prehistory as well as a history, with both indeed relevant to the understanding of the human capacity for more than one language.

Notes

(1) I would like to thank Marianne Gullberg and Camiel Hamans for their help in regard to this project. Thanks also to Rosa Alonso Alonso for encouraging me in the project. Naturally I take sole responsibility for any problems in the chapter.
(2) The 1875 version of the Ahlqvist book is a translation of a work originally published in Swedish in 1871. In the foreword to the German edition, Ahlqvist notes that the translator was a native speaker of German.
(3) Selinker (personal communication) notes that contrastive analysis is not in itself a theory of learning, so in effect it is unrealistic to see any crosslinguistic comparison as a model of acquisition even though such comparisons can contribute much to a sound model.

References

Ahlqvist, A. (1871) *Det vestfinska språkets kulturord*. Helsinki: Frenckell.
Ahlqvist, A. (1875) *Die Kulturwörter der westfinnischen Sprachen*. Helsinki: Warsenius.
Bloomfield, L. (1933) *Language*. New York: Holt, Rinehart and Winston.
Blumenthal, A. (1985) Psychology and linguistics. In S. Koch and D. Leary (eds) *A Century of Psychology as Science* (pp. 804–824). New York: McGraw-Hill.
Carroll, J. (1968) Contrastive linguistics and interference theory. In J. Alatis (ed.) *Report of the Nineteenth Annual Meeting on Linguistics and Language. Georgetown University Monograph Series on Language and Linguistics* (pp. 113–122). Washington, DC: Georgetown University Press.
Chesterman, A. (1991) *On Definiteness: A Study with Special Reference to English and Finnish*. Cambridge: Cambridge University Press.
Chomsky, N. (1959) Review of Skinner (1957). *Language* 35, 26–58.
Corder, S. (1983) A role for the mother tongue. In S. Gass and L. Selinker (eds) *Language Transfer in Language Learning* (pp. 85–97). Rowley, MA: Newbury House.
Dulay, H., Burt, M. and Krashen, S. (1982) *Language Two*. New York: Oxford University Press.
Elliott, A.M. (1886) Speech mixture in French Canada, Indian and French. *Transactions and Proceedings of the Modern Language Association of America* 2, 158–186.
Ellis, N. (2008) Usage-based and form-based language acquisition. In P. Robinson and N. Ellis (eds) *Handbook of Cognitive Linguistics and Second Language Acquisition* (pp. 372–405). New York: Routledge.
Ellis, N. and Robinson, P. (2008) An introduction to cognitive linguistics, second language acquisition, and language instruction. In P. Robinson and N. Ellis (eds) *Handbook of Cognitive Linguistics and Second Language Acquisition* (pp. 3–24). New York: Routledge.
Ellis, R. (1985) *Understanding Second Language Acquisition*. Oxford: Oxford University Press.
Elston-Güttler, K. and Williams, J. (2008) L1 polysemy affects L2 meaning interpretation: Evidence for L1 concepts active during L2 reading. *Second Language Research* 24, 167–87.
Foley, C. and Flynn, S. (2013) The role of the native language. In J. Herschensohn and M. Young-Scholten (eds) *The Cambridge Handbook of Second Language Acquisition* (pp. 97–113). Cambridge: Cambridge University Press.
Fries, C. (1945) *Teaching and Learning English as a Foreign Language*. Ann Arbor: University of Michigan Press.
Graham, G. (2010) Behaviorism. In E. Zalta (ed.) *Stanford Encyclopedia of Philosophy*. Stanford: Metaphysics Research Lab. See http://plato.stanford.edu/entries/behaviorism/

Hammarberg, B. and Hammarberg, B. (2009) Re-setting the basis of articulation in the acquisition of new languages: A third language study. In B. Hammarberg (ed.) *Processes in Third Language Acquisition* (pp. 74–85). Edinburgh: Edinburgh University Press.

Han, Z. (2010) Grammatical inadequacy as a function of linguistic relativity: A longitudinal case study. In Z. Han and T. Cadierno (eds) *Linguistic Relativity in Second Language Acquisition: Evidence of First Language Thinking for Speaking* (pp. 154–182). Bristol: Multilingual Matters.

Haugen, E. (1953) *The Norwegian Language in America*. Philadelphia: University of Pennsylvania Press.

Hoijer, H. (1954) The Sapir-Whorf Hypothesis. In H. Hoijer (ed.) *Language and Culture* (pp. 92–105). Chicago: University of Chicago Press.

Jarvis, S. and Pavlenko, A. (2008) *Cross-linguistic Influence in Language and Cognition*. New York: Routledge.

Kelly, L. (1969) *25 Centuries of Language Teaching*. Rowley, MA: Newbury House.

Kupferberg, I. and Olshtain, E. (1996) Explicit L2 instruction facilitates the acquisition of difficult L2 forms. *Language Awareness* 5, 149–165.

Lado, R. (1957) *Linguistics across Cultures*. Ann Arbor: University of Michigan Press.

Lakoff, G. and Johnson, M. (1999) *Philosophy in the Flesh: The Embodied Mind and its Challenge to Western Thought*. New York: Basic Books.

Langacker, R. (2008) Cognitive grammar as a basis for language acquisition. In P. Robinson and N. Ellis (eds) *Handbook of Cognitive Linguistics and Second Language Acquisition* (pp. 66–88). New York: Routledge.

Larsen-Freeman, D. and Long, M. (1991) *An Introduction to Second Language Acquisition Research*. London: Longman.

Lehrer, A. (1983) *Wine and Conversation*. Bloomington: Indiana University Press.

Levelt, W. (2013) *A History of Psycholinguistics* Oxford: Oxford University Press.

Lucy, J. (1992) *Grammatical Categories and Cognition*. Cambridge: Cambridge University Press.

Morgan, C. and King, R. (1971) *Introduction to Psychology*. New York: McGraw-Hill.

Odlin, T. (1989) *Language Transfer*. Cambridge: Cambridge University Press.

Odlin, T. (2008) Conceptual transfer and meaning extensions. In P. Robinson and N. Ellis (eds) *Handbook of Cognitive Linguistics and Second Language Acquisition* (pp. 306–340). New York: Routledge.

Odlin, T. (2012) Nothing will come of nothing. In B. Kortmann and B. Szmrecsanyi (eds) *Linguistic Complexity in Interlanguage Varieties, L2 Varieties, and Contact Languages* (pp. 62–89). Berlin: de Gruyter.

Odlin, T. (2014) Rediscovering prediction. In Z. Han and E. Tarone (eds) *Interlanguage 40 Years Later* (pp. 27–45). Amsterdam: John Benjamins

Odlin, T. and Yu, L. (2016) Introduction. In L. Yu and T. Odlin (eds) *New Perspectives on Transfer in Second Language Learning*. Bristol: Multilingual Matters.

Osgood, C. (1949) The similarity paradox in human learning: A resolution. *Psychological Review* 36, 132–143.

Osgood, C. and Sebeok, T. (eds) (1965) *Psycholinguistics: A Survey of Theory and Research Problems*. Bloomington: Indiana University Press.

Otwinowska-Kasztelnic, A. (2010) Language awareness in using cognate vocabulary: The case of Polish advanced students of English in light of the theory of affordances. In J. Arabski and A. Wojtaszek (eds) *Neurolinguistic and Psycholinguistic Perspectives on SLA* (pp. 175–190). Bristol: Multilingual Matters.

Reed, D., Lado, R. and Shen, Y. (1948) The importance of the native language in foreign language learning. *Language Learning* 1, 17–23.

Ringbom, H. (2007) *Cross-linguistic Similarity in Foreign Language Learning*. Clevedon: Multilingual Matters.
Sapir, E. (1921) *Language*. New York: Harcourt, Brace, Jovanovich.
Sapir, E. (1929) The status of linguistics as a science. *Language* 5, 207–214
Schuhardt, H. (1883) Kreolische Studien IV: Über das Malaiospanische der Philippinen. *Sitzungberichte der kaiserlichen Akademie der Wisssenschaften zu Wien (philosophisch-historische Klasse)* 105, 111–150.
Schuhardt, H. ([1884] 1971) *Slawo-deutsches und Slawo-italienisches* [with reprinted reviews of the work by A.M. Elliott, H. Paul, and others]. Munich: Wilhem Fink.
Selinker, L. (1972). Interlanguage. *International Review of Applied Linguistics* 10, 209–231.
Selinker, L. (1992) *Rediscovering Interlanguage*. London: Longman.
Selinker, L. (2006) Afterword: Fossilization or 'Does your mind mind?' In Z. Han and T. Odlin (eds) *Studies of Fossilization in Second Language Acquisition* (pp. 201–210). Clevedon: Multilingual Matters.
Selinker, L. (2014) Interlanguage 40 years on: Three themes from here. In Z.H. Han and E. Tarone (eds) *Interlanguage: Forty Years Later* (pp. 221–246). Amsterdam: John Benjamins.
Singley, M. and Anderson, J. (1989) *The Transfer of Cognitive Skill*. Cambridge, MA: Harvard University Press.
Skinner, B. (1957) *Verbal Behavior*. New York: Appleton-Century-Crofts.
Slobin, D. (1996) From 'thought and language' to 'thinking for speaking'. In J. Gumperz and S. Levinson (eds) *Rethinking Linguistic Relativity* (pp. 97–114). Cambridge: Cambridge University Press.
Stockwell, R., Bowen, J.D. and Martin, J. (1965) *The Grammatical Structures of English and Spanish*. Chicago: University of Chicago Press.
Thomas, M. (2004) *Universal Grammar in Second Language Acquisition: A History*. London: Routledge.
Thomas, M. (2006) Robert Lado, 1915–1995. In K. Brown (ed.) *Encyclopedia of Language And Linguistics, Volume 6* (pp. 301–302). Amsterdam: Elsevier.
Thomason, S. and Kaufman, T. (1988) *Language Contact, Creolization, and Genetic Linguistics*. Berkeley: University of California Press.
Wardhaugh, R. (1970). The contrastive analysis hypothesis. *TESOL Quarterly* 4, 123–30.
Weinreich, U. (1953a) *Languages in Contact*. The Hague: Mouton.
Weinreich, U. (1953b) Review of *The Study of Language* by John Carroll. *Word* 9, 277–279.
Weinreich, U. (1963) The semantic structure of language. In J. Greenbaum (ed.) *Universals of Language* (pp. 142–216). Cambridge, MA: MIT Press.
Weiss, A. (1925) Language and psychology. *Language* 1, 52–57.
Whitney, W.D. (1881) On mixture in language. *Transactions of the American Philological Association* 12, 5–26.
Whitney, W.D. ([1881] 1971) On mixture in language. In M. Silverstein (ed.) *Whitney on Language* (pp. 170–191). Chicago: University of Chicago Press
Whorf, B.L. (1956) *Language, Thought, and Reality*, J. Carroll (ed.) Cambridge, MA: MIT Press.
Winford, D. (2003) *An Introduction to Contact Linguistics*. Oxford: Blackwell.

2 Transfer and the Relationships Between the Languages of Multi-Competence

Vivian Cook

This chapter treats transfer as one of the central relationships between languages in the second language (L2) user's mind, rather than as social interaction or language contact. It draws on developments in the multi-competence perspective since its first appearance in Cook (1991), in particular a paper entitled 'Is transfer the right word?', given at the IPRA conference in Budapest (Cook, 2000), which concluded 'Transfer is not enough as a term because it restricts L2 users to the position of cumulative monolinguals rather than seeing the richness of the L2 mind.' The present chapter elaborates and develops this theme, particularly in connection with the current interest in how L2 users think differently from monolinguals – bilingual cognition.

From Transfer and Interference to Crosslinguistic Influence

What distinguishes second language acquisition (SLA) research from other language disciplines is that it is concerned with the acquisition and use of language by people who already know one language. This may seem so obvious it doesn't need stating: it is a truism to say that second language research is about second languages.

Yet this axiom is effectively ignored every time we treat second language acquisition without reference to the first language (L1) already present in the person's mind. If SLA research pays no heed to the first language, deprived of its one unique element, L2 acquisition becomes a shadow projected from L1 acquisition. Ignoring the first language effectively dismisses it as irrelevant to SLA research, equivalent to studying how people with two legs manage to hop on one.

Some SLA research indeed treats the first language as an integral part of the picture. For example, the generative SLA researchers of the

1990s debated the relative importance of the first language grammar and Universal Grammar for the second language (L2) grammar through Full Access (Epstein et al., 1996), Full Transfer/Full Access (Schwartz & Sprouse, 1996) or Failed Functional Features (Hawkins & Chen, 1997) hypotheses, sometimes called the war of the hypotheses.

Nevertheless, the vast bulk of SLA research has undoubtedly minimised the role of the first language in second language acquisition, particularly in the 1970s when an influential faction saw transfer merely as a communication strategy, for example, Krashen (1982). One reason might be the belief that all L2 users are coordinate bilinguals, keeping the languages in separate compartments of the mind (Weinreich, 1953). The coordinate assumption has indeed been a commandment in language teaching since the 1880s, enforced by many educational systems, with the classroom effectively an L2 ghetto from which the L1 is excluded. The claim of coordination needs to be the outcome of research, not a presupposition: it now seems highly unlikely in view of the massive evidence for links between the languages in the mind, described in say Jarvis and Pavlenko (2009). A second reason might be the view that L2 users are all the same: L2 learning is L2 learning regardless of the pairs of languages involved, a universal process, so the L1 can be disregarded. Again this needs to be tested empirically rather than presupposed; recent thinking suggests that, at best, universality may apply to certain highly abstract areas of language such as structure dependency (Hauser et al., 2002).

In the 1950s, the relationship between the two languages was conceptualised as interference created by contact between two languages in one person (Weinreich, 1953): the forms of the first language influence the new forms being acquired in the second. Weinreich (1953: 8), for instance, talks of the Russian Subject Object Verb order yielding *I him see* in Russian learners of English. *Transfer* was a general term for this relationship: elements from the first language were transferred to the second, invisibly when they were the same as those in the second language (positive transfer), visibly when they were different (negative transfer). Much SLA research came down to investigating how the L2 was affected by the L1, leading to generations of theses on different pairs of languages as L1 and L2, originally concerned with syntax and phonology but now extending to areas such as spelling and gestures: Japanese learners, for example, transfer their Consonant Vowel syllable structure to English, generating the epenthetic vowels of *adavantage* and *dificulity*.

As the term *transfer* had so many associations with the scorned behaviourist theories of language acquisition, Kellerman and Sharwood-Smith put forward the more neutral alternative *crosslinguistic influence* (CLI) as 'the interplay between earlier and later acquired languages', which has indeed become the most established term (Kellerman & Sharwood-Smith, 1986).

The transfer relationship between the languages in the mind can, however, go in both directions. The Voice Onset Time (VOT) for the plosive consonant /t/ is longer for French speakers who know English than for French speakers who don't – in their first language (Flege, 2002); the meaning of the Japanese word bosu ('gang-leader') is different for Japanese people who speak English ('boss') than for those who don't – in Japanese (Tokumaru, 2002); English-speaking children learning heritage Cherokee over-regularise English past tense forms such as *taked* more than their monolingual contemporaries (Hirata-Edds, 2011). In other words, the L2 has discernible effects on the L1.

This 'reverse' transfer was indeed inherent in Weinreich's first formulation of interference – 'those instances of deviation from the norms of either language which occur in the speech of bilinguals as a result of their familiarity with more than one language' (Weinreich, 1953: 1). Yet until recently few people have taken this point on board (Cook, 2003); the research into L2 on L1 effects amounts to a tiny fraction of that into L1 on L2 effects. (One might speculate an unconscious motivation was that this could undermine the status of bilinguals as proper native speakers of their L1.)

Now, much research has gone beyond people who know second languages to the other languages that multilinguals may speak. A third language (L3) may be influenced by the L2 or by the L1; Kulundary and Gabriele (2012) found that the most influence on the acquisition of L3 English relative clauses by speakers of L1 Tuvan came from L2 Russian. Similarly, an L3 may influence an L2 or an L1: Wrembel (2011) has for instance shown that L3 VOTs are affected by both L1 and L2. And so on, up to the indefinite number of languages (Ln) a particular multilingual may know. The complexity of relationships dealt with in SLA research is ever increasing, leading to research questions about which languages have most influence on others, such as the Cumulative Enhancement Model which sees all previous language learning as contributing to L3/Ln learning (Flynn *et al.*, 2004).

A further crucial distinction made by Weinreich (1953) was between crosslinguistic influence during actual speech and as part of language knowledge; parole versus langue: 'In speech interference is like sand carried by a stream; in language it is the sedimented sand deposited on the bottom of a lake' (Weinreich, 1953: 11). This was restated in De Groot's definition as 'The influence of the non-selected language on the selected language in language use by bilinguals (and multilinguals) or the influence of an earlier acquired language (e.g. the L1) on the acquisition of a new language (e.g. L2)' (De Groot, 2010: 449), the first clause summing up use, the second acquisition. This distinction has not, however, been made in most research on crosslinguistic influence; it is absent from Odlin's definition: 'Transfer is the influence resulting from similarities and differences between the target language and any other language that has been previously (and perhaps imperfectly) acquired' (Odlin, 1989: 27), or indeed from Hu's: 'Transfer refers to how previous learning influences current and future learning' (Hu, 2013: 732).

SLA research thus usually refers to transfer as an influence on acquisition, not on the speech process, even if most research data are directly products of the speech or writing process, and only indirectly of learning. Perhaps the researchers no longer accept a distinction between speech and language knowledge or between langue and parole, seeing it as a version of Chomsky's competence and performance (Chomsky, 1965). Nevertheless, the logical default is surely that the relationships between languages that shape their systems in the mind are different from the relationships manifested in speech production: arguments need to be provided for the abolition of this learning/use distinction.

The key element in SLA research is the relationships between the languages in the mind. Transfer is one type of relationship, conceived in one particular way. The rest of this chapter will explore some issues with whether transfer is the central relationship between the languages in the L2 user's mind and with how other relationships can be taken into account.

Multi-competence and Transfer

The concept of multi-competence initially complemented the independent grammars assumption that learners create languages of their own, crystallised in the term 'interlanguage'. Rather than inefficiently imitating the target language, L2 learners create their own language out of the resources they have available to them, such as their learning strategies, the language provided by their teacher and indeed their first language (Selinker, 1972): they do not have a defective copy of the L2 in their minds so much as an interlanguage of their own making. An L2 learner thus possesses an L1 and an L2 interlanguage. But there was no overall term for the totality of [L1 + interlanguage] in their minds, only for its component elements, the L1 and the interlanguage. Multi-competence was proposed as a way of referring to the sum of these elements, initially defined as 'the compound state of a mind with two grammars' (Cook, 1991).

This definition has developed over the years into the current 'the overall system of a mind or a community that uses more than one language' (Cook, 2015), extending its scope to the community as well as the individual, and to any other languages that are known beyond the first, and talking more generally about the language system rather than the grammar. Multi-competence is not so much a theory or a model as a perspective, viewing second language acquisition from the L2 user's standpoint rather than from the native speaker's.

In a sense, the crucial point is what is left out of the definition of multi-competence – the native speaker. An L2 user has an independent language system of their own, not a combination of two monolingual states. In Grosjean's terms (Grosjean, 2008), it is a bilingual 'wholistic' interpretation of bilingualism as opposed to a monolingual 'fractional' interpretation. The proficiency, or lack of it, of the L2 user is defined in their own terms, not in terms of how successfully they mimic monolingual native speakers. Interesting comparisons can be made between L2 users and monolingual native speakers – both are after all examples of human language acquisition – just as it is interesting to compare apples and pears, but this is incidental rather than the core issue. What cannot be claimed is that L2 users are deficient compared to native speakers, since this assumes the native speaker to be the norm rather than the multi-competent speaker, any more than one can say that an apple is a rather inferior pear. Measuring the L2 user against the native speaker at best reveals the similarities and differences but not the unique qualities of the L2 user, any more than describing a pear in terms of an apple captures the unique essence of pears.

An important element in the multi-competence perspective described in Cook (2015) is thus the premise that 'multi-competence concerns the total system for all languages (L1, L2, Ln) in a single mind or community and their inter-relationship'. This asserts that all the languages in the individual mind or community form a whole system at some level. Since bilinguals do not have two heads, this is trivially true; the question is at what level, if any, does the whole system divide into two or more languages?

Multi-competence therefore emphasises the dynamic inter-relationship between the languages in the mind. To take some examples: if L2 users are shown pictures of objects named in one language, their eyes are attracted by objects that have similar names in the other (Spivey & Marian, 1999, 2003); producing cognates activates both phonological systems (Hermans *et al.*, 2011; Friesen & Jared, 2011). L2 users never switch off either language entirely; the word *coin* has different meanings in English and French, however, whichever language you are speaking, you cannot turn off the meaning in the other (Beauvillain & Grainger, 1987). The question of which language to use in speech is not a question of either/or but of more/less, whether conceived positively as activation of one language or negatively as deactivation of one language (Green, 1998).

Seeing the relationships between the languages in the mind as evolving in both the short and long terms brings multi-competence within the same compass as dynamic systems theory (DST). Here, the main characteristic of the system is that it is always in a state of flux, changing from minute to minute and day to day: any description is a single frame taken from a continuous movie, as described by De Bot (2015). This does not mean that it is impossible to describe, simply that its workings are always fluid and changeable; a snapshot is an arbitrary moment in time stolen from a continuous process.

Aronin and Singleton (2012: 59) have put forward the idea of Dominant Language Constellation (DLC): 'A complex of languages shared on a day-to-day basis by an entire community ...'. The relationships between the languages of multi-competence form an inner constellation of languages in active use, surrounded by a repertoire of other languages the person knows but does not currently use, surrounded in turn by languages the person is merely aware of to some degree. DLC presents a complex set of relationships between three or so main languages, another four or five minor languages and an indefinite number of peripheral languages. DLC is one useful way of looking at multilingualism from a multi-competence perspective.

Other Relationships in Multi-competence

The overall question which naturally arises for multi-competence is 'How do the relationships between the languages of multi-competence affect them?' Under the rubric of transfer/crosslinguistic influence, these relationships were defined in terms of direction – L1 affects L3, L2 affects L1 and L3, and so on – and in terms of positive and negative effects.

The metaphor involved in the term *transfer* creates a particular problem (Cook, 2000). The central dictionary meaning of *transfer* is 'To convey or take from one place, person, etc. to another' (OED, 2009). In other words, *transfer* means something moving from Point A to Point B, as reflected in the titles of articles such as 'Transfer to somewhere' (Andersen, 1983) and 'Transfer to nowhere' (Kellerman, 1995). The English verb *transfer* typically has four arguments, namely an Actor, an Object, a source location and a destination; *John transferred his account from the NatWest to Barclays*. The verb reifies three distinct objects – the source language, the destination language and the linguistic entity that is transferred – and one process – the act of transferring. (The analysis of the dictionary meanings of *transfer* is developed further in Dechert, 2006.)

So, when someone transfers language, they move some of the properties of one language to another. While the term *crosslinguistic influence* may substitute *influence* for *transfer*, it still accepts the same pair of L1 and L2 objects. But the transferred object does not actually move and leave a gap where it came from. The metaphor does not work literally – when you transfer your funds from one bank to another, you don't leave funds behind. Rather, some kind of copy is made and stored in the other language. In Odlin (1989), this is indeed used to distinguish the meaning of *transfer* in behaviourist psychology, where the original becomes extinct, from that in SLA research where the first language does not vanish – when it does, it is called *attrition*, not *transfer*, as we see below.

A further logical difficulty occurs when what is transferred is the lack of something in one language that exists in another. Chinese does not have articles and inflections; the effects of this on the learning of English by Chinese speakers are readily evident in sentences such as *I used to be cook in peking hotel* and *computer take the new life into our world*. To Weinreich, what is transferred is rarely just an item, a discrete object: 'a language is a system of oppositions' (Weinreich, 1953: 8): it is a structure or system. A lack of articles, for instance, can be transferred as part of a grammatical system, not as an individual object.

Let us now turn to relationships between the languages of multi-competence other than transfer, such as code switching and attrition. In codeswitching, the L2 user employs two languages in the same discourse, as in the advertising slogan for Stella Artois: *Into a chalice not a glass. C'est cidre not cider.* Code switching has been studied from many angles: what they have in common is the attempt to relate the two languages in the user's mind, whether through vocabulary *chalice/glass*, syntax *C'est cidre not cider*, or many other areas of language.

Code switching is important because it is unlike anything that a monolingual can do. Two languages combine together to produce one sentence; the relationship between the languages extends to every aspect. It is an extreme case of Grosjean's bilingual mode (Grosjean, 2008) in which the person has access to both languages simultaneously rather than the monolingual mode in which they have access to only one language, whether the first or the second. Code switching in itself shows the necessity for studying both languages in the L2 user's mind rather than the second language in isolation.

Attrition is defined as 'the non-pathological decrease in a language that had previously been acquired by an individual' (Kopke & Schmid, 2004: 5): parts of a language are 'lost' to the user, whether L1 or L2. L2 attrition is perhaps all too familiar to school language learners: school Latin becomes a dim memory apart from a few tags from Horace. Attrition has become a major field of research of its own, concentrating more on describing the complexity of factors that affect it rather than the over-riding importance of any single common factor (Seton & Schmid, 2015), the underlying cause being 'a lack of inhibitory control' between the two languages, i.e. a malfunction in the relationship between the languages.

The idea of transfer does not then include decline; taking something from A and putting it in B is different from something dying out. Multi-competence includes this possibility by insisting on a complex network of relationships between languages, among which transfer is only one. The attrition relationship of multi-competence allows language growth and decline in the network. Transfer, on the other hand, denotes a relationship between existing elements, not bringing a language into being or into non-existence.

So what is it that changes in first language attrition? We have seen that the transfer relationship goes in both directions and involves systems rather than items. Under pressure from the VOT in one language, the VOT in the other language changes; 'any of the languages in a multilingual system may change' (Opitz, 2013: 753). This is a change in the system, not a loss. But how far can such change go before it constitutes loss, before the person can no longer be said to command their first language or other attriting language?

Meanings of Language and Transfer

De Saussure once remarked, 'D'autres sciences opèrent sur des objets donnés d'avance et qu'on peut considérer ensuite à différents points de vue; dans notre domaine, rien de semblable' (De Saussure, 1915/1976: 23) (trans 1959: 8: 'Other sciences work with objects that are given in advance and that can then be considered from different viewpoints; but not linguistics.'). Everything in SLA research therefore depends upon what is meant by *language*, as argued in Cook (2010): *language* is not a primitive term given in advance. The *language* used in studying bilingual networks (Li Wei, 1994) is hardly the same as that in psycholinguistics research like Sebastián-Gallés and Bosch (2005), post-modern studies of discourse such as Block (2007), Vygotskyan studies such as Lantolf (2000) or procedural/declarative models like Ullmann (2001). The differences between generative-based multilingualism research (Cabrelli Amaro *et al.*, 2012) and usage-based theorists (Ellis, 2002) are irreconcilable because of their different understanding of language itself.

According to Chomsky, language is a derived notion – an epiphenomenon: 'The grammar in a person's mind/brain is real ... The language (whatever that may be) is not' (Chomsky, 1982: 5). To refer to something in the mind as *language* is a convenient shorthand label for whatever this mental representation consists of – rules, items, patterns or whatever. In this sense, *language* is a countable noun, so the mind might contain many languages. The word *language* is needed to be able to talk about first language, second language and so on. This does not establish these 'languages' as discrete components in the whole language system in the mind, where they may in fact be totally intertwined; it is a convenience in order to be able to distinguish subsystems within the whole. Claiming that existing 'language' A in the L2 user's mind has a crosslinguistic influence on emerging 'language' B or vice versa does not commit one to a belief that these language systems are countable objects in the mind.

In another sense, the word *language* labels an abstract system independent of the mind of the speaker, reflected in published grammars and dictionaries of English, not the individual mind. In this sense, a language belongs to Popper's third world of abstract ideas (Popper, 1972) or the linguistic realism of Katz and Postal (1991); it is language in an ideal form, which does not even require a community of speakers, as in 'dead' languages like Latin. This is the meaning of *language* that became associated in 18th-century Europe with ideas of national identity (Anderson, 1983); French is a proud possession of the French, German of the Germans. The notions of two languages in the mind and two languages in the world of ideas are radically different, yet both are covered by *language*. A person who speaks English and French does not possess the essentially unknowable abstractions of the English and French languages. Transferring something from English to French is not a matter of relating an item recorded on page 295 of someone's grammar of English to one on page 342 of someone's grammar of French, but rather of seeing how a node in one subsystem in the mind affects a node in another subsystem: the two meanings of *language* and the two processes are not commensurate.

Neither of these meanings, however, brings in the meaning of *language* as 'an instrument used by the members of the community to communicate with each other' (Labov, 1972: 277). Language is for interacting with other people, at the same time communicating information and building and maintaining social relationships with them, 'making sense of our experience, and acting out social relationships', the ideational and interpersonal metafunctions (Halliday & Mattheissen, 2013: 30). The relationship between two languages in this sense is then that the L2 user can carry out these functions with more than one community of speakers. Some of this communicative ability may be transferrable from one language to another, some may not; in Halliday's terms, unlike the native child, the L2 learner does not have to learn how to mean (Halliday, 1973).

It is clear that any theory of transfer has to specify just what aspect of 'language' is involved. Traditionally, transfer has been seen as the carrying over of mental elements of the language from one language to another. But this is not carrying over elements from one abstract language to another: it is fatal to assume that the English grammatical structures in the mind are the same as those in the English in the grammar book.

The relationships between mental languages in the mind of the L2 user are then difficult to pin down. Transfer is not taking an item from Language A and putting it in Language B, moving it from one pigeonhole in the mind to another. Attrition is not an item vanishing from Language A; code switching is not taking an item from Language A and putting it in Language B. Rather they are all aspects of an overall system in the mind.

Creating New Aspects of Cognition

So far we have seen the relationships between the languages in the mind as links between some kinds of mental entities, which increase or decrease in strength in diverse ways. This means that the entire relationship can be stated in terms of things that already exist; if we can fully describe what someone knows in the first language and in their other languages, we can see everything as interactions between them. Nothing new needs to be added as it is all describable somewhere within the existing overall system. In a sense, transfer is not about the acquisition of new knowledge or behaviour, i.e. learning, but about the rejigging of existing knowledge or behaviour into new configurations. It is a partial explanation of second language acquisition and use because it cannot account for the acquisition of new information or for the loss of old information, or as we see below, for the unique state of L2 users unrelated to L1 or L2.

What does this mean for the increasingly important area of bilingual cognition – how people who know more than one language think? A test case can be how people see colours, a topic pioneered in SLA research by Athanasopoulos (2009). In Bassetti and Cook (2011) four possible scenarios for L2 users are spelt out, as illustrated in Figure 2.1. Suppose that we are dealing with monolingual native speakers of a language that recognises two distinct colours, for example Greek *ble*, in English a light Cambridge blue, and *ghalazio*, in English a dark Oxford blue (Athanasopoulos, 2009). What happens when they acquire a language with a single colour spanning both their colours, like English *blue*?

(i) **The one-concept scenario.** In this, people do not think differently when they learn another language; the same concept is used across

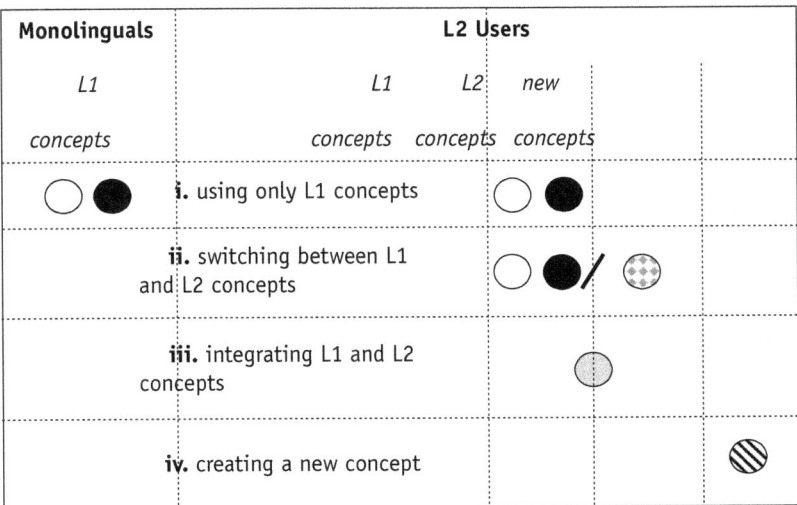

Figure 2.1 Concepts in L2 users

languages regardless of which they are speaking: the original, L1-related concept is used in both languages. So a Greek person who has learnt English will still think in terms of two colours equivalent to *ble* and *ghalazio* even when using the English word *blue*.

(ii) **The double-concepts scenario.** In this, L2 users switch concept according to the language they are speaking, using L1-related concepts when speaking the first language, L2-related concepts when using the second. Their minds hold two sets of concepts, which come into play when required. So the Greek/English speaker will think in terms of two blues when using Greek but one blue when speaking English.

(iii) **The one-integrated-concept scenario.** Here the speakers adopt a single concept that integrates the L1-related concept and the L2-related concepts. Their thinking differs from monolingual native speakers of both languages. So the Greek/English speaker will have neither the two Greek blues nor the single English blue but a colour that is a compromise between the two.

(iv) **The original-concept scenario.** The final logical possibility is that L2 users devise a new concept that is not so much intermediate between the L1-related and L2 concepts as something different. The Greek/English speaker will not think of blue in terms of the dark/light difference, say, but might have a blue that is characteristic of neither first language. Indeed, the Greek-English L2 users have a concept of 'ghalazio' ('light blue') that is lighter than Greek monolinguals (Athanasopoulos, 2009).

These four scenarios portray four different outcomes to the relationship between L1 and L2 concepts. In (i) the user is unaffected by the L2 concepts, in (ii) the user switches between the L1 and the L2 concepts and in (iii) the L1 and the L2 concepts are merged so that the L2 user does not think like an L1 user whichever language is used. All of these are indeed statable in terms of the relationship between the existing concepts in the mind, so we can talk of transferring a concept, of losing a concept and switching between concepts.

Scenario (iv) however is different: something is created that is not predictable from the relationships between L1 and L2: something new has come into being. The interesting problem for SLA research is describing things that cannot be anticipated from the given, the cases when $2 + 2 = 5$. We have seen that measuring the L2 by the L1 of monolinguals gives an unfair result; we now see that accounting for the joined L1 and L2 of the L2 user in terms of the combined L1 and L2 is also inadequate as the unique constructs of the L2 user elude an analysis built only on the L1 and L2; comparison is not enough.

Conclusions

This chapter has tried to explore different issues in incorporating transfer within the multi-competence perspective. It has succeeded mostly in raising difficulties with the typical use of transfer as a relationship in which something in one language affects something in another. Transfer needs to be seen as more than a one-way relationship between the first and second language and instead as consisting of multiple directional relationships between multiple languages. It also means seeing transfer as one among several relationships between the languages of multi-competence, such as attrition and codeswitching. Additionally, it concerns the very nature of language as a reality in the L2 user's mind. Crucially, the study of the relationships between the languages of multi-competence involves seeing how the state of multi-competence is not the same as two monolinguals combined but something of its own, not statable solely in terms of the thinking or language of monolinguals.

References

Andersen, R. (1983) Transfer to somewhere. In S. Gass and L. Selinker (eds) *Language Transfer in Language Learning* (pp. 177–201). Rowley, Mass: Newbury House.

Anderson, B. (1983) *Imagined Communities.* New York: Verso.

Aronin, L. and Singleton, D. (2012) *Multilingualism.* Amsterdam: John Benjamins.

Athanasopoulos, P. (2009) Cognitive representation of colour in bilinguals. *Bilingualism, Language and Cognition* 12 (1), 83–95.

Bassetti, B. and Cook, V. (2011) *Language and Cognition.* The second language user. In V. J. Cook and B. Bassetti (eds.) *Language and Bilingual Cognition* (pp. 143–190). Oxford: Psychology Press.

Beauvillain, C. and Grainger, J. (1987) Accessing interlexical homographs: Some limitations of a language-selective access. *Journal of Memory and Language* 26, 658–672.

Block, D. (2007) *Second Language Identities.* London: Continuum.

Cabrelli Amaro, J., Flynn, S. and Rothman, J. (eds) (2012) *Third Language Acquisition in Adulthood.* Amsterdam: John Benjamins.

Chomsky, N. (1965) *Aspects of the Theory of Syntax.* Cambridge, MA: MIT Press.

Chomsky, N. (1982) *Some Concepts and Consequences of the Theory of Government and Binding.* Cambridge, MA: MIT Press.

Cook, V.J. (1991) The poverty-of-the-stimulus argument and multi-competence. *Second Language Research* 7 (2), 103–17.

Cook, V.J. (2000) Is transfer the right word? Unpublished paper given at IPRA 2000 in Budapest, available at http://homepage.ntlworld.com/vivian.c/Writings/Papers/Transfer2000.htm.

Cook, V.J. (ed.) (2003) *Effects of the L2 on the L1.* Clevedon: Multilingual Matters.

Cook, V.J. (2010) Prolegomena to second language learning. In P. Seedhouse, S. Walsh and C. Jenks (eds) *Conceptualising Language Learning* (pp. 6–22). Basingstoke: Palgrave MacMillan.

Cook, V.J. (2015) Premises of multi-competence. In V.J. Cook and Li Wei (eds) *The Cambridge Handbook of Linguistic Multi-competence.* Cambridge: Cambridge University Press.

De Bot, K. (2015) Multi-competence and dynamic/complex systems. In V.J. Cook and Li Wei (eds) *The Cambridge Handbook of Linguistic Multi-competence*. Cambridge: Cambridge University Press.

De Groot, A. (2010) *Language and Cognition in Bilinguals and Multilinguals*. Hove: Psychology Press.

De Saussure, F. (1915/1976) *Cours de Linguistique Générale*, edited by Bally, C., Sechehaye, A. and Reidlinger, A. Reprinted (1976) Paris: Payot. Translation by W. Baskin (1959) *Course in General Linguistics*. London: Peter Owen.

Dechert, H.W. (2006) On the ambiguity of the notion 'transfer'. In J. Arabski (ed.) *Cross-Linguistic Influences in the Second Language Lexicon* (pp. 3–11). Clevedon: Multilingual Matters.

Ellis, N.C. (2002) Frequency effects in language processing – a review with implications for theories of implicit and explicit language acquisition. *Studies in Second Language Acquisition* 24, 143–188.

Epstein, S.D., Flynn, S. and Martahardjono, G. (1996) Second language acquisition: Theoretical and experimental issues in contemporary research. *Brain and Behavioral Sciences* 19 (4), 746–752.

Flege, J.E. (2002) Interactions between the native and second language phonetic systems. In P. Burmeister, T. Piske and A. Rohde (eds) *An Integrated View of Language Development* (pp. 217–244). Trier: Wissenschaftliche Verlag.

Flynn, S., Foley, C. and Vinnitskaya, I. (2004) The Cumulative-Enhancement Model for language acquisition: Comparing adults' and children's patterns of development in first, second and third language acquisition of relative clauses. *International Journal of Multilingualism* 1 (1), 3–16.

Friesen, D.C. and Jared, D. (2011) Cross-language phonological activation of meaning: Evidence from category verification. *Bilingualism: Language and Cognition* 15 (1), 145–156.

Green, D.W. (1998) Mental control of the bilingual lexico-semantic system. *Bilingualism: Language and Cognition* 1, 77–82.

Grosjean, F. (2008) *Studying Bilinguals*. Oxford: Oxford University Press.

Halliday, M.A.K. (1975) *Learning how to Mean*. London: Edward Arnold.

Halliday, M.A.K. and Mattheissen, C. (2013) *An Introduction to Functional Grammar* (4th edn) London: Hodder Educational.

Hauser, M.D., Chomsky, N. and Fitch, T.M. (2002) The faculty of language: what is it, who has it and how did it evolve. *Science* 298, 1569–1579.

Hawkins, R. and Chen, C. (1997) The partial availability of Universal Grammar in second language acquisition: The 'failed functional features' hypothesis. *Second Language Research* 13 (3), 187–226.

Hermans, D., Ormel, E., van Besselaar, R. and van Hell, J. (2011) Lexical activation in bilinguals' speech production is dynamic: How language ambiguous words can affect cross-language activation. *Language and Cognitive Processes*, DOI:10.1080/01690965.2010.530411.

Hirata-Edds, T. (2011) Influence of second language Cherokee immersion on children's development of past tense in their first language, English. *Language Learning* 61 (3), 700–733.

Hu, A. (2013) Transfer. In M. Byram and A. Hu (eds) *The Routledge Encyclopedia of Language Teaching and Learning* (pp. 732–734). Abingdon: Routledge.

Jarvis, S. and Pavlenko, A. (2009) *Crosslinguistic Influence in Language and Cognition*. Abingdon: Routledge.

Katz, J.J. and Postal, P.M. (1991) Realism vs. Conceptualism in linguistics. *Linguistics and Philosophy* 14 (5), 515–554.

Kellerman, E. (1995) Crosslinguistic influence: Transfer to nowhere. In W. Grabe (ed.) *Annual Review of Applied Linguistics* 15, 125–150.
Kellerman, E. and Sharwood-Smith, M. (eds) (1986) *Crosslinguistic Influence and Second Language Acquisition*. Oxford: Pergamon Press.
Kopke, B. and Schmid, M. (2004) Language attrition: The next phase. In M. Schmid, B. Kopke, M. Keijzer and L. Weilemar (eds) *First Language Attrition* (pp. 1–43). Amsterdam: John Benjamins.
Krashen, S. (1982) *Principles and Practice in Second Language Acquisition*. Oxford: Pergamon Press.
Kulundary, V. and Gabriele, A. (2012) Examining the role of L2 syntactic development in L3 acquisition: a look at relative clauses. In J. Cabrelli Amaro, S. Flynn and J. Rothman (eds) (2012) *Third Language Acquisition in Adulthood* (pp. 1–6). Philadelphia/Amsterdam: John Benjamins.
Labov, W. (1972) *Sociolinguistic Patterns*. University of Pennsylvania Press.
Lantolf, J. (ed.) (2000) *Sociocultural Theory and Second Language Learning*. Oxford: Oxford University Press.
Li Wei (1994) *Three Generations, Two Languages, One Family: Language Choice and Language Shift in a Chinese Community in Britain*. Clevedon: Multilingual Matters.
Odlin, T. (1989) *Language Transfer: Cross-Linguistic Influence in Language Learning*. Cambridge: University Press.
Oxford English Dictionary (2009) Oxford: Oxford University Press, online at http://www.oed.com/
Opitz, C. (2013) A dynamic perspective on late bilinguals' linguistic development in an L2 environment. *International Journal of Bilingualism* 17 (6), 701–715.
Popper, K.R. (1972) *Objective Knowledge*. Oxford: Clarendon Press.
Schwartz, B. and Sprouse, R. (1996) L2 cognitive states and the Full Transfer/Full Access model. *Second Language Research* 12 (1), 40–72.
Sebastián-Gallés, N. and Bosch, L. (2005) Phonology and bilingualism. In J.F. Kroll and A.M.B. de Groot (eds) *Handbook of Bilingualism: Psycholinguistic Approaches* (pp. 68–87). Oxford: Oxford University Press.
Selinker, L. (1972) Interlanguage. *International Review of Applied Linguistics* X, 3, 209–231.
Seton, B. and Schmid, M. (2015) Multi-competence and first language attrition. In V.J. Cook and Li Wei (eds) *The Cambridge Handbook of Linguistic Multi-competence*. Cambridge: Cambridge University Press.
Spivey, M.J. and Marian, V. (1999) Cross talk between native and second languages: partial activation of an irrelevant lexicon. *Psychological Science* 10, 181–84.
Spivey, M.J. and Marian, V. (2003) Competing activation in bilingual language processing: Within- and between-language competition. *Bilingualism: Language and Cognition* 6 (2), 97–115.
Tokumaru, Y. (2002) Cross-linguistic influences of L2 English on L1 Japanese in Japanese-English bilinguals. *ACTAS/Proceedings II Simposio Internacional Bilingüismo*, 399–406.
Ullman, M. (2001) The neural basis of lexicon and grammar in first and second language: the declarative/procedural model. *Bilingualism: Language and Cognition* 4 (1), 105–122.
Weinreich, U. (1953) *Languages in Contact*. The Hague: Mouton.
Wrembel, M. (2011) Crosslinguistic influences in third language acquisition of Voice Onset Time. *ICPhS* XVII, 2157–2160.

3 Comprehension, Learning and Production of Foreign Languages: The Role of Transfer

Håkan Ringbom

Differences Between Comprehension and Production

A main difference between L2 comprehension and L2 production concerns the difference between data-driven and self-activated mechanisms. Comprehension and production are modes of use relying on different retrieval procedures. Comprehension starts out from an input: an utterance with linguistic form to which the learner assigns a meaning. In production, on the other hand, the starting point is a pre-verbal intention to which various phonological and grammatical procedures are applied. There is, however, constant interaction between comprehension and production, and the learning aspect further complicates distinguishing between the processes, as communication and learning processes also interact; they 'operate at different levels of consciousness. If the wish to communicate is in focus ... there may be a process of learning taking place simultaneously' (Faerch *et al.*, 1984: 186). However, relating an item to prior knowledge in comprehension does not automatically involve a change in competence (receptive learning). One difference between comprehension and production concerns their relationship to learning. Comprehension must have taken place before learning occurs, and at least some comprehension must occur before production (cf. Clark, 1993). When learning has occurred, the new information can be used for production. The consequence of this chronology is that comprehension, which has been much less studied than production, should be given more attention in research. Only when a sufficiently good picture of the processes underlying comprehension has been achieved, the development of the learning processes can be understood. Second language research has mainly focused on the production processes and in doing so has neglected the study of comprehension. The term learning has also been applied to both receptive and productive aspects of language proficiency, but then the differences between the mechanisms of comprehension and production as well as the lack of symmetry between comprehension and production are ignored (see Clark, 1993; Clark & Hecht, 1983).

There are certain corollaries that follow from the differences between comprehension and production which need to be considered before the role of transfer is discussed. A general difference concerns the approximate nature of all comprehension. But even if comprehension is only approximate, communication, aided by linguistic and situational context, may still work: it is not necessary to understand every detail and shade of meaning of a message in order to understand its general content. For production, on the other hand, definite sentence plans for the message are required. Production places much greater demands on specificity and accuracy than comprehension.

While linguistic accuracy is important for production, it is less so for comprehension. If, for example, inflectional affixes or function words are left unnoticed or unanalysed, a text may still be at least approximately understood. The concept of redundancy existing in language thus has a different role for L2 comprehension, compared with L2 production. A target language (TL) may, for instance, have grammatical categories such as articles and prepositions which do not exist in the learner's L1, and this will easily lead learners at the initial stages to unconsciously regard such words as redundant. Thus, learners having an L1 without articles have been found to omit articles in their L2 production much more than learners with an L1 where there are articles (see e.g. Ringbom, 2007: 69; Sajavaara, 1983: 78). The same is true about inflectional affixes and prepositions. Learners seem to impose their native standards of efficiency on their production: elements perceived as redundant on the basis of prior linguistic knowledge are frequently omitted. In the L2, comprehension redundancies do not seem to have any major influence.

In production, to what extent are the underlying linguistic structures new or merely modified on the basis of perceived similarities? The use of the potential knowledge of cognates that a learner has of a related target language is easily accessible, as it only needs to be tagged 'OK for L2 as well, perhaps slightly modified.' (Sharwood Smith, 1986: 248). L1 procedures need to be only slightly modified for retrieving a word which is both phonologically and semantically similar, and the process is facilitated by their being automatised. For L2 comprehension, the learner has established links between new information (items) and prior knowledge on the basis of perceived similarities. For production, the direction of these linkings has been reversed, as a process of learning has first taken place in that a new or modified item has been stored in the brain.

What are the underlying processes for comprehending an L2 text? The main requirement is to have a sufficient knowledge of the vocabulary of the language. Apart from relying on context, the learner can avail of different cues to infer the meaning of unfamiliar words. Comprehension relies on three types of information: input (linguistic and other communicative), context (linguistic and situational), which will often prevent erroneous interpretation of items, and knowledge. Knowledge is linguistic knowledge, which comprises both declarative knowledge, 'knowledge that', where processing is slow and under attentional control, and procedural knowledge, 'knowledge how', where processing is faster and often automatised. Declarative knowledge develops suddenly, from being told, whereas procedural knowledge is acquired only gradually. The asymmetry normally existing between comprehension and production (you can understand much more than you can produce) is affected by both crosslinguistic distance and the amount of linguistic input. When learning a totally unrelated language only in a classroom setting where there is limited linguistic input, this asymmetry likely does not exist.

Some words are more easily inferred than others, and apart from crosslinguistic similarity of the word or parts of it, there are other inherent factors in the word itself affecting the relative ease or difficulty of comprehension. Such factors are the length of the word, the degree of abstractness or concreteness, prototypicality and the compatibility between the sound and meaning patterns of the word (see Laufer, e.g. 1997). There is, however, considerable variation among learners even within the same L1 background on how easily and naturally they can make relevant associations.

Some previous studies (Bergh, 1986; Kolers, 1966) have found that there is more interdependence, that is, mutual dependence between L1 and L2 in comprehension than in production. The consequence of this is that there is more transfer, more use of crosslinguistic similarities in L2 comprehension than in L2 production.

Related versus Unrelated Languages: The Importance of Formal Similarities

Ability to produce an L2 presupposes some previous mastery of the underlying systems of phonology, grammar and lexis, while ability to comprehend does so to a much more limited extent. However, if the target language (TL) and the L1 are closely related, some basis for at least minimal comprehension already exists before learning has started. The importance of formal similarities is basic here. Even at the earliest stages of learning, formal similarities between words can be perceived, and this facilitates comprehension.

The natural thing for a learner to do is to try to connect the new information of a foreign language text with prior knowledge in order to make sense of it. Prior knowledge in this case means the language(s) already mastered, and it generates expectations which guide language processing. We try to associate new elements with the linguistic elements, items and structures already stored in our mind. Existing knowledge structures are more easily activated by the linguistic cues of incoming data if similarities between the items can be perceived by the learner. Vocabulary knowledge is of crucial importance for comprehension of written texts. L1 words perceived to be similar are activated, while this does not normally happen with grammatical structures, at least not consciously. The learner's expectation is that the words of a new language are different from the languages already known, but until there is information to the contrary, the system of this new language is expected to work more or less in the same way as the L1 or some other known language (cf. Odlin, 1989: 142). This assumption will, of course, have to be modified when learning progresses and a more comprehensive knowledge about the new language is achieved, but at the beginning it is natural to try to establish one-to-one translation equivalences between items in order to arrive at some approximate comprehension of a text. If some formal similarity to L1 items can be perceived, i.e. if the L2 items are transparent for the learner, it is a great help in establishing crosslinguistic equivalences. L2 learners at the early stages of learning therefore try to establish crosslinguistic links between items, providing a bridge between input and prior knowledge. Initially, comprehension of a word normally means that a new TL item can be matched with an existing L1 item. It is natural for a learner to assume that if a word in another language is formally similar to an L1 word, it will also have an identical, or at least a similar meaning. However, equivalence between items may be difficult to perceive without an existing underlying equivalence between linguistic categories. Such equivalences normally exist across closely related languages. As the process of production is reversed compared with comprehension, crosslinguistic formal similarities do not have the same significance for production as they have for comprehension.

Learners of a related language, a language perceived to have useful similarities to the L1, have a smaller learning burden than learners of a distant language. There is simply less that they need to learn.

Listening versus Reading

There are some differences between listening and reading. In listening, the importance of formal similarity may not be as strong. The potential lexical knowledge a learner has is of less direct use to listening than to reading because of the more holistic approach required for listening, where the situational context with gestures and tone of voice plays an essential part. In listening, the use of transfer is transfer of L1-procedures rather than transfer of L1 items. The subskill of vocabulary recognition is, of course, useful in listening, but it is not as useful as in L2 reading where a long way can be gotten by relying on lexical knowledge only. Comprehension of spoken items requires a quick application of cognitive flexibility and automatisation of subskills, while in the written modality, cognitive speed is a lesser issue and learners have more time to apply their knowledge-based resources and engage in 'linguistisches Probabilitätskalkûl' (Berthele, 2008: 92; Vanhove, 2014: 99; cf. Reves & Levine, 1988). In comprehension, information of different kinds (form and frequency) and from different languages can more efficiently be integrated when guessing the meaning of written cognates (Vanhove, 2014).

Perceived and Assumed Similarity

An important distinction in transfer research is that of the difference between perceived and assumed similarity. In comprehension, similarities are perceived on the basis of formal linkings between L2 and L1, while in production similarities are merely assumed, though they may be based on previously perceived similarities in comprehension. The degree of perceived similarities varies depending on psychotypology. In comprehension of unrelated languages learners can perceive few formal similarities between items. Such an absence of positive transfer often leads to an erroneous assumption of semantic and pragmatic (i.e. non-formal) similarities, which are normally only assumed, not perceived. The tendency to assume non-formal crosslinguistic similarities can be seen in learners producing typologically distant languages: there is covert crosslinguistic influence meaning that the learner has not been able to perceive crosslinguistic similarities, but assumes that such similarities, lexical and grammatical, exist. The relative lack of formal similarities facilitating bottom-up processes means that learners of distant languages have to rely too much on assumed similarities, i.e. top-down processes, which is not very different from guessing (cf. Haastrup, 1991: 342). While the process of transfer is neutral, i.e. neither positive nor negative, the result of transfer can be either positive or negative. What lies behind negative transfer is the absence of relevant concrete positive transfer. This leads to erroneous assumptions of crosslinguistic similarities. Positive transfer can then be described as 'the application of at least partially correct perceptions or assumptions of crosslinguistic similarity'. Transfer as a communication process is more complicated in production than in comprehension in that procedural knowledge, not only declarative knowledge, is more in the foreground for production, while declarative knowledge can take the learner a long way in comprehension, especially reading comprehension. Together with a facilitating context, declarative lexical knowledge helps at least approximate comprehension. Lexical crosslinguistic similarity facilitates the learner in linking words to other, formally similar words. This process facilitates comprehension, but it does not work in exactly the same way for learning or production. Context is essential for the process of comprehension, which precedes learning, but not so much for the learning process itself. The result of (repeated use of) transfer in comprehension is transfer in learning.

When it comes to the difference between learning related versus unrelated languages, a main difference is that the learner of a related language perceives crosslinguistic similarities, while the learner of an unrelated language, who can establish few or no crosslinguistic links, merely assumes them. If there is formal crosslinguistic similarity, when the form of a target language word can be linked to an equivalent L1 word relatively easily, it is natural to assume semantic/functional similarity as well. Syntactic congruence also has a key role. Across related languages, L1 procedures work reasonably well for comprehension and the main task for the learner is to acquire a sufficiently large vocabulary of high-frequency words in order to make sense of a simple L2 text. As long as the two grammatical systems are basically congruent, the learner can approach the reading comprehension task primarily by making out the meaning of words, without having to worry about their syntactic relationships (see Swain, 1985). If, on the other hand, the target language has grammatical categories that are absent in the L1, learners have to have acquired some knowledge of their functions for satisfactory comprehension to occur. This process of acquiring a basic receptive competence takes time and effort, which the learner of a related language does not have to spend.

Crosslinguistic similarities, formal and functional, can be perceived at the phonological, grammatical or lexical levels. Vocabulary is the area where transfer is most easily detectable, while the study of grammatical transfer requires intricate research designs (Falk & Bardel, 2010). Formal crosslinguistic similarity of a word is especially relevant at the earliest stages of learning, when the learner has little else to rely on than his prior knowledge of L1 or other languages. How easily words can be matched with existing L1 words largely determines the relative ease or difficulty of L2 comprehension.

Learning for Comprehension versus Learning for Production: Items and Systems

Cruttenden (1981) was the first to make the distinction between item learning and system learning, relating it to L1 acquisition. Before systems can be learnt, a number of items have to be known. In the SLA context, L2 items are linked to already known items in the L1: a one-to-one relationship is established. Items are not only words, lexical items, they can just as well be phonemes, morphemes, syntactic units or phrases. Initially, learning takes place on an item-by-item basis in all areas of language: phonological, morphological, syntactic, lexical and phraseological. In the closed systems of phonology and morphology, the learner does not normally dwell very long at the stage of item learning, at least not if he can fall back on some kind of reference frame. In the open system of lexis, on the other hand, both item learning and system learning are important throughout: learning both new words and the complex ways in which old and new items are linked to other items provides a challenge at all stages of learning.

We can distinguish four different types of learning: (1) item learning for comprehension; (2a) item learning for production; (2b) system learning for comprehension; and (3) system learning for production. Item learning for comprehension is the starting point, while item learning for production and system learning for comprehension follow. The reason for labelling the stages (2a) and (2b) rather than (2) and (3) is that they normally develop in parallel, not successively, though learners may primarily pay more attention to either of them, depending on the aims, the learning situation, individual learner characteristics and other variables.

The starting point for learners is item learning for comprehension. The existence or absence of crosslinguistic similarities lies behind the difference in task magnitude between learning a related language and learning an unrelated one. Learners who can make use of positive transfer to facilitate learning can free many cognitive resources for other aspects of receptive learning (cf. Odlin, 2003: 441).

System learning for comprehension means that oversimplified one-to-one relationships are gradually modified. There is a development from partial towards precise understanding and the learner gradually expands the lexical network by learning more about the different sense relations a word has to other words (cf. Henriksen, 1999; Henriksen & Haastrup, 1998). In system learning, the crosslinguistic similarities are functional or semantic, while formal similarity plays a subordinate role, if any.

In item learning for production, errors are more likely to occur than in comprehension, partly because of the absence of a context in production that would rule out the wrong interpretations that formal similarities can induce. The conversion of receptive knowledge into productive knowledge is still not very well understood.

The final learning stage is system learning for production, where pragmatic aspects also enter the picture. Here, learners gradually learn to make use of the many different linguistic means for expressing similar meanings, thus expanding their lexical network. Known words are used in new senses, collocational restrictions are considered and links to other words are established. As learning progresses towards advanced proficiency, crosslinguistic similarity loses importance at the same time as intra-lingual similarity becomes more important. This corresponds to what studies of the organisation of the mental lexicon have found: that as learning progresses, learners rely less on phonological similarity and more and more on semantic similarity (Kroll & De Groot, 1997; Ringbom & Jarvis, 2009: 114; Singleton, 1994, 1999).

L1 Transfer versus Lateral Transfer

Transfer, or crosslinguistic influence, can occur not only between L1 and the TL, but also between two non-native languages (lateral transfer). Lexis is the area where lateral transfer is most clearly seen. Interaction between source languages may also occur, but it is difficult to investigate. In principle, the same processes are applied in lateral transfer as in L1 transfer, but there are also some differences. In production, phonological transfer is of less importance where two non-native languages are concerned. The reason is probably the same as for pragmatic CLI: the sounds as well as the pragmatic aspects of the L1 are too deeply integrated in the mind to be easily modified, though a good non-native proficiency may also provide a useful basis. Formal crosslinguistic item similarities can, however, be established between the TL and LN, at least if the LN is closely related to the TL, but the activation of an LN is generally not as automatised and natural. In vocabulary, the associative network involving individual items has not as wide a coverage in a non-native language as it has in the L1. Especially in comprehension, superficial formal similarities between the TL and the LN may lead learners astray as they may not be able to make as efficient use of the contextual constraints and the underlying linguistic structures. The grammatical system of an LN is apparently not as easily accessible for modification as the L1 system. This can be seen from there being relatively little clear evidence of lateral grammatical transfer. The role of background languages in L3 acquisition has been the subject of recent investigations by e.g. De Angelis (2007), Hammarberg (2009) and Lindqvist (2010).

Item Transfer and Procedural (system) Transfer: Lateral Transfer in Comprehension

Transfer has many different shapes (see the discussion in Jarvis & Pavlenko, 2008: 20 ff.) and if a reasonably full treatment is attempted, it should be concerned with at least psychotypology, the distinction between similarity of form and similarity of function/meaning, the difference between items and systems and the different modes of comprehension and production.

Transfer in comprehension is overt transfer, where similarities have been perceived between L2-input and existing L1-knowledge, which is potential L2-knowledge. It thus occurs primarily across related languages. The greater the crosslinguistic distance between L1 and the TL, the less (positive) transfer there is in comprehension, as there are much fewer crosslinguistic similarities to be perceived.

A distinction between item transfer and procedural transfer (system transfer) needs to be made. Items in item transfer are not only words, they can just as well be phonemes, morphemes, syntactic units or phrases. Item transfer is based on a crosslinguistic one-to-one relationship. Simplified linguistic one-to-one correspondences between items are established at the early stages of learning to reduce the learner's workload. In comprehension, item transfer is basic, while it has been more difficult to point out concrete instances of system transfer. If there is both (positive) transfer of form and (positive) transfer of meaning, comprehension and learning will be facilitated, as Laufer has shown (1997). The extent to which the learners' assumptions that L1 procedures actually work for L2 comprehension determines whether the effect is positive or negative. When L1 procedures are used to fill gaps in L2 competence, communication errors are often the result, but across closely related languages L1 procedures are generally appropriate and tend to work well for comprehension.

In procedural transfer, abstract principles of organising information are transferred. Since these principles are often the same, or at least very similar, across closely related languages, communication generally works here, but more easily and naturally if the source language is L1 than if it is a non-native language. Whether advanced learners or near-native speakers can profit as much from the crosslinguistic similarities as native speakers needs to be investigated further, although results from previous studies seem to indicate that at least in production, native proficiency helps more than merely native-like proficiency.

In production, a language the learner knows only superficially is not normally involved in procedural transfer, although assumed item similarities often cause negative lexical item transfer. The title of Selinker and Baumgartner-Cohen's paper (1995) is illustrative: 'Multiple language acquisition: "Damn it, why can't I keep these two languages apart?"' But this paper is only concerned with item transfer at the lexical level (a roughly corresponding term used by Corder (1983) being borrowing). Apparently, grammatical rules and semantic properties must be well internalised, perhaps even fully automatised, before they can be successfully transferred in production. Thus, L2 proficiency, together with the psychotypology of the different languages involved, plays an important role in the use of lateral transfer. Lateral transfer has been studied primarily in production, but a question that should be asked is: What happens in comprehension, as comprehension precedes production?

One way of studying transfer in comprehension is to give learners a text in a totally unfamiliar language and ask them to make sense of both the text and individual words and to provide comments on their strategies (see e.g. Gibson & Hufeisen, 2003; Vanhove, 2014). Learners with a totally unrelated L1 will not normally understand much of such a text. The greater the crosslinguistic distance is, the less (positive) transfer there is in comprehension. However, learners often know another non-native language, which may be closer to the TL than their L1. To what extent this knowledge is useful for the learner also depends on how good a proficiency he has in L2 and L3. A large number of studies have found that previous knowledge of English (or French) influences the learning of French (or English) more than the learners' African or Asian L1. (See e.g. the surveys by Cenoz, 2001 and Ringbom, 2007: 78.) Formal similarities between L2 items and L3 items can be perceived even at early stages of learning, but as the associative lexical network in non-native languages is not as well developed as in native speakers, it is apparently harder to make crosslinguistic connections. L2 words have a smaller number of shared associates with L3 words than would be the case with an L1 lexicon (cf. Meara, 1996). Lateral transfer tends to be not procedural transfer, but lexical item transfer, which is triggered by formal similarity. If formal similarities cannot be established, the role of context comes more into the fore in the process of comprehension. There may thus be differences between native and non-native speakers in understanding words within a text versus understanding L3 words in isolation. For comprehension of words given without a full supporting context, the native speaker may be able to access unconscious knowledge which a non-native speaker cannot generally make use of, at least not to the same extent. As for context, on the other hand, there may well be non-native speakers who, relying on context, are just as good as native speakers in making sense of at least part of a text. A reasonable hypothesis could be that native speakers will be much better than non-natives at comprehending words in isolation, but that if the same words occur in a text, the differences may not be as great.

Prototypicality

One feature relevant for transfer research is prototypicality. Kellerman's comment is that 'the less representative of the prototypical meaning a usage of a given form is, the lower its transferability' (Kellerman, 1987, quoted in De Angelis, 2007: 23). This concept refers to L2 users' perceptions concerning the degree to which a structure or meaning is prototypical (central, typical, universal, core meaning) versus aprototypical (noncentral, atypical, language-specific, peripheral meaning). Prototypicality has not been investigated much in transfer research, but Kellerman (e.g. 1978) and Ijaz (1986) are relevant here. Their research has focused on L2 production, but the concept may well be applied to L2 comprehension as well, especially if it is combined with formal similarity. If an L2 item encountered is perceived to be functionally/ semantically equivalent to a formally similar L1 item which in this particular situation has a core or prototypical meaning, this probably facilitates comprehension and also, at a later stage, learning. This point is also made by Jarvis for production: 'Learners' assumptions concerning which L1 and L2 words are translation equivalents are generally based on which L1 and L2 words have the closest central meanings, regardless of their peripheral meanings and semantic ranges' (1997: 344; cf. Jarvis & Pavlenko 2008: 186 ff.).

English and Estonian as Target Languages in Finland

My discussion of transfer so far is largely based on the results of a long-term project investigating differences between Finns and Swedish-speaking Finns in the learning of English (Ringbom, 1987, 1992, 2007). Studies of second language acquisition in Finland have generally had English as their target language, sometimes also some other Indo-European language (Swedish, German or French). Researchers investigating Fenno-Ugric languages have constantly faced a situation where the literature concerning language learning and teaching has been based on Indo-European languages. The results could not always be applied to Fenno-Ugric languages. One difference is that in Finnish, a synthetic, agglutinative language, the word as linguistic unit contains much more (grammatical) information than a word in English or Swedish (Karlsson, 1977). There is thus a need to look at target languages from other language families, and an ongoing project focuses on the comprehension of Estonian in Finland and of Finnish in Estonia. This project involves researchers from the universities of Tallinn, Eastern Finland and Jyväskylä, and the ultimate aim is to develop a situation of receptive multilingualism between Finns and Estonians, where everybody could speak their own L1 and understand the speakers from the neighbouring country. Similar projects have been the EuroCom (see e.g. Duke *et al.*, 2004) as well as the study of the Scandinavian situation, where Swedes, Norwegian and Danes can generally understand each other's (standard) language (see further Delsing, 2007; Zeevaert, 2007). Relevant control groups are Finland-Swedish speakers in Finland and Russian speakers in Estonia. One aspect to be considered here is the relevance of attitudes to the languages involved: do Russian speakers in Estonia have the same positive attitudes to the learning of Estonian as Swedish speakers in Finland generally have to the learning of Finnish? If there are differences, how are they reflected in the understanding of a target language unrelated to their L1? Also, there may be differences in how easily L2 lexical items can be linked to counterparts in the L1. The long period of the Swedish and Finnish languages existing together in Finland has made it easier to establish one-word linkings between Swedish and Finnish than between English and Finnish, where the languages do not have the same cultural and administrative background. Russian and Estonian are languages where there is no such long-lasting common cultural background, and the Russian learner of Estonian may not find it as easy to establish natural one-to-one links as can be found between Finnish and Swedish. A Swedish learner of Finnish (and Estonian) may thus have an advantage compared to the Russian learner of Estonian (and Finnish).

Estonian and Finnish are related languages, but they are not close enough to be mutually intelligible, as the Scandinavian languages are. Apart from vocabulary, differences are found in phonology and morphology, while the syntactic differences appear to be too slight to affect comprehension. Without guidance, Finnish teenagers were found to understand about 30% of isolated Estonian sentences out of context (Paajanen & Muikku-Werner, 2012). Isolated Estonian words were also tested (Muikku-Werner & Heinonen, 2012) and, as expected, comprehension was not as successful (cf. Albert & Obler, 1978: 41: 'When L1 and L2 categories are largely congruent, lexical items are easier to comprehend in context, though not necessarily in isolation, where similarity in form is crucial.'). In particular, the false friends between Estonian and Finnish posed problems when the words were presented in isolation, as there was no facilitating context to rule out wrong interpretations.

The subjects in these tests of Estonian were teenagers still at school. University students of Finnish with a fair knowledge of linguistics, but no knowledge of Estonian, have also been tested by Muikku-Werner (2013) and Kaivapalu (forthcoming). Here, the investigations focused on how much the subjects could understand of a relatively simple coherent text. It was found that they could make good use of the crosslinguistic similarities, as well as the context, in order to arrive at a reasonably good comprehension. They also made some interesting comments on the strategies they used.

Future results from the Finnish-Estonian project can be compared in particular with the existing results from Finland where Finnish-speaking and Swedish-speaking Finns' knowledge of English was studied. Comparing the language groups, a reasonable hypothesis is that Swedish speakers in Finland, who generally have a good, though non-native knowledge of Finnish, will not comprehend Estonian as well as Finns. Their non-native knowledge of Finnish is not expected to work as well for comprehension of Estonian as native proficiency in Finnish. In particular, the comprehension of isolated words will pose more problems than for native speakers of Finnish. The extensive body of research existing for the comparison between Finns and Swedish Finns in the learning of English has shown that Finns with a non-native knowledge of Swedish do not reach the same standard as native speakers of Swedish in tests of both comprehension and production of English. Exactly what differences can be established between native and non-native proficiency in the comprehension of a related language will be interesting to find out in the comprehension of Fenno-Ugric languages: whether the results can confirm previous transfer studies in Finland and how lateral transfer differs from L1 transfer quantitatively and qualitatively.

Note

(1) Håkan Ringbom passed away during the elaboration of this volume. The paper has undergone no modifications or reviews. It has been left as it stood in his original draft.

References

Albert, M.L. and Obler, L.K. (1978) *The Bilingual Brain*. New York: The Academic Press.
Bergh, G. (1986) The Neuropsychological Status of Swedish-English Subsidiary Bilinguals. *Gothenburg Studies in English* 61. Gothenburg University.
Berthele, R. (2008) Dialekt-Standard Situationen als embryonale Mehrsprachigkeit. Erkenntnisse zum interlingualen Potenzial des Provinzlerdaseins. *Sociolinguistica* 22: 87–107.
Cenoz, J. (2001) The effect of linguistic distance, L2 status and age on cross-linguistic influence in third language acquisition. In J. Cenoz, B. Hufeisen and U. Jessner (eds) *Cross-linguistic Influence in Third Language Acquisition* (pp. 8–20). Clevedon: Multilingual Matters.
Clark, E.C. (1993) *The Lexicon in Acquisition*. Cambridge: Cambridge University Press.
Clark, E.C. and Hecht, B.F. (1983) Comprehension, production and language acquisition. *Annual Review of Psychology* 34, 325–349.
Corder, S.P. (1983) A role for the mother tongue. In S. Gass and L. Selinker (eds) *Language Transfer in Language Learning* (pp. 85–97). Rowley, MA: Newbury House.
Cruttenden, A. (1981) Item-learning and system-learning. *Journal of Psycholinguistic Research* 10, 79–88.
De Angelis, G. (2007) *Third or Additional Language Acquisition*. Clevedon: Multilingual Matters.
Delsing, L.O. (2007) Scandinavian intercomprehension today. In J.D. ten Thije and L. Zeevaert (eds) *Receptive Multilingualism. Linguistic Analyses, Language Policies and Dialectic Concepts* (pp. 231–246). Amsterdam: John Benjamins.
Duke, J., Hufeisen, B. and Lutjeharms, M. (2004) Die sieben Siebe des EuroCom für den multilingualen Einstieg in die Welt der germanischen Sprachen. In H.G. Klein and D. Rutke (eds) *Neuere Forschungen zur europäischen Interkomprehension* (pp. 109–134). Aachen: Shaker Verlag.
Faerch, C., Haastrup, K. and Phillipson, R. (1984) *Learner Language and Language Learning*. Clevedon: Multilingual Matters.
Falk, Y. and Bardel, C. (2010) The study of the role of the background languages in third language acquisition. The state of the art. *International Review of Applied Linguistics in Language Teaching. IRAL* 48: 2–3: 185–220.
Gibson, M. and Hufeisen, B. (2003) Investigating the role of prior foreign language knowledge. In J. Cenoz, B. Hufeisen and U. Jessner (eds) *The Multilingual Lexicon* (pp. 87–102). Dordrecht: Kluwer.
Haastrup, K. (1991) *Lexical Inferencing Procedures or Talking about Words: A Book about Receptive Procedures in Foreign Language Learning with Special Reference to English*. Tübingen: Gunter Narr.
Hammarberg, B. (2009) *Processes in Third Language Acquisition*. Edinburgh: Edinburgh University Press.
Henriksen, B. (1999) Three dimensions of vocabulary development. *Studies in Second Language Acquisition* 21, 303–317.
Henriksen, B. and Haastrup, K. (1998) Describing learners' lexical competence across tasks and over time: A focus on research design. In K. Haastrup and Å. Viberg (eds) *Perspectives on Lexical Acquisition in a Second Language: Travaux de l'Institute de Linguistique de Lund* 38 (pp. 61–95). Lund: Lund University Press.

Ijaz, I.H. (1986) Linguistic and cognitive determinants of lexical acquisition in a second language. *Language Learning* 36, 401–451.
Jarvis, S. (1997) The role of L1-based concepts in L2 lexical reference. PhD dissertation, Indiana University.
Jarvis, S. and Pavlenko, A. (2008) *Crosslinguistic Influence in Language and Cognition*. New York: Routledge.
Kaivapalu, A. (forthcoming in *Lähivõrdlusi/Lähivertailuja*) Reseptiivinen monikielisyys: miten suomenkielinen oppija ymmärtää viroa äidinkielensä pohjalta? (Receptive multilingualism: how do Finnish learners understand Estonian on the basis of their L1).
Karlsson, F. (1977) Morphotactic structure and word cohesion in Finnish. In K. Sajavaara and J. Lehtonen (eds) *Contrastive Papers. Jyväskylä Contrastive Studies* 4, 59–74. University of Jyväskylä.
Kellerman, E. (1978) Giving learners a break: Native language intuitions as a source of predictions about transferability. *Working Papers on Bilingualism* 15, 59–92.
Kolers, P. (1966) Reading and talking bilingually. *American Journal of Psychology* 79, 357–376.
Kroll, J. and de Groot, A. (1997) Lexical and conceptual memory in the bilingual: Mapping form to meaning in two languages. In A. de Groot and J. Kroll (eds) *Tutorials in Bilingualism. Psychological Perspectives* (pp. 169–199). Mahwah, NJ: Lawrence Erlbaum.
Laufer, B. (1997) What's in a word that makes it hard or easy: Some intralexical factors that affect the learning of words. In N. Schmitt and M. Mc Carthy (eds) *Vocabulary: Description, Acquisition and Pedagogy* (pp. 140–155). Cambridge: Cambridge University Press.
Lindqvist, C. (2010) Lexical cross-linguistic influences in advanced learners' French L3 oral production. *International Review of Applied Linguistics in Language Teaching. IRAL* 48: 2–3, 131–157.
Meara, P. (1996) The dimensions of lexical competence. In G. Brown, K. Malmkjaer and J. Williams (eds) *Performance and Competence in Second Language Acquisition* (pp. 35–50). Cambridge: Cambridge University Press.
Muikku-Werner, P. (2013) Vironkielisen tekstin ymmärtäminen suomen kielen pohjalta. (English summary: Understanding Estonian texts on a Finnish language base). *Lähivõrdlusi/Lähivertailuja* 23, 210–237.
Muikku-Werner, P. and Heinonen, M. (2012) *Lumesadu* – 'tarina' vai 'lumikasa' vai ei kumpikaan? Suomalaiset lukiolaiset viron sanoja tunnistamassa. (English summary: *Lumesadu* – 'tarina' or 'lumikasa' or something completely different? How Finnish senior high school students try to recognize Estonian words) *Lähivõrdlusi/Lähivertailuja* 22, 157–187.
Odlin, T. (1989) *Language Transfer: Cross-Linguistic Influence on Language Learning*. Cambridge: Cambridge University Press.
Odlin, T. (2003) Cross-Linguistic Influence. In C.J. Doughty and M.H. Long (eds) *The Handbook of Second Language Acquisition* (pp. 436–486). Malden, MA: Blackwell Publishing.
Paajanen, I. and Muikku-Werner, P. (2012) *Tee on kitsas* – onko 'tee kitkerää' vai oletteko 'te saita'? Suomalaiset opiskelijat viroa ymmärtämässä. (English summary: *Tee on kitsas* – is 'tea bitter' or are 'you penny-pinching'? Finnish students comprehending Estonian.) *Lähivõrdlusi/Lähivertailuja* 22, 219–257.
Reves, T. and Levine, A. (1988) The foreign language receptive skills: Same or different? *System* 16, 327–336.
Ringbom, H. (1987) *The Role of the First Language in Foreign Language Learning*. Clevedon: Multilingual Matters.
Ringbom, H. (1992) On L1 transfer in L2 comprehension and L2 production. *Language Learning* 42, 85–112.

Ringbom, H. (2007) *Cross-linguistic Similarity in Foreign Language Learning*. Clevedon: Multilingual Matters.
Ringbom, H. and Jarvis, S. (2009) The importance of cross-linguistic similarity in foreign language learning. In M.H. Long and C. Doughty (eds) *The Handbook of Language Teaching* (pp. 106–118). Chichester: Wiley-Blackwell.
Sajavaara, K. (1983) The article errors of Finnish learners of English. In C.C. Elert and A. Seppänen (eds) *Finnish-English Language Contact: Papers from a Workshop. Umeå Papers in English 4* (pp. 72–87). Umeå: Umeå University.
Selinker, L. and Baumgartner-Cohen, B. (1995) Multiple language acquisition. 'Damn it, why can't I keep these two languages apart?'. *Language, Culture and Curriculum* 8, 115–121.
Sharwood Smith, M. (1986) Comprehension versus acquisition: Two ways of processing input. *Applied Linguistics* 7, 238–256.
Singleton, D. (1994) Learning L2 lexis: A matter of form? In G. Bartelt (ed.) *The Dynamics of Language Processes: Essays in Honor of Hans W. Dechert* (pp. 45–57). Tübingen: Gunter Narr.
Singleton, D. (1999) *Exploring the Second Language Mental Lexicon*. Cambridge: Cambridge University Press.
Swain, M. (1985) Communicative competence: Some roles of comprehensible input and comprehensible output in its development. In S. Gass and C. Madden (eds) *Input in Second Language Acquisition* (pp. 235–253). Rowley, MA: Newbury House.
Vanhove, J. (2014) *Receptive Multilingualism across the Lifespan. Cognitive and Linguistic Factors in Cognate Guessing*. PhD Thesis. University of Fribourg (Switzerland).
Zeevaert, L. (2007) Receptive multilingualism and inter-Scandinavian semicommunication. In J.D. ten Thije and L. Zeevaert (eds) *Receptive Multilingualism. Linguistic Analyses, Language Policies and Dialectic Concept* (pp. 103–135). Amsterdam: John Benjamins.

4 The Implications of Linguistic Relativity for Language Learning

John A. Lucy

In recent years there has been increasing interest in the relationship between second language learning and linguistic relativity (Cook & Bassetti, 2011; Han & Cadierno, 2010; Jarvis & Pavlenko, 2008; Pavlenko, 2011). In some ways this is a natural development since both lines of inquiry concern themselves with how meaning systems in language affect behaviour. But the two traditions differ in the behaviours they attend to. In the case of language learning, the interest is in how the meaning systems in a first language might affect speakers' learning of and ultimate attainment in a second language. In the case of linguistic relativity, the interest is in how the meaning systems in a language might affect thought about reality more generally, that is, speakers' cognitive processes and views of reality. Thus, bringing the two lines of inquiry into dialogue requires not only attending to how they treat meaning systems, but also articulating the relation between second language learning and how speakers think about reality.

The current paper focuses on how the emergence of linguistic relativity during middle childhood holds implications for the ability to learn a second language. The first section will characterise linguistic relativity and highlight a few important theoretical distinctions. The second section will describe the emergence of linguistic relativity during child development, including the associated changes in first language acquisition. Finally, the third section will outline the implications of these developmental changes for second language learning, including the challenges of distinguishing relativity effects from other effects on language learning.

Linguistic Relativity Characterised

Linguistic relativity can be characterised in several distinct ways. First, it can be distinguished externally from other types of language influences on thought. Second, it can be defined internally in terms of the formal elements it brings together into a proposed relationship so as to distinguish it from closely related, but distinct proposals.

Types of language influence on thought

The potential influences of language on thought can be classed into three types or levels (Lucy, 1996).

The first, or semiotic, level concerns how speaking any natural language at all may influence thinking. The question is whether having a code with a symbolic component (versus one confined to iconic and indexical elements) transforms thinking in certain ways. If so, we can speak of a *semiotic relativity* of those aspects of thought with respect to other species or individuals lacking such a code. For example, here we would include not only animal comparisons, but also studies showing cognitive deficits arising from lack of access to verbal input during early periods of life (e.g. among the deaf) as well as the cognitive advantages for classification and memory abilities arising from the mere presence of a verbal or other symbolic label. The influence of language on thought at this level has long been recognised, although much remains to be learnt about the specific mechanisms.

The second, or structural, level concerns how speaking one or more particular natural languages (e.g. Hopi versus English) may influence thinking. The question is whether quite different morphosyntactic configurations of meaning affect some aspects of thinking about reality. If so, we can speak of a *structural relativity* of thought with respect to speakers using different language codes. This has been the level traditionally associated with the term *linguistic relativity* and will be the focus here. Long deemed to be controversial, the existence of cognitive effects is now widely recognised, although controversies still exist over how profound they are in terms of process type or behavioural impact (Lucy, 2014). But the overall trend of the evidence is clear.

The third, or functional, level concerns whether using language in a particular way (e.g. schooled, scientific) may influence thinking. The question is whether verbal discursive practices affect some aspects of thinking either by modulating structural influences or by directly influencing the interpretation of interactional context. If so, we can speak of a *functional relativity* of thought with respect to speakers using language differently. This level can be conveniently referred to as *discursive relativity*. Although there is an abundance of evidence that training in these functional regimes has effects, there is much disagreement as to whether the effects are due to social or cognitive factors, especially in the context of schooling. Claims about discursive relativity assert that in addition to any social factors, some functional practices actually enhance the cognitive power of language with regard to certain goals.

So when we consider whether linguistic relativity has an influence on second language learning, we are asking specifically about structural relativity, that is, whether general cognitive effects arising from first language structure are affecting second language learning. Do speakers see language and its referents as aspects of reality like any other aspect, that is, through the lens of cognitive categories engendered by the morphosyntactic structure of their first language? It is also true that the other two levels of relativity can also be relevant to second language learning. For example, semiotic relativity may emerge when we entertain the possibility of age of onset effects and functional relativity may emerge when second language learning occurs in school and other social contexts. Indeed, the three types of language influences on thought are not functionally independent and always interact in important ways. Thus, the emergence of symbolic signs enables the complex and diverse morphosyntactic systems based on them, which provide in turn the essential means for the discursive interactions central to all cultures. Or inversely, thinking functionally, the impetus to engage in discourse drives linguistic development, which in turn drives the development of the symbolic capacity. Ultimately, then, investigation of structural relativity leads to a consideration of the other two levels. Likewise, the implications of linguistic relativity for second language learning will raise questions as to whether second language issues at other levels (e.g. age of onset, schooling effects), might also be mediated by relativity effects.

Formal aspects of linguistic relativity

Linguistic relativity proposals claim that each language embodies interpretations of reality and that these interpretations can influence thought about that reality (Lucy, 1992a, 1997). The interpretations arise from the selection of substantive aspects of experience and their formal arrangement into systems of referential meaning in the verbal code. Such selection and arrangement is, of course, necessary for language, so the crucial emphasis here is that each language involves a particular interpretation, not a common, universal one. Influences on thought ensue when the particular interpretations guide or support cognitive activity and hence the beliefs and behaviours dependent on it. Accounts vary in the specificity of the proposed mechanisms of influence and the degree of power attributed to them, but in all cases, claims for linguistic relativity require a demonstration that speaking a specific language influences thinking generally.

We now have evidence for such general effects on thought from grammatical categories such as tense, number, gender, complement constructions, causal forms, etc.; from referential domains such as colour, object construal, causation, space and motion, counterfactuals, etc.; from constructions such as metaphors in the areas of music and time, terminology in mathematics, co-speech gesture, etc. (e.g. Boroditsky, 2003; Casasanto, 2008; Levinson, 2003; Lucy, 1996, 1997, 2011; Niemeier & Dirven, 2000; Wolff & Holmes, 2011). The patterns of thinking affected include attention and perception, similarity judgements and classification, short and long term memory, and learning and reasoning, and these effects are evidenced in everyday experiences, specialised contexts or ideational traditions.

We can illustrate this type of finding with an example from my own work comparing the speakers of American English and Yucatec Maya (Lucy, 1992b; Lucy & Gaskins, 2003). The two languages differ in the way they mark number for nouns referring to a stable object (e.g. *candle*) in comparison to a malleable object (e.g. *clay*): English requires plural marking for multiple stable object referents whereas Yucatec does not, and Yucatec requires numeral unitisers for them whereas English does not. Thus, in acts of referring, English speakers attend more to the number and unit (or shape) of referent, whereas Yucatec speakers ignore number and unit (or shape) and focus instead on material. These differences yield reliable cognitive differences: English speakers reliably attend more to number and shape in nonverbal classification and memory tasks than do Maya speakers. But where the two languages are the same in their number marking, that is, in the treatment of malleable objects, they show no cognitive differences. Thus, the specific number marking patterns both across and within languages predict the specific cognitive responses. And this particular pattern recurs in a wide range of languages of similar types (Lucy, 2014).

The concept of 'thinking for speaking' is often confused with linguistic relativity, but is analytically distinct. This distinction was made clear in the original formulation where 'thinking for speaking' meant 'a special form of thought that is mobilized for communication' in one's native language 'while we are speaking' and which may therefore affect 'one's mastery of the grammatical categories of a foreign language' (Slobin, 1987: 436). So in the first instance, the concept was confined to language effects on language learning, rather than language effects on cognition more generally as in the relativity case. Second, even in considering second language effects, special emphasis was put on categories that 'cannot be experienced directly in our perceptual, sensorimotor, and practical dealings with the world' but which language alone requires us to make (Slobin, 1996: 91). By distancing possible effects from our conceptual or practical dealings with the world, it is clear that the concept does not refer to a general impact of language on experience. Eventually, evidence has emerged (e.g. Slobin, 2006) showing that thinking for speaking can in fact lead to broader cognitive effects, that is, to linguistic relativity. Nonetheless, it remains important to keep the two concepts distinct because it remains highly likely that some thought associated with speaking remains confined to language use. More generally, similar arguments about crosslinguistic influence, transfer or interference (Jarvis & Pavlenko, 2008) typically need not appeal to category effects beyond language use itself. By contrast, linguistic relativity proposals claim that the referential categories of language affect our cognitive engagement with the world generally and it is this broader pattern of engagement that has its own implications for second language learning.

Linguistic Relativity and First Language Acquisition

One key question in linguistic relativity research is when and how cognitive effects emerge in development. Knowing this developmental trajectory can confirm that the language patterns precede the cognitive ones, an important step in establishing the causal priority of language in the association of language and thought. And it can also illuminate the general process of child development by revealing when and how language-specific categories become important in cognition. In terms of the levels outlined in the first section, we are using semiotic developments to inform our analysis of structural relativity and our analysis of structural relativity to inform our understanding of semiotic developments. In the present context we are concerned with the second aspect, that is, what the onset of linguistic relativity can tell us about the child's language development. The main issues are the age of onset of cognitive effects, the co-occurring language developments and the possible mechanisms linking the two.

Emergence of linguistic relativity in childhood

Language-specific effects on general cognition first appear in middle childhood, around age eight (Lucy & Gaskins, 2001, 2003). Before age seven, children speaking different languages perform in very similar ways to each other on the cognitive measures used with adults. By age nine, they have shifted such that each group performs more like adult speakers of their language. That is, where the adult groups differ, so do the older children, and where the adult groups are the same, so are the older children. So children go from being more like each other across language communities to being more like adults in their own language community.

Again, an example can clarify the pattern here. Returning to the contrast of American English versus Yucatec Maya discussed above, Figure 4.1 presents the results of a nonverbal sorting task involving stable objects that assesses preference for shape versus material by age.

As the figure makes clear, at age seven, both groups favour classifying stable objects on the basis of shape. Yet by age nine the two groups have

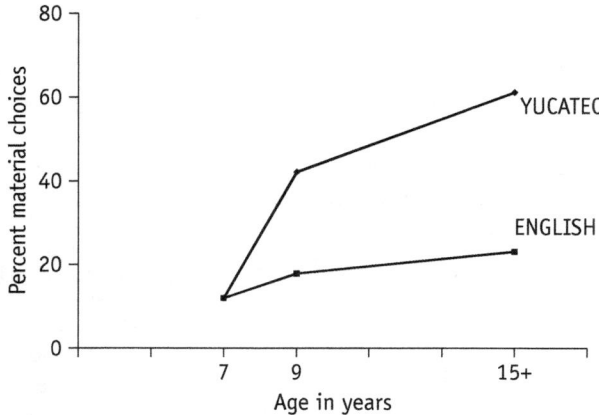

Figure 4.1 Developmental pattern for English and Yucatec nonverbal classification preferences with stable objects: Material versus shape (from Lucy, 2004: 13)

diverged as the Maya move toward favouring classification on the basis of material, in line with the adult pattern. There is no change in the English preference in this case because the adult preference accords with the childhood preference. (In other cases, as in the development of memory for stable objects, it is the English children who change their behaviour.)

Continuing this example, Figure 4.2 shows the results of a nonverbal sorting task involving malleable objects, where the two languages agree in their referential patterns. As the figure makes clear, in sorting these malleable objects, both groups favour material at about the same rate at all ages and there is no reliable difference in sorting preference by age, despite

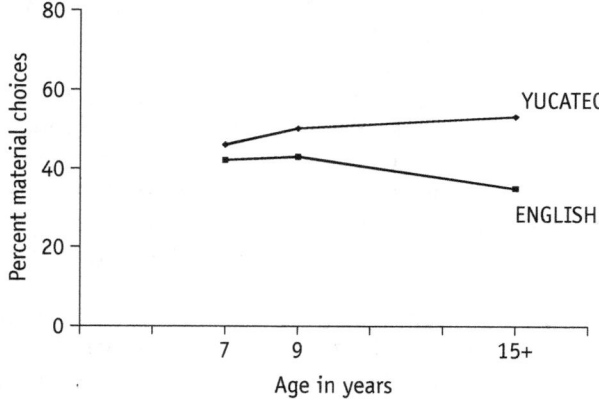

Figure 4.2 Developmental pattern for English and Yucatec classification preferences with malleable objects: Material versus shape (from Lucy, 2004: 15)

the slight drift toward more shape preferences by adult English speakers. In short, the childhood preference pattern fits both languages and thus requires no cognitive reorganisation during development.

Before this period, there are language-specific effects on the language learning process itself, but not on the general cognitive measures used with adults. Such language-internal effects appear throughout the period between two and eight in comprehension and production, in the ability to keep two languages separate, in the treatment of novel forms, etc. For example, to continue with our number marking task, children start to show sensitivity to number marking patterns in novel word learning tasks by age four, but not in their nonverbal sorting behaviour (e.g. Imai, 2000; see also Imai & Gentner, 1997; Li *et al.*, 2009). Such patterns confirm the importance of recognising that there may be effects on language learning that operate independently of linguistic relativity.

Clearly, early language learning in itself is not sufficient to create relativity effects. Indeed, children already speak quite well by age seven and have been applying and extending the basic categories in their languages for years. In the case of number marking, for example, English-speaking children have substantial command of plurals by age seven and Yucatec-speaking children have substantial command of numeral classifiers by this age. Children in both groups reliably comprehend and use the appropriate forms and will judge constructions misusing them as faulty. Although they have yet to master all the details, there is no question whatsoever that the basic structural characteristics of each number marking system are firmly in place and have been in routine habitual use for many years. So something more is required for relativity to emerge. This late emergence of linguistic relativity thus directs our attention to the later language development in relation to cognitive changes during the middle childhood period.

First language developments in middle childhood

During middle childhood (ages six to twelve) there are substantial changes in the structure and use of a child's first language (Nippold, 1998; Romaine, 1984). These changes appear in measures of verbal comprehension and production and they collectively strengthen and exploit language-internal structural relationships to support new narrative and discursive effects.

The structural changes occur at several levels. The lexicon expands rapidly and the child becomes more sensitive to the system-structural values of these forms (Lucy, 2010; Vygotsky, 1987). Likewise, grammatical categories achieve fuller functionality and the child becomes increasingly sensitive to argument tracking (e.g. case marking) (Chomsky, 1969) and predicate coordination (e.g. time marking) (Berman & Slobin, 1994). Of course, children are sensitive to structural effects well before this age (Bowerman, 1982). What seems to change is their willingness and ability to attend to a structural entailment and then merge it with the concrete world knowledge embodied in denotational regularities. That is, an existing awareness is recruited in such a way as to reconcile conflicts between what interlocutors say and what the child knows or to create and express a novel stance on events.

Building on these structural changes, various functional transformations appear as well, that is, the functional level mentioned above becomes relevant to the discussion. Narratives become more textually cohesive and discursive interaction becomes more interactionally appropriate and pragmatically effective (e.g. Berman & Slobin, 1994). Again, the child has been narrating and interacting for years, so the change again is one of recruiting existing devices to achieve new capabilities. Since the changes often operate across larger segments of speech in interaction, the difference can be difficult to detect with simplified sentence-based situations focused on a single speaker (Karmiloff-Smith, 1980). As a consequence, these changes have been much less studied, with the exception of studies concerned with school instruction. Mediating many of these functional changes are a set of indexical forms, or 'shifters' (Jakobson, 1971 [1957]), such as pronouns and tense markers that change from mostly indexing aspects of the surrounding context to also indexing aspects of the discourse itself.

To illustrate the operation of these developments, we can look at the acquisition of definite and indefinite articles (e.g. English *a* and *the*), which sit at the intersection of lexical number (e.g. count/mass status), grammatical number (singular/plural status) and discourse presupposition (e.g. pronominal/definiteness systems). Children begin using these forms in the second year of life and some would thus say they have been acquired by that age. But their use of the forms remains heavily confined to the immediate denotational context. When asked to respond to more complex questions requiring appropriate consideration of the communicative context, they continue to make errors well into middle childhood. Thus, for example, Karmiloff-Smith (1979) presented the following sort of probe to children at different ages:

Experimenter: In the forest lots of squirrels and cats were chasing each other. There were lots and lots of them. Suddenly one of the animals ran up a tree. Guess who it was.
Child: **A** squirrel/cat **/or/ one of the** squirrels/cats (**expected response**)

On this probe, young children tend to give responses using the definite article (e.g. **The** squirrel) and only give up this sort of response at age ten, and even then about ten percent of them still do not correctly use the indefinite article. The same pattern recurs in the reverse contexts where the definite article would be preferred and across a variety of probe types. Likewise, Berman and Slobin (1994) track the slow emergence of appropriate narrative uses of these forms in a task that has a child narrate a picture book for a listener. Here is a sample narrative from a five-year-old:

> When **the** boy and **the** dog were asleep **the** frog jumped out of **the** jar. And then **the** boy and **the** dog woke up. **The** frog was gone. Then **the** boy got dressed, and **the** dog stuck **his** head in **the** jar. (Example 25; bold added)

This child does not recognise that newly introduced referents need to be marked as such, since listeners who hear the definite article will expect some prior reference in the discourse. Contrast this with a sample narrative form a nine-year old where this context is correctly acknowledged:

> **There's a** boy who has **a** pet frog and **a** pet dog, and **one** night after **he** goes to bed **the** frog sneaks out. And **he** wakes up and **it**'s gone. So **he** and **his** dog look all over **the** place for **it**. (Example 29; bold added)

The mere possession of a form, whether lexical or grammatical, does not indicate that the child has mastered the full structural range of its use, and some of these critical uses arise only during middle childhood. Similar developments have been noted in other indexical forms (e.g. Hickmann, 1993, 2002; Berman & Slobin, 1994). Collectively, they enable a set of new functions: higher levels of narrative organisation (e.g. temporal sequencing), metalanguage (e.g. definitions), source marking (e.g. reported speech) and stance taking (e.g. humour, sarcasm).

Linking mechanisms

This growth in structural sensitivity brings to the fore fundamental tensions in language between those aspects of meaning derived from denotational regularities associated with language-external realities and those based on sense relations associated with language internal structural patterns (Lyons, 1977). When the two sources of meaning conflict, the children can reconcile them by reshaping their understanding of either their language-external realities or their language-internal patterns. When they reshape their view of external reality, we have the source of linguistic relativity. When they reshape their view of internal patterns, we have the source of language change. It is the relativity effects that concern us here.

Again, some examples can help clarify how the tensions can be reconciled. The seven-year-old Yucatec-speaking child is cognitively distinguishing stable and malleable objects but grammatically treating them alike. This potentially creates analogical pressure either to draw a corresponding distinction in the language so it matches cognition or to refigure their cognition so as to see the two types of objects as alike in some way. The cognitive evidence suggests that this pressure is indeed felt and that it is the reality that is reshaped in this case: children realise that those lexical items in their language referring to stable objects actually denote in the same way as those referring to malleable objects, and so they also start sorting the stable objects by their material rather than their shape. The developmental data on word extension mentioned above suggests that sensitivity to the structural entailments of the language emerges earlier, but the altered cognitive performance in nonverbal contexts suggests that the structural implications later become much more powerfully felt, prompting a realignment of language and cognition. The English-speaking child faces similar pressures. Correct use of the indefinite article, which increases after age seven, requires the child to distinguish stable and malleable objects (*a chair* versus *some clay*) and to mark plural reliably for the stable objects. It is in this context that their relative memory for number of stable objects increases even in nonverbal contexts. The Yucatec child need not draw any such distinction in the world. In both cases then, the socially shared meaning system in the language becomes more salient for the child at this age and induces a shift in the cognitive system in the child.

A similar transformation characterises cognitive development in general. During this period, children complete a shift from dependence on more spontaneous, perceptual strategies to reliance on more systematically organised, conceptual ones. This shift too can be difficult to detect in naturalistic settings but reveals itself when assessed carefully (Piaget & Inhelder, 1969; Vygotsky, 1987 [1934]). Given that cognitive development during this period also exhibits language-specific influences, it seems likely this broader cognitive shift depends on the associated language changes in some intimate way. But even if this proves not to be the case, the more general point would hold: not only does a first language change during this period but so also does cognition. It is this dual shift that also holds implications for second language learning.

Implications for Second Language Learning

Since relativity effects appear in middle childhood, it is to this period that we must look for any effects of them on second language learning. Language learning before this may of course show influences from another language through such processes as transfer, interference, entrainment, thinking for speaking, etc. And there may well be maturational factors, both linguistic and cognitive, that govern when and how these effects operate

(Newport, 1990). But to call any second language learning effect a linguistic relativity effect, it should be mediated by a general cognitive orientation associated with first language development. Inversely, after the onset of linguistic relativity, we need to ask whether maturational or interference effects on second language learning might better be accounted for in terms of linguistic relativity. And finally, we can ask whether second language learning might alter first language relativity effects.

Language learning and understandings of reality

With the rise of linguistic relativity around age eight comes a cognitive or ontological commitment to certain aspects of reality. Once such a commitment is made, it can conflict with acquisition of a second language because it makes denotation awkward and violates structural expectations. The categories of the new language just do not seem to fit well with one's reality, making it difficult to understand or accept the proper meaning and use of a form. Elsewhere I have used the term *semantic accent* (in contrast to 'thinking for speaking') to capture these relativity effects that arise when working with a second language in order to emphasise the referential entailments for experienced reality, the continuities across verbal and nonverbal modalities, and the evaluative component (Lucy, 2003, 2004, 2010, 2011).

One gets a sense of the power and vitality of these commitments when language learners regard the category meanings of the second language as illogical, arbitrary, unnecessary, clumsy or crazy. These are not judgements about what the category means or how it is used, or even that it is different, but rather judgements about its very appropriateness to the world. And such judgements have long operated to evaluate other languages as inferior, less capable of full and adequate reference, less suitable to science and advanced thought, substandard, etc. (Lucy, 2011; Whorf, 1956). Basically, the conventional treatment of the world found in such a speaker's first language has been given ontological status. The language fits ideally with the world precisely because the world has been reimagined to accord with the language.

The practical difficulties of altering one's view of reality during second language learning can be profound. To take another number marking example, Han (2010) conducted a longitudinal case study of an adult Chinese speaker's difficulty with plurals and articles. Despite years of experience with English and a high level of attainment before the study and increased exposure and use over the eight years of the study, these difficulties persisted. Chinese number marking resembles Yucatec, exhibiting almost no pluralisation and requiring obligatory unitisers when counting objects; and adult speakers of Chinese show relativity effects similar to those of Yucatec speakers (Li *et al.*, 2009). In this case, the speaker's errors stemmed from applying English number marking forms using a heuristic based on marking of 'specificity' in Chinese, which diverges from English number and definiteness marking. Thus, English noun phrases that contained an explicit quantifying expression (e.g. *two, several, much*, etc.) were regarded as specific and hence pluralised. Utterances lacking such an expression, for example, generic constructions, were systematically left unmarked. Likewise, when Chinese would include a demonstrative or number word, the construction was construed as specific, and the appropriate article applied, but not otherwise. This Chinese-based heuristic allowed the speaker to approximate the correct patterns yet fell short of genuine mastery of English. In Han's (2010: 178) view, overcoming his difficulties would require a 'conceptual *restructuring*' that 'entails not just mapping individual forms onto individual meanings, but rather, integrated mapping of a cohort of forms.' This seems right, but actually undertaking such a remapping of forms would also involve understanding how the English lexicon itself is structured with respect to quantification, including how it construes objects in the world (e.g. distinct individuation of stable versus malleable objects), and then how both lexicon and world interact with the requirements of grammatical number marking and discourse definiteness. Such an 'integrated mapping' thus entails a full grasp of the worldview embodied in the English lexicon. It remains an interesting question as to which contexts or interventions can promote such a fundamental remapping.

Language analysis and understandings of reality

These difficulties in understanding a second language can emerge unwittingly even among linguists when they rely on translation equivalents to characterise the forms of another language carrying their own ontological commitments with them (Lucy, 2000). In such cases, the second language itself has been taken as an aspect of reality and is subject to the same judgements about what is natural, appropriate, etc.

The unitisers discussed above for languages like Yucatec provide a good example. These unitisers provide a necessary unit when one wants to count a referent. Such a form is needed when the lexical form does not contain any unit as part of its inherent lexical meaning. The application of such a unitiser seems natural to an English speaker with a lexeme denoting a malleable object like *clay*, where one cannot say *two clays* but requires something like *two sticks of clay, two balls of clay*, etc. But its application seems anomalous for a lexeme denoting a stable object like *candle* where one can simply say *two candles* without any need to specify a unit. But the Maya requires a unitiser to count 'candles' in this way. Since candles clearly have a unit ('long thin' or 'stick' or 'cylindrical') as part of their very being as objects, the unitiser appears to be referentially superfluous. Here for example is a typical English definition from *Webster's Seventh New Collegiate Dictionary* (1965: 121): '1: a long slender cylindrical mass of tallow or wax containing a loosely twisted linen or cotton wick that is burned to give light. 2: something resembling a candle in shape or use.' This rendering of what a candle *is* focuses on its 'slender cylindrical mass' and on its function. In this context, adding unit or shape information seems redundant. This then leads to the view that rather than adding meaning, the unitiser merely agrees with a meaning value already in the lexeme. Thus, the numeral unitisers in such contexts are called numeral classifiers to indicate that they classify lexemes (or their referents) in terms of their inherent shape, rather than adding any real meaning value. In this way, the unitisers are divided into two classes – mensural and sortal – those that truly unitise or measure (as with 'clay') and those that merely sort (as with 'candle').

But deeper analysis of Yucatec reveals the lexeme *kib'*, which is routinely used to refer to candles, actually means 'wax' and can be used equally well for wax in any of the various shapes it comes in: candles, honey combs, drips, blocks, etc. To count candles then, an appropriate unitiser must be added (e.g. *ká'a ts'íit kib'* 'two long-thin wax'). So the imagined translation equivalence between *k'ib* and *candle* is only half right: there is indeed denotational overlap but there is no sense equivalence. In Yucatec the unit is required and not merely agreeing or redundant with the noun. In this way, an inappropriate analysis of the language form has ensued because analysts took for granted that the lexeme that Yucatec uses to refer to something has the same ontological alignment as a denotationally similar lexeme in English.

This type of error is surprisingly common among linguists, especially when they rely on translation equivalents in trying to compare languages. And it reaches its apogee in efforts to apply the categories of standard language, highly elaborated so as to match closely the base language's construal of reality, in the description and evaluation of other languages, whether vernacular or standard.

Language learning and effects on first language relativity

In seeking to establish the causal role of language in relativity effects, another line of research has looked at second language learners to see whether the learning of a new language alters the cognitive responses. The argument is that if learning a second language shifts speakers' cognition in accordance with its categories, then we would have direct evidence that language-specific categories can affect cognition. And such effects have indeed been found (see below), providing clear evidence of language as the driving force in the cognitive change. However, in the present context, we are interested in two other aspects of such work. First, to the extent that the second language affects cognition, it suggests that first language linguistic relativity effects are neither so strong nor so durable as to preclude effective second language learning. And second, such work may help us distinguish whether relativity effects arise from simple repeated exposure to alternatives or from the development of a more fundamental structural understanding. To date, we only have evidence on the first of these two issues.

The cognitive effects of learning a second language with a contrasting structure can again be illustrated in the area of number marking. Athanasopoulos (2006, 2007, 2011) studied Japanese speakers learning English. Japanese is similar to Yucatec in the ways it treats number marking. Overall, Japanese bilingual responses moved in the direction of monolingual English speakers on both attentiveness to number as a function of object type and in attentiveness to shape versus material. And more advanced learners, especially in immersion contexts, showed stronger effects than intermediate learners. Athanasopoulos concludes that the results clearly 'support the view that language influences cognitive dispositions by directing speakers' attention to specific features of stimuli' (2006: 95). And these results from increasing proficiency were not dependent on the language used in the assessment or on general cultural exposure.

What remains unclear in such work is whether the cognitive patterns of the more proficient language learners simply reflected increasing levels of exposure or whether they evidenced discrete structural reorganisation. Nor does it seem likely that this question can be answered only by cross-sectional comparisons of groups at different proficiency levels since it can be difficult to create groups that are equivalent at the outset and, in any event, the aggregate patterns tend to obscure individual discontinuities. What will likely be needed then will be longitudinal studies where it is possible to identify individual moments of reorganisation and link them with concurrent cognitive shifts. Something like this sort of longitudinal analysis, following individual learner's patterns of structural organisation, has been achieved with second language learning (e.g. Perdue & Klein, 1992), but it has not been attempted with studies of linguistic relativity. What is clear is that studies of second language acquisition can not only be informed by linguistic relativity but that the study of second language learning can contribute to our understanding of linguistic relativity.

Summary and Conclusions

The study of linguistic relativity is one aspect of the study of the relation of language and thought, one that concerns the effects of language-specific structures on general cognition. The evidence for such effects is now abundant, though questions remain about their broader significance.

One such question about the broader significance of linguistic relativity is its relationship to language learning. In first language development, relativity effects arise in middle childhood and are associated with an array of changes in language form and function during that period that likely give rise to them. In particular, it seems that young children become increasingly attentive to the structural meaning values latent in the language, elaborating and drawing on them to organise their speech and ultimately their understandings of reality. These changes in turn seem to enable the child to undertake an array of new function activities that depend on exploiting these meanings and shared view of the world. These meanings and the associated cognitive construals they entail may play a role in the learning and understanding of a second language. Characteristic of such effects would be their impact on general cognition and on learner appeals to reality in order to understand and evaluate categories in the second language. Such linguistic relativity effects mediated by ontological commitments should be understood as distinct from other forms of influence such as transfer and interference that are confined largely to the process of speaking. That said, relativity effects likely work in tandem with these other forces. And it remains to be seen whether some other first language influences on second language learning can be better understood as relativity effects or vice versa. A major task will be to develop measures capable of distinguishing these factors.

Finally, it seems that second language learning can create relativity effects as well, suggesting both the potency of verbal communication for cognition and the possibility that first language effects are not immutable. And, of course, there remains the intriguing question of what happens in terms of relativity when two languages are acquired simultaneously in early childhood, something about which we know almost nothing at this point.

It remains to comment briefly on the larger significance of these developments in middle childhood. Children are essentially drawing together into a unified package their language categories, their cognitive categories, their ontological commitments and their discursive understandings. Insofar as these are all adjusted to harmonise with each other, the totality becomes a durable psychological organisation. Learning a second language involves alteration in the whole package. That such alteration is possible no doubt stems from the fact that the child retains some access to the various individual elements before their integration. But breaking apart the whole and constructing another reality, another way of being, will always be a challenging task. In the end, it may be that the threads cannot ever be entirely unwoven and hence our feeling that our own language categories are natural, even inevitable. From this vantage the categories of other languages acquired later in life can look impoverished or enriched, illogical or poetic, but they do not look natural. And the root source of that sense of naturalness lies in the linguistic relativity effect, when a first language is knit together with thought and reality by the young child. Understanding this process will be central to our understandings of language learning in all its aspects.

References

Athanasopoulos, P. (2006) Effects of the grammatical representation of number on cognition in bilinguals. *Bilingualism: Language and Cognition* 9, 89–96.

Athanasopoulos, P. (2007) Interaction between grammatical categories and cognition in bilinguals: The role of proficiency, cultural immersion, and language of instruction. *Language and Cognitive Processes* 22, 689–699.

Athanasopoulos, P. (2011) Cognitive restructuring in bilingualism. In A. Pavlenko (ed.) *Thinking and Speaking in Two Languages* (pp. 29–65). Bristol: Multilingual Matters.

Berman, R.A. and Slobin, D.I. (1994) *Relating Events in Narrative: A Crosslinguistic Developmental Study*. Hillsdale, NJ: Lawrence Erlbaum Associates.

Boroditsky, L. (2003) Linguistic Relativity. In L. Nadel (ed.) *Encyclopedia of Cognitive Science* (pp. 917–921). MacMillan Press: London, UK, pages.

Bowerman, M. (1982) Reorganizational processes in lexical and syntactic development. In E. Wanner and L.R. Gleitman (eds) *Language Acquisition: The State of the Art* (pp. 319–346). Cambridge: Cambridge University Press.

Casasanto, D. (2008) Who's afraid of the Big Bad Whorf? Crosslinguistic differences in temporal language and thought. *Language Learning* 58 (Supplement 1): 63–79.

Chomsky, C. (1969) *The Acquisition of Syntax in Children from 5 to 10* (Research monograph no. 57). Cambridge, MA: The MIT. Press.

Cook, V.J. and Bassetti, B. (eds) (2011) *Language and Bilingual Cognition*. Abingdon: Routledge, Taylor and Francis Group.

de Villiers, J. and de Villiers, P. (2003) Language for thought: Coming to understand false beliefs. In D. Gentner and S. Goldin-Meadow (eds) *Language in Mind: Advances in the Study of Language and Thought* (pp. 335–384). Cambridge, MA: MIT Press.

Han, Z. (2010) Grammatical morpheme inadequacy as a function of linguistic relativity: A longitudinal case study. In Z. Han and T. Cadierno (eds) *Linguistic Relativity in SLA: Thinking for Speaking* (pp. 154–182). Bristol: Multilingual Matters.

Han, Z. and Cadierno, T. (eds) (2010) *Linguistic Relativity in SLA: Thinking for Speaking*. Bristol: Multilingual Matters.

Hickmann, M. (1993) The boundaries of reported speech in narrative discourse: some developmental aspects. In J.A. Lucy (ed.) *Reflexive Language: Reported Speech and Metapragmatics* (pp. 63–90). Cambridge: Cambridge University Press.

Hickmann, M. (2002) *Children's Discourse: Person, Space and Time Across Languages*. Cambridge University Press: Cambridge Studies in Linguistics 98.

Imai, M. (2000) Universal ontological knowledge and a bias toward language-specific categories in the construal of individuation. In S. Niemeier and R. Dirven (eds) *Evidence for Linguistic Relativity* (pp. 139–60). Amsterdam and Philadelphia: John Benjamins.

Imai, M. and Gentner, D. (1997) A cross-linguistic study of early word meaning: Universal ontology and linguistic influence. *Cognition* 62, 169–200.

Jarvis, S. and Pavlenko, A. (eds) (2008) *Crosslinguistic Influence in Language and Cognition*. New York: Routledge.

Jakobson, R. (1971 [1957]) Shifters, verbal categories, and the Russian verb. In *Selected Writings, Vol. 2: Word and Language* (pp. 130–147). The Hague: Mouton.

Karmiloff-Smith, A. (1983) Language development as a problem-solving process. *Papers and Reports on Child Language Development* 22, 1–23.
Karmiloff-Smith, A. (1979) *A Functional Approach to Child Language: A Study of Determiners and Reference*. Cambridge: Cambridge University Press.
Karmiloff-Smith, A. (1980) Psychological processes underlying pronominalization and non-pronominalization in children's connected discourse. In E. Ojedo (ed.) *Papers from the Parasession on Pronouns and Anaphora* (pp. 222–250). Chicago IL: Chicago Linguistics Society.
Li, P., Dunham, Y., and Carey, S. (2009) Of substance: The nature of language effects on entity construal. *Cognitive Psychology* 58, 487–524.
Levinson, S.C. (2003) *Space in Language and Cognition: Explorations in Cognitive Diversity*. Cambridge: Cambridge University Press
Lucy, J.A. (1992a) *Language Diversity and Thought: A Reformulation of the Linguistic Relativity Hypothesis* [Studies in the Social and Cultural Foundations of Language 12]. Cambridge: Cambridge University Press.
Lucy, J.A. (1992b) *Grammatical Categories and Cognition: A Case Study of the Linguistic Relativity Hypothesis* [Studies in the Social and Cultural Foundations of Language 13]. Cambridge University Press
Lucy, J.A. (1996) The scope of linguistic relativity: An analysis and review of empirical research. J.J. Gumperz and S.C. Levinson (eds) *Rethinking Linguistic Relativity* (pp. 37–69). Cambridge: Cambridge University Press,
Lucy, J.A. (1997) Linguistic relativity. *Annual Review of Anthropology* 26, 291–312. Palo Alto: Annual Reviews Inc.
Lucy, J.A. (2000) Systems of nominal classification: A concluding discussion. In G. Senft (ed.) *Systems of Nominal Classification* (pp. 326–341). Cambridge: Cambridge University Press.
Lucy, J.A. (2003) Semantic accent and linguistic relativity. Unpublished manuscript from a Conference on Cross-linguistic Data and Theories of Meaning, Catholic University of Nijmegen, The Netherlands, 20 May.
Lucy, J.A. (2004) Language, culture, and mind in comparative perspective. In M. Achard and S. Kemmer (eds) *Language, Culture, and Mind* (pp. 1–21). Stanford: Center for the Study of Language and Information Publications [distributed by the University of Chicago Press].
Lucy, J.A. (2010) Language structure, lexical meaning, and cognition: Whorf and Vygotsky revisited. In B. Malt and P. Wolff (eds) *Words and the Mind: How Words Capture Human Experience* (pp. 268–288). Oxford: Oxford University Press.
Lucy, J.A. (2011) Language and cognition: The view from anthropology. In V. Cook and B. Bassetti (eds) *Language and Bilingual Cognition* (pp. 43–68). Abingdon: Routledge, Taylor and Francis Group.
Lucy, J.A. (2014) Methodological approaches in the study of linguistic relativity. In Luna Filipović and Martin Pütz (eds) *Multilingual Cognition and Language Use: Processing and Typological Perspectives* (pp. 17–44). Amsterdam, NL: John Benjamins.
Lucy, J.A. and Gaskins, S. (2001) Grammatical categories and the development of classification preferences: A comparative approach. In S. Levinson and M. Bowerman (eds) *Language Acquisition and Conceptual Development* (pp. 257–283). Cambridge: Cambridge University Press.
Lucy, J.A. and Gaskins, S. (2003) Interaction of language type and referent type in the development of nonverbal classification preferences. In D. Gentner and S. Goldin-Meadow (eds) *Language in Mind: Advances in the Study of Language and Thought* (pp. 465–492). Cambridge, MA: MIT Press.
Lyons, J. (1977) *Semantics. Volume 1*. Cambridge: Cambridge University Press.
Niemeier, S. and Dirven, R. (2000) (eds) *Evidence for Linguistic Relativity*. Amsterdam and Philadelphia: John Benjamins

Newport, E.L. (1990) Maturational constraints on language learning. *Cognitive Science* 14, 11–28.
Nippold, M.A. (1998) *Later Language Development: The School-Age and Adolescent Years* (2nd edn). Austin, TX: Pro-Ed
Pavlenko, A. (ed.) (2011) *Thinking and Speaking in Two Languages*. Bristol: Multilingual Matters.
Perdue, C. and Klein, W. (1992) Why does the production of some learners not grammaticalize? *Studies in Second Language Acquisition* 14, 259–272
Piaget, J. and Inhelder, B. (1969) *The Psychology of the Child*. New York: Basic Books.
Romaine, S. (1984) *The Language of Children and Adolescents: The Acquisition of Communicative Competence*. New York: Basil Blackwell.
Slobin, D.I. (1987) Thinking for speaking. *Proceedings of the Annual Meeting of the Berkeley Linguistic Society* 13, 435–445.
Slobin, D.I. (1996) From 'thought and language' to 'thinking for speaking'. In J.J. Gumperz and S.C. Levinson (eds) *Rethinking Linguistic Relativity* (pp. 70–96). Cambridge: Cambridge University Press.
Slobin, D.I. (2006) What makes manner of motion salient? Explorations in linguistic typology, discourse, and cognition. In M. Hickmann and S. Robert (eds) *Space in Languages: Linguistic Systems and Cognitive Categories* (pp. 59–81). Amsterdam: John Benjamins.
Vygotsky, L.S. (1987 [1934]) Thinking and speech. In R.W. Rieber and A.S. Carton (eds) *The Collected Works of L.S. Vygotsky*. Vol. 1: *Problems of General Psychology* (N. Minnick trans.) (pp. 37–285). New York: Plenum.
Webster's Seventh New Collegiate Dictionary (1965) Springfield, MA: G. and C. Merriam.
Whorf, B.L. (1956) *Language, Thought, and Reality: Selected Writings of Benjamin Lee Whorf* (J.B. Carroll, ed.). Cambridge, MA: MIT Press.
Wolff, P. and Holmes, K.J. (2011) Linguistic relativity. *Wiley Interdisciplinary Reviews: Cognitive Science* 2, 253–265

5 Crosslinguistic Lexical Influence: Cognate Facilitation

Rena Helms-Park and Vedran Dronjic

Introduction

This chapter centres on cognate facilitation, an aspect of lexical transfer that greatly interests psychologists and neuroscientists investigating the organisation and functioning of the bilingual lexicon since the links between L1 and L2 cognates, especially ones identical in form and meaning, are the tightest that can exist between the two lexicons. Cognate facilitation is also greatly relevant to language pedagogy since it holds the potential of accelerating lexical acquisition when the target language is related to a previously learnt one (Ringbom, 1987). In addition, the existence of 'false cognates' (homographs or homophones with unrelated meanings) and 'false friends' (historically related items that are semantically divergent in current usage), in the midst of facilitative cognates, often necessitates 'negative evidence' to offset overgeneralised L1-to-L2 transfer. Likewise, in lexical testing for evaluative or research purposes, a common concern is the extent to which cognates inflate the scores of certain language groups (Cobb, 2000) or need to be eliminated in experimental studies in order to control for variables that could bias L2 results (e.g. Ard & Homburg, 1983).

Within psycholinguistic and neurolinguistic research contexts, cognates are generally considered to be phonetically related words that share a meaning (Carroll, 1992), a definition that shifts the focus of research from an etymological one to a synchronic investigation of how speakers and readers store and process words that share form and meaning. Psycholinguistic research frequently addresses the question of whether cognates (e.g. *wasser* and *water* in German and English respectively), unlike L1-L2 translation equivalents (e.g. पानी *paani* /pɑːni/ and *water* in Hindi and English respectively), share one lexical entry in the bilingual lexicon based on shared morphology (Davis *et al.*, 2010; Lotto & de Groot, 1998) or, alternatively, have two discrete morphological entries even when identical (e.g. the orthographic form of *radio* in French and English) (Peeters *et al.*, 2013). A further question, and one relevant to both cognate facilitation in processing within the steady-state lexicon or to the acquisition of cognates, is whether the main locus of activation is the semantic, lexical/morphological or sublexical (phonological or orthographic) level of representation (Costa et al., 2005), with sublexical activation or a combination of sublexical and semantic activation winning the greatest empirical support. A related issue is linked to modality: is it the visual (orthographic) or the auditory (phonetic) characteristics of cognates in specific language pairings that make cognates conducive to automatic recognition? Where recognition is not automatic (for example, because of certain phonological or orthographic impediments, or because of the learner's age or proficiency in the languages in question), the question that arises is whether or not certain interventions are effective in facilitating cognate recognition and retention.

This chapter first discusses what cognates are and are not, depending on the research context. The chapter goes on to examine empirical research on cognate facilitation in behavioural research in psycholinguistics, recent electrophysiological research and classroom-based L2 research; this section also summarises empirical findings in frequency and genre-based L2 lexical testing. The second half of the chapter considers the possible mechanisms driving cognate facilitation and examines the effectiveness of classroom intervention in situations where cognate recognition is not automatic or when L2 lexemes are inaccurately linked with L1 lemmas as a result of overgeneralised L1-to-L2 transfer.

What are Cognates?

Related languages feature a certain proportion of word pairs in their vocabularies which trace their origin to the same word in their ancestor language. Thus, the Finnish and Hungarian words for 'water', *vesi* and *víz*, respectively, are both derived from the reconstructed Proto-Uralic word **weti* (Janhunen, 1998). Word pairs of this type are called cognates. Apart from word pairs directly descended from an ancestral form, the term 'cognate' could be extended to include instances of a language borrowing vocabulary from another language, as is the case with Serbo-Croatian *fotelja* ('armchair'), from French *fauteuil*. Similarly, the term would encompass words which two languages, related or not, borrowed from a third language (to which they may or may not be related). For example, Hungarian and Malay both feature a version of the Latin word *trānsāctiō* ('transaction'), the former as *tranzakció* and the latter as *transaksi*. In some circles, the term 'cognate' is extended to even more recent borrowings between genetically unrelated languages, as has become common in today's world of global communication, for instance, Japanese サーモスタット /saːmosɯtatto/ from English *thermostat* /'θɚmoʊstæt / (Shirai, 2012).

There are other ways in which two languages may end up with pairs of similar-sounding words with roughly the same meanings. As is often remarked, the connection between the form of a word and its meaning is typically arbitrary (e.g. Modern Greek represents 'water' as *νερó* /

ne'ro/, Mandarin as 水 *shuǐ*/ʂwei̯˧˩˧/, and Ojibwe as *nibi* /nɪˈbɪ/ (Nichols & Nyholm, 2002)). However, iconicity frequently creates some crosslinguistic similarities among words, as in onomatopoeia (e.g. the sound of a dog's barking is rendered as הַב־הַב/'hav 'hav/ in Hebrew, *bow-vow* in English, *au-au* in Basque and भऊभऊ /bʱa'uː bʱa'uː/ in Hindi). Similarly, a subtler process such as sound symbolism can result in crosslinguistic resemblances, as when the prosody of independently derived words for 'butterfly' captures the fluttering motion of a butterfly's wings (see Beeman, 2000), as in פרפר /paʁ'paʁ/ in Hebrew and *farfalla* in Italian. Iconic words that resemble each other are not considered cognates. Likewise, pairs of similar words in unrelated languages owing their existence to the nature of the language acquisition process and the physiology and anatomy of the infant speech tract are not cognates. Typical examples are kinship terms, especially the words for 'mother' and 'father'. Thus, the Persian word for 'daddy' or 'papa', بب/bɒˈbɒ/ and its Mandarin counterpart 爸爸 /pa\pa/, are not cognates, but likely the result of adults' misattribution of meaning to infants' early reduplicated babbling productions, which are well known not to be referential in nature.

Another way in which unrelated languages may end up with similar-sounding words is through chance resemblance. Hawaiian and Ancient Greek, for instance, feature a number of pairs of similar words: 'Eagle' is *'aeko* /ʔaˈeto ~ ʔaˈeko/ in Hawaiian and αἰετός /aieˈtos/ in Ancient Greek, while 'honey' is *meli* in Hawaiian and μέλι /ˈmeli/ in Ancient Greek (data adapted from Trask, 1996). The odds of such resemblances occurring in unrelated languages are actually much higher than one would expect. The likelihood of finding a six-way chance resemblance among a set of ten arbitrarily selected languages is approximately 1 in 180; the odds of finding additional chance match-ups in the same set is even higher if we also allow for seven-way, eight-way, nine-way and ten-way match-ups (Ringe, 1992; Trask, 1996).

If we adopt an etymological definition of the term, cognates are pairs of words that share common ancestry, and therefore the examples seen above are referred to as **false cognates** despite sharing form and meaning. A complicating factor when we consider etymology, however, is that cognates typically exhibit varying degrees of semantic overlap due to the process of semantic drift. Thus, Belarussian *галава* /ɣalaˈva/ and Slovene *glava* ('head') are both descended from Proto-Slavic **golva*, and their meanings overlap to a very high degree; they are solid **translation equivalents**. At the opposite end of the spectrum would be Serbo-Croatian *obraz* and Slovene *obraz*, which, while both descended from Proto-Slavic **obrazъ*, mean 'cheek' and 'face', respectively, while Serbo-Croatian *lice* and Slovene *lice*, both originating in Proto-Slavic **lice*, mean 'face' and 'cheek', respectively. In other words, due to an extreme case of semantic drift, the words *lice* and *obraz* appear to have exchanged places in these two languages. Words of this type (whether cognate or not), which might easily seduce a second language learner into a false sense of comprehension, are called **false friends**. Between true cognates and cognate false friends, there is a full range of greater or lesser degrees of semantic overlap: for instance, the Romanian verb *a intoxica* means 'to poison by having someone ingest bad food or a noxious substance', while the poisoning in the present-day English meaning of the verb *intoxicate* is restricted to ingesting alcohol (while the other meanings are archaic).

A Psycholinguistic Approach to Cognate Relationships

The etymological aspect of cognateness is an issue of central concern to historical linguists. On the other hand, psycholinguists, neurolinguists, language acquisition researchers, as well as clinical and applied linguists are mostly interested in cognates from a psycholinguistic standpoint. From a theoretical perspective, we might ask how cognates are represented in the bilingual brain, how they are processed and how they are acquired. From an applied perspective, we might want to know what implications the representation, processing and acquisition of cognates may have for a variety of practical enterprises such as language pedagogy, language testing or speech-language therapy. For instance, it would be reasonable for a language teacher to assume that it should be easier for students to learn an L2 word that has a readily recognisable cognate in the L1. A person creating a language test might need to consider whether a test, say of Italian vocabulary, would favour an examinee who spoke French or Catalan, as opposed to one who spoke Vietnamese or Japanese (Cobb, 2000). A speech-language pathologist treating a patient who has suffered a stroke and is experiencing asymmetrical difficulties in accessing lexical representations in their two languages might wish to know whether access to words in the more heavily affected language could be boosted via encouraging access to their cognates in the better preserved language (e.g. Costa *et al.*, 2005).

Since the psycholinguistic approach to cognates is concerned with how cognates are organised in the brain, an issue of crucial importance in this context is the extent to which the forms, meanings and usage patterns of two cognates overlap, as this will crucially influence acquisition, representation, word recognition, lexical access and use. It is reasonable to assume that a cognate will be more easily recognised by an L2 learner the more similar its spoken or written form is to the L1 word (Dijkstra *et al.*, 2010). Thus, a Spanish speaker learning Italian will have no difficulty recognising the Italian words *madre* ('mother') and *padre* ('father'), since they are written identically and pronounced with phonetically similar segments as in the L1.

There are also instances where cognates are easier to recognise in either the visual or the auditory form. For example, it is extremely easy for a Norwegian speaker to recognise Danish *kirke* ('church') as the equivalent of Bokmål Norwegian *kirke* (identical meaning) in writing; however, the two words' pronunciations have diverged sufficiently to render recognition in the auditory modality more difficult: in Oslo, *kirke* is pronounced / ˈçɪrkə/, while in Copenhagen it is /ˈkiɐ̯gə/. Conversely, it might be the spelling that obscures the connection between two cognates; for instance, a speaker of Rioplatense Spanish may recognise the Portuguese word *chama* /ˈʃɐmɐ/ ('flame') as the equivalent of the L1 word *llama* /ˈʃama/ relatively easily in its spoken form, but the relationship is obscured by the orthographic representations of the initial sound. It should be noted, however, that in both the Norwegian-Danish and Rioplatense Spanish-Portuguese cases, contextual information will often facilitate the recognition of cognates where phonology and orthography interfere.

With respect to how the recognition of cognates would proceed in real time when formal overlap is less than ideal, as is the case with the aforementioned spoken forms of Danish and Norwegian *kirke*, it has been posited that, until a language learner has developed a lexical representation for the new word, access would happen by abstracting the rules of correspondence between L1 and L2 words and correcting the L2 input algorithmically to match existing L1 representations (Bannert, 1981 in Warter, 2001; Warter, 1995, 2001). Success would clearly depend on a speaker's experience with the L2. In light of what is known about the serial nature of lexical access in the auditory modality, similarity between cognates at word onsets is particularly important (Marslen-Wilson, 1987, 1990; McClelland & Elman, 1986); dissimilar word onsets can be expected to result in more difficulties in cognate recognition compared to dissimilarities further downstream. To a lesser extent, this would also be true of the visual modality. Thus, for an English speaker, Irish *salann* would be easier to recognise as a cognate of *salt* than Welsh *halen*.

The foregoing implies that researchers interested in psycholinguistic aspects of cognateness would do well to adopt a definition that states that COGNATE = [+ FORMAL OVERLAP + SEMANTIC OVERLAP], while FALSE FRIEND = [+ FORMAL OVERLAP - SEMANTIC OVERLAP], allowing for the fact that both formal and semantic overlap exist on a continuum, as seen above. This has the practical implication that, psycholinguistically, a pair of real and readily recognisable cognates, such as Hawaiian and Tuvaluan *lua* ('two') (Greenhill *et al.*, 2008), will be more similar to a false cognate pair such as Hawaiian *meli* and Modern Greek μέλι /ˈmeli/ in a bilingual mind than to a true cognate pair that was altered beyond recognisability through language change, such as Irish *cú* and

English *hound*. In language learning, false friends, such as Spanish *pronto* ('soon') and Italian *pronto* ('ready'), often present learners with difficulties at first encounter.

Any psycholinguistic model of cognate recognition needs to explicitly address the issue of how similarity is to be measured and what degree of similarity will suffice in order for a word pair to be considered 'psycholinguistically cognate'. One example of such a decision is Roberts and Deslauriers' (1999) 70% feature overlap criterion, which was imposed following a systematic comparison of L1 and L2 phonemic inventories on feature similarity and a calculation of their distance. Kondrak (2003) recommends the use of an algorithm based on feature salience with a rationale that certain phonetic features are perceptually more relevant than others. Measures of graphemic difference between cognates also exist, which can be used to gauge the visual similarity of two cognates (see Gooskens & van Bezooijen, 2006).

In summary, the concept of cognateness is defined differently in historical and psycholinguistic approaches to the study of language. Historical definitions emphasise shared etymology regardless of the degree of formal and meaning overlap existing synchronically, as even false friends and dissimilar-sounding or looking pairs of words are considered cognate if they share the same ancestry. On the other hand, in psycholinguistic terms, word pairs that share elements of form and meaning are expected to be treated similarly by the brain regardless of whether they are etymologically related.

Cognate Facilitation: Online and Offline Evidence

The cognate facilitation hypothesis puts forward the view that when formal similarities between L1 and L2 lexical items coincide with semantic overlap between these items, L2 lexical acquisition is facilitated; likewise, when bilingualism is examined cross-sectionally, as a 'steady state', cognates are processed more rapidly, for instance in translation or lexical decision tasks (Costa *et al.*, 2000; Cristoffanini *et al.*, 1986; Davis *et al.*, 2010; de Groot & Nas, 1991; de Groot & Keijzer, 2000; Dijkstra *et al.*, 1999; Dijkstra *et al.*, 1998; Dijkstra *et al.*, 2010; Hall, 2002; Kroll & Sunderman, 2003; Lotto & de Groot, 1998; Sánchez-Casas *et al.*, 1992; van Hell & Dijkstra, 2002; Voga & Grainger, 2007). The cumulative findings of behavioural research conducted during the last few decades, as well as more recent electrophysiological research (e.g. Christoffels *et al.*, 2007; Midgley *et al.*, 2011; Peeters *et al.*, 2013) provide plentiful evidence in support of the cognate facilitation hypothesis.

The bulk of findings point to cognates being learnt more quickly and also being more robust in the face of attrition than non-cognate translation equivalents (de Groot & Keijzer, 2000). They are also recognised and translated faster than non-cognates, particularly when there is a frequency mismatch across a bilingual's two languages (frequent in the better-known language and relatively infrequent in the target language) (Dijkstra et al., 1999; Kroll & Sunderman, 2003; Lotto & de Groot, 1998; Peeters et al., 2013). This contrasts with non-cognate homographs across a bilingual's languages, such as English *mace* and Serbo-Croatian *mace* ('kitties'), which may or may not be recognised faster than words without a cognate equivalent in the other language (Dijkstra et al., 1998). Cognates are also less likely to be subject to temporary retrieval problems in processing than non-cognates (Gollan & Acenas, 2004).

The following sections examine these issues in online laboratory-based research as well as offline classroom-based research, which is ecologically more reflective of most L2 learning and testing contexts than online research.

Online research

Behavioural studies

Primed lexical decision has been used extensively to investigate cognate representation and processing in the bilingual brain. Priming is an experimental psycholinguistic technique in which one stimulus (the prime, e.g. *sugar*) is presented before another stimulus (the target, e.g. *cake*) and the time taken to respond to the target is measured (e.g. the participant has to decide whether the target is a real word, which is termed a lexical decision task). The participant may be aware of the prime ('unmasked priming'); when the prime is immediately preceded by a visual mask (typically a series of '#'s) and is presented visually for a very brief period of time (e.g. 40 milliseconds) before the target appears, but most participants are not consciously aware of its presence ('masked priming'). Of interest to the researcher is whether the presentation of a prime, which may be phonologically/orthographically, morphologically or semantically related or unrelated to the target, affects the response to the target by either speeding it up (which is termed facilitation) or slowing it down. Thus, for instance, our example prime, *sugar*, would typically speed up the lexical decision to the target *cake*, an effect known as semantic priming.

Early priming research on cognates mostly consisted of visual priming without masking. Studies with stimulus-onset asynchronies (SOAs, the time period which elapses between the onset of the prime and the onset of the target) over 300 milliseconds (ms), which is considered long, tended to find facilitation with cognate translation equivalents (Gerard & Scarborough, 1989), while no facilitation was evident for non-cognate translation equivalents (Cristoffanini et al., 1986; Kirsner et al., 1980; Scarborough et al., 1984). Conversely, studies using SOAs shorter than 300 ms have found facilitation for both cognate and non-cognate translation equivalents (e.g. de Groot & Nas, 1991; Sánchez-Casas & Almagro, 1999, cited in Sánchez-Casas & García-Albea, 2005). Since long SOAs favour form priming and short SOAs are conducive to both form and semantic priming, it would follow from the above that formal similarity, as opposed to semantic overlap, is what sets cognates apart from other types of translation equivalents in the bilingual mental lexicon (see also Costa et al., 2005). This point is further reinforced by a study conducted by Sánchez-Casas, Suárez-Buratti and Igoa (1992, cited in Sánchez-Casas & García-Albea, 2005) with Spanish-English bilinguals. On a translation recognition task featuring pairs of words, cognate translations with full and partial semantic overlap take equal amounts of time to verify, while their non-cognate counterparts are identified as translations more rapidly only with full semantic overlap.

Bearing in mind that studies of cognate processing tend to be carried out in the visual modality and would, consequently, have implications for the overlap between orthographic and semantic components of cognates, but not necessarily the phonological and semantic components, Dijkstra, Grainger and van Heuven (1999) conducted a study with Dutch-English bilinguals which presented visual stimuli controlled for phonological similarity. In a progressive demasking and lexical decision task, they found a facilitative effect of orthographic and semantic overlap, but an inhibitory effect of phonological overlap. Phonologically similar forms are known to compete in lexical access, but to assist in production. It is thus unsurprising that a strong facilitation effect is present for cognates in picture-naming tasks (Costa et al., 2000). It is worth noting that, while highly relevant in online processing, this contradiction between the effects of phonological and orthographic similarity could well disappear in offline tasks, where one could reasonably expect both kinds of formal similarity to result in facilitation (leading to awareness of cognate status), an issue that has a bearing on offline L2 lexical testing in classroom settings, as will be discussed below.

Masked priming has also been used to investigate cognate facilitation due to its potential to circumvent most episodic and strategic processing effects (as a vast majority of participants, approximately 98%, are not able to report the masked stimulus when the SOA is 40 ms). Typically, lexical decision studies with masked primes have found facilitation for cognates, but not non-cognates (Duyck & Warlop, 2009; Sánchez-Casas et al., 1992), with the exception of studies where the masking is not complete due to stimulus properties (e.g. de Groot & Nas, 1991).

ERP studies and cognates

The last decade has seen a steady increase in electrophysiological studies focusing on cognate facilitation. Event-Related Potentials (ERPs) are measurable changes in the brain's electrical activity related to cognitive events and are measured through electroencephalography (EEG) as changes in electrical charges in the scalp. The findings generally support those of the behavioural studies cited above but also add more time precision and detail to the analyses of responses. Facilitation via cognates is generally shown through a less pronounced peak in the negative wave in the 400 ms window (the N400 component, a negative-going change in the electrical charges related to semantic processing) than is the case with corresponding words that require deeper semantic processing (Bessen et al., 1992), for example, non-cognate translation equivalents or controls with no formal or meaning overlap with targets. Generally, words in these experiments are organised in language-specific blocks in order to tap language-selective or language non-selective processing unambiguously (but see use of mixed blocks as well as language-specific blocks in Christoffels et al., 2007).

Working with German L1-Dutch L2 asymmetrical bilinguals completing a picture-naming task in their L1 or their L2 (with L1 blocked), Christoffels et al. (2007) found evidence in their behavioural data of bidirectional cognate facilitation. Their ERP data yielded weaker but reliable evidence of bidirectional facilitation (though stronger in the L1-to-L2 direction). Likewise, Midgley et al. (2011), testing English L1-French L2 bilinguals via a lexical decision task in L1 and L2 blocks, found evidence of bidirectional cognate facilitation in their ERP data but, once again, with more pronounced effects in the L1-to-L2 direction than vice versa. Working with late French L1-English L2 bilinguals, Peeters et al. (2013) also found bidirectional facilitation in both behavioural (reaction time) and ERP data, but interestingly, their most disproportionally powerful evidence materialised when cognates were orthographically identical rather than near-identical, and when the non-target French L1 cognates were high frequency and their target English L2 counterparts low frequency.

The roles of proficiency level and frequency in cognate facilitation

A review of online cognate processing experimentation reveals that L2 proficiency at the lowest levels seems to be a moderating factor in cognate facilitation. The findings of online studies on cognates seem to indicate that there could well be a certain threshold level of proficiency (likely related to the size of the mental lexicon and its interconnectivity) below which cognate facilitation in online processing will not occur. Beyond the threshold, however, there seems to be little difference between balanced and unbalanced bilinguals in terms of cognate facilitation. Thus, in a study which featured balanced and unbalanced English-Spanish and Spanish-English bilinguals (with the unbalanced group featuring individuals with high and with very low L2 proficiency), Davis et al. (2010) found comparable priming effects in both groups, in both directions (L1-to-L2 and L2-L1), irrespective of the degree of orthographic overlap within the cognate pairs used as stimuli (e.g. *rich-rico*; *tower-torre*). The only exception was the low L2 proficiency group, in which the priming effects were unidirectional (from the L1 to the L2). The foregoing notion of a proficiency threshold extends to L3 situations as well: cognate facilitation can take place in the L3-L1 direction but only when L3 proficiency is high enough (van Hell & Dijkstra, 2002).

We should note, however, that this hypothesised threshold cannot be easily quantified or defined since it is a function of the L1-L2 combination in question as well as the host of personal and environmental factors that have shaped a participant's mental lexicon. However, without defined thresholds in a given study, any argument that facilitation is bidirectional because of adequate proficiency is tautological. Thus, in many cases, facilitation results related to proficiency can be ambiguous. Nakayama, Sears, Hino and Lupker (2013), for instance, concluded that their L1 Japanese-L2 English bilinguals' loanword cognate priming advantages were bidirectional 'irrespective of proficiency', but this could well be because the bilinguals were more proficient than the hypothesised threshold. In a different context, Duyck and Warlop's (2009) L1 Dutch-L2 French bilinguals experienced bidirectional cognate facilitation despite being in an L1-dominant milieu. Here, too, the results might hinge not on the linguistic context but on whether or not L2 proficiency is beyond the threshold. We recommend that a more precise identification of this threshold (e.g. through quantification) be a goal for future efforts in research on online cognate facilitation.

Cross-script priming

As suggested by various studies discussed above, shared orthography provides powerful visual cues in online cognate facilitation. A unidirectional cognate effect, that is, in an L1-to-L2 direction rather than in reverse, has also been observed in cases where the L1 and L2 do not share a script, suggesting that, apart from a lexical proficiency threshold, there may be a similar orthographic decoding proficiency threshold for cognate facilitation. In a masked translation priming task using orthographic primes in Hebrew L1 and English L2 scripts, Gollan *et al.* (1997) found cognate facilitation only in the L1-to-L2 direction. A similar study by Dimitropoulou, Duñabeitia and Carreiras (2011), but with low proficiency and late Greek L1-Spanish L2 bilinguals, also uncovered facilitation only in the L1-to-L2 direction. The existence of an orthographic threshold, like the lexical one discussed above, as well as any interaction between the two thresholds, remains to be confirmed empirically.

One exception to the L1-to-L2 unidirectional cognate facilitation is Nakayama *et al*'s. (2013) masked translation priming study involving L1 Japanese-L2 English bilinguals. Here loanword cognate priming advantages were bidirectional despite the fact that the L1 stimuli were presented in katakana. Note that in this study facilitation was also impervious to L2 proficiency and word frequency, suggesting that loanword cognates in Japanese might not behave like typical cognates. In Jones' (2014) classroom-based study too, Japanese-speaking beginner-level learners of English seemed to have little difficulty recognising the English counterparts of English-sourced Japanese loanwords. Our conjecture is that Japanese speakers are highly conscious of foreign borrowings since these are written in katakana (used for foreign words) and also because they encounter many of the English equivalents in the media or elsewhere (e.g. リスト /ɾi.sɯ.to/ 'list', from Shirai, 2012). The potential impediment that script can pose in cognate recognition in L2 classroom situations will be discussed further below.

Offline studies

L2 lexical tests

To examine cognate facilitation in L2 lexical tests, Helms-Park *et al.* (2009) collected data from two groups of English L2 undergraduates. The experimental group consisted of undergraduate speakers of Romanian ($n = 41$), a language which shares a profusion of Latin-based cognates with English. The control group consisted of undergraduate speakers of Vietnamese ($n = 24$), a language with only a few phonologically nativised borrowings from French and English. Romanian and Vietnamese share a Latinate script, eliminating the confound of script when testing involves visual (orthographic) word recognition.

The participants completed various levels of the Schmitt (2000) Vocabulary Levels Test (VLT) as well as a newly created version of the size test consisting of very low-frequency (uncommon) words in English. The rationale for using these tests was that these could reveal how cognate facilitation might vary with word frequency or with words from academic versus non-academic registers. Using these tests was further motivated by Cobb's (2000) finding that cognate facilitation could seriously skew the results of lexical tests for the purposes of placement in programmes. His Francophone participants, for example, managed to perform well on Nation's (1990) VLT because of the Latinate words in English, while failing to comprehend many basic Germanic words in English. Conversely, there is an equally legitimate view that L2 tests should accurately reflect cognate frequency in real corpora (e.g. Elgort, 2012; Eyckmans, 2004).

As is to be expected, the Academic Level of the VLT has a preponderance of cognates between Romance languages and English, and in the specific case of Romanian, 24 out of 30 test items here are semantically congruent cognates of Romanian words (e.g. *sumă* 'sum' or *a converti* 'convert'). As expected, the Romanian group outperformed the Vietnamese group despite the fact that both groups performed very close to ceiling (Romanians at 98.86% and Vietnamese at 96.7%). The difference was due to the Romanian group's better performance on cognate items, as both groups performed comparably on non-cognates. Thus, even when the words being tested belong to a register that is well known to participants, as was the case with academic vocabulary here, a cognate facilitation effect is observable.

The magnitude of the cognate facilitation effect increases in the 10,000-word level, which has words that are fairly low frequency but generally outside an academic corpus (e.g. Coxhead, 2000). Twelve of the words are cognate with Romanian and 18 are not. Scores for the Romanian speakers were significantly higher, with a large effect size, for cognates than non-cognates, as well as being significantly higher than the Vietnamese speakers' scores for cognates and non-cognates respectively. The cognate and non-cognate scores for the Vietnamese speakers were statistically indistinguishable.

To test for cognate facilitation at even lower frequency levels (ranging from the 12,000 to 20,000 level), we created a new section of the VLT with Romanian-English cognates (e.g. *peregrination, extirpation*) and non-cognate distractors (e.g. *squib, gerrymander*). Within the lowest frequency bands, the effects of cognate facilitation were even more pronounced, with the Romanian group ($n = 24$) once again outperforming the Vietnamese one ($n = 17$) on the cognates and also scoring better on cognates than on non-cognates, with large effect sizes. The Romanian group performed as well as a group of native English speakers ($n = 22$), and the pattern of results shows that this is due to better performance on cognates. The difference between cognates and non-cognates was only significant for Romanian-speaking participants, and not for Vietnamese and English speakers. In light of the rarity of some of the words in question, it is likely that the Romanian speakers had not yet encountered some of these words in English and could yet arrive at their meanings.

These findings not only highlight the lexical advantage that L2 learners of genetically related L1s have but also underline the role of word frequency in cognate facilitation. The special advantage of the 'high frequency L1 versus low frequency L2' formula highlighted in Peeters *et al.*'s (2013) experiment is congruent with these VLT results. However, the explanation for these parallel results requires much closer scrutiny since the mechanisms at play in online and offline tasks can be assumed to be dissimilar to a large extent.

In a second study, Petrescu and Helms-Park (2014) used a Yes-No test to further probe the impact of cognate facilitation on L2 test results. The Yes-No instrument, an unpaced version of a lexical decision task, is frequently used in language teaching units for quick placement of students in a language programme. Once again, in this study the experimental group consisted of L1 Romanian-L2 English undergraduates ($n = 33$) and a corresponding Vietnamese L1-English L2 comparison group ($n = 30$). The test contained 138 mixed-frequency items, of which 40 items were semantically congruent Romanian-English cognates with full or partial formal overlap (e.g. *maniac – maniac* and *mamut – mammoth*); 17 items were 'quasi-cognates' (partially overlapping in meaning, as in *intoxicate* or *notorious*); 21 items were 'misleading cognates' (e.g. *preservative* and *pregnant*); 20 items were pseudo-cognates (as defined by Hall, 2002, e.g. Romanian *anormal* for *abnormal*); 20 items were non-cognate real words; and 20 items were nonce words that did not resemble Romanian-English cognates.

An analysis of the class-by-class scores revealed that the Romanian group outperformed the Vietnamese group only in the recognition of semantically congruent cognates with formal overlap. This advantage disappeared for word pairs with only partial semantic overlap (irrespective of form) as well as for all of the distractors. The findings suggested that advanced-level Romanian speakers block pseudo-cognates such as *anormal* as potential L2 lexical items, possibly because they have been expunged by attested words such as *abnormal*. Interestingly, the Vietnamese speakers also excluded such pseudo-cognates, possibly for the same reasons as the Romanians or because these were *not* attested in the input. Most importantly, the findings indicated that semantically and formally congruent cognates have a special status in the bilingual lexicon, possibly because a stimulus activates both semantic and orthographic/phonological aspects of the cognate in both of the languages.

In summary, online and offline psycholinguistic experimentation points to a conclusion that cognates constitute a special class of words in bilingual mental lexicons, as they are processed faster and more efficiently and forgotten less easily than other kinds of L2 words. It is likely that in order for cognate facilitation to become detectable in online performance, the learner needs to reach a certain, yet undefined, lexical proficiency threshold, as well as a certain minimal level of orthographic decoding and spoken word recognition facility. Establishing this threshold is a yet unresolved matter of theoretical and pedagogical importance. The findings involving L2 lexical tests highlight the lexical advantages that cognates bestow on advanced-level learners with L1s that are related to their L2s. However, in this limited research context at least, this advantage is most pronounced when (i) cognates in the L2 are very low frequency or (ii) high levels of semantic and formal overlap exists between cognates. Notably, contrary to the online studies reviewed in the previous section, our offline findings indicate that a high degree of formal overlap alone is unable to override less-than-perfect semantic overlap in situations where untimed tests are being used to assess bilinguals' lexical knowledge. On the basis of these results, we recommend that learners' performance on cognates and non-cognates be viewed both together and separately, or, where this is too cumbersome, assessors take some note of learners' L1s when evaluating individual results.

Representation, Activation Patterns and Pedagogical Implications

Representation and activation patterns

Whether examining the processing of cognates within a steady-state lexicon or the processing of input during the acquisition of cognates, the issue of lexical activation remains front and centre. If we were to assume that only the selected or context-relevant lexicon is activated and the other inhibited (Scarborough *et al.*, 1984), cognate facilitation could not be explained satisfactorily. Only access to both of the lexicons ('non-selective' activation) can account for empirical evidence of inter-lexical influence. A study by de Groot and Nas (1991) that revealed that cognates, but not non-cognates, exhibited interlingual associate priming effects can be explained in no other way. (For instance, English *baker* primed Dutch *brood* 'bread', but English *blanket* did not prime Dutch *laken* 'sheet'.) Similarly, studies demonstrating cognate facilitation across three languages cannot be accommodated by a theory positing selective activation.

A minority of online studies argue in favour of related intralingual and interlingual cognates being morphological variants of a single entry in the bilingual lexicon; in this scenario, only non-cognates have language-specific representations (Lotto & de Groot, 1998; Sánchez-Casas & García-Albea, 2005). Acquisition is said to be simple because no new entry need be created. Activation of the shared morphological representation of the cognates (the 'etymological root'), enhanced through input from both languages, is said to result in the kind of cognate facilitation witnessed in online tasks. However, an array of online studies, including many of those discussed in above, demonstrate that (i) there is a reaction-time difference (in favour of cognates) between a target word primed by a morphologically related non-cognate prime and a cognate prime; and (ii) reaction times in L2 lexical decision tasks decrease as orthographic overlap between cognates increases (e.g. Dijkstra *et al.*, 2010; Voga & Grainger, 2007). In fact, as mentioned earlier, in Peeters *et al.*'s (2013) study, identical cognates provided disproportionally greater processing advantages than near-identical ones. Furthermore, Peeters and colleagues contend that separate morphological representations account for language-specific characteristics (e.g. in inflectional behaviour, interaction with syntax, frequency, and register and style) as well as the fact that L1 and L2 cognates are almost always acquired in different contexts.

Collectively, these studies put forward the view that similarities in phonological/orthographic form are crucial to the co-activation of cognates.

This activation, in turn, is heightened by similarities in semantic content. In cases of relatively quick cognate recognition, phonological neighbours are activated in both of the bilingual's languages, leading to a realisation that (i) there is a lexeme in the L1 that has a similar phonological structure; and, when further exposed to this lexeme, (ii) it carries the same meaning as its L1 counterpart (Carroll, 1992). Such a mechanism could also lead to the assumption, often correct but sometimes not, that congruent L1 and L2 lexemes have the same meaning ('lemma mediation', Jiang, 2000). Where there is some discrepancy in the two meanings, it is only after receiving rich positive evidence, and likely some negative evidence, that the inaccuracy is corrected.

The implications for pedagogy are that crosslinguistic morphological approaches to cognate acquisition have limited value, as has long been witnessed in the L2 classroom. In general, examining crosslinguistic ties requires a high level of metalinguistic awareness, linguistic knowledge and lexical sophistication, even when the interlingual morphological variants are not drastically different in shape, for example, French *loup* ('wolf') and English *lupine* connected via an etymological morpheme such as *lup-*. In complex cases involving variants that are very different in shape, the learner would need even greater sophistication, as in Latin *aurora* and Serbo-Croatian *zora*. Looking for morphological links within the target language itself, for example, among words such as *economic, economy, economist* and *economical* offers far more promise. Although there are situations where cognates share morphological structure in a relatively transparent fashion (e.g. English *mother+ly* and Danish *moder+lige*), a general conclusion is that the learner's attention is more profitably directed to what online studies have uncovered as key levels of representation: phonological and/or orthographic form and meaning.

Difficulties posed by cognates and pedagogical interventions

While there is a steadily growing corpus of findings to support cognate facilitation, positive L1-to-L2 transfer in this regard is not always successful. One of the most reported problems is that of learners being trapped by semantically misleading transfer (Carroll, 1992; Daulton, 2008; Horst et al., 2010). During the acquisition process delineated above, an L2 phonological form in the input could activate an L1 phonological neighbour, which then could be mistakenly assigned an L1 meaning, as when English speakers assume that Spanish *sopa* is *soap* (instead of *soup*). More complicated are cognates that overlap only partially in meaning since they are frequently treated as identical, as when Romanian *a intoxica* and English *intoxicate* are considered synonymous (see above), giving rise to utterances in Romanian speakers' English such as *the children were intoxicated by bad seafood* (Maria Claudia Petrescu, personal communication). Similarly, the

Japanese loanword *mansion* continues to represent a dwelling place (viz. a condominium), without the additional semantic component of 'grandiosely large'; such a meaning can be easily carried over to English because of the misleading semantic overlap (Jones, 2014).

Less serious problems are transference of L1 syntax and collocations as well as a stilted style resulting from an infrequent item in the L2 being overproduced because of its high L1 frequency. Another relatively minor side effect (at least in our opinion) of the close links between L1 and L2 cognates lies in pronunciation. Due to their formal similarity, cognates are particularly likely to 'short-circuit' in word production and cause phonetic transfer (Paterson & Goldrick, 2008). Amengual (2012), for instance, found that various types of Spanish-English bilinguals pronounced the /t/ in the Spanish counterpart of an English cognate with a longer VOT (voice onset time), as they would in English; this was not the case with non-cognates.

A different type of difficulty relates to L2 speech perception. In a best-case scenario, cognates in auditory form are recognised automatically. However, when there is partial overlap of form, inexperienced listeners often fail to identify a cognate word since they are still undergoing a process of habituation to the L1-L2 correspondence rules. When learners are able to 'correct' the L2 input during online speech perception and when they encounter a cognate frequently, they have an increased chance of recognising the item as a cognate and form a separate lexical representation for it (Warter, 1995, 2001).

Research in the United States demonstrates that in the junior grades (e.g. Grade 4) students often have difficulty recognising Spanish-English cognates. Children's sensitivity to orthographic cognates is dependent on many intersecting variables that often cluster with age and grade level, such as reading and academic skills and level of L1 ability (including previous knowledge of the word/concept in the L1), as well as the degree of visual and phonological correspondence between the item and its cross-language translation equivalent (García, 1991; Nagy *et al.*, 1993; Kelley & Kohnert, 2012; Leacox, 2011).

Classroom instruction has been found to give learners, especially new ones, an enormous boost even when the orthographic or phonological systems of the two languages make cognate status relatively transparent. In the case of closely related languages such as Spanish and English, many advocate inductive techniques. Garrison (1990), for example, recommends providing paradigmatic examples, such as *civilization* ~ *civilización* and *nation* ~ *nación,* and then asking students to determine what the Spanish equivalents of *investigation* and *transportation* are. Similarly, Horst *et al.* (2010) used inductive strategies for discovering English-French cognates expeditiously, for example, by asking francophone learners of English if *rice* in the video version of Maurice Sendak's *Chicken Soup and Rice* (1962) was the same as *riz* ('rice') in French, or if *crocodile* meant the same in the two languages. (Both answers are in the affirmative.)

One area where online and offline research has been unclear is how auditory and visual stimuli in the L2, either discretely or in tandem, facilitate or impede cognate recognition. Caplan-Carbin (2006) illustrates how mindful instructors need to be of modality in this regard; for example, in auditory mode without the articulation of /t/, the English word *often* could easily be (incorrectly) paired with German *ofen* 'oven', but in visual mode, the word would have a better chance of being (correctly) matched with *oft*. Caplan-Carbin also highlights the benefits of pointing out systematic diachronic changes leading to differences in cognate realisation, for example, *ss/ß* /s/ in German often alternates with *t* /t/ in English, seen in German-English pairs such as *Wasser* and *water*, or *Straße* and *street*.

Research also reveals that having the same script but with dissimilar orthographic and phonological systems prevents learners from discovering cognates expeditiously, as in the cases of Polish-English cognates such as *egzystencja* and *menedżer* ('existence' and 'manager' respectively). In Otwinowska-Kasztelanic's (2009) classroom-based study with advanced Polish-speaking learners of English, both experimental and control groups were informed about the existence of Polish-English cognates as well as well-attested vocabulary learning strategies. However, only the experimental group was given explicit instruction on cognates and encouraged to process Polish-English cognates in an elaborative way. At the end of the treatment, the experimental group recognised a significantly larger number of cognates in a text and produced more cognates in a composition than the control group did, suggesting that even advanced Polish-speaking learners of English needed considerable awareness training to benefit from the existence of the sizeable number of semantically helpful cognates that are shared by Polish and English.

The issue of modality becomes the crux of cognate recognition in cases where the two related languages do not share the same script. Helms-Park and Perhan (forthcoming) found that recognition (through activation of orthographic/phonological neighbours) is frequently delayed when cognates appear in different scripts since there are no visual cues to signal the relationship between cognate pairs. In the case of Ukrainian, which uses the Cyrillic script, while English uses the Latin one, many of the participants in the study were not aware that the two Indo-European languages contained a wide range of related words. Script differences, compounded by differences in the languages' sound systems, seemed to not only camouflage cognate status but also make phonological decoding of newly encountered 'academic' words laborious. In cases involving both sound and script differences, it appears that making explicit connections between cognates is especially advantageous since induction generally delays cognate recognition unnecessarily.

Helms-Park and Perhan (forthcoming) determined that explicit instruction (e.g. making learners aware of Ukrainian-English cognates through a quick history of Ukrainian and examining the internal structure of cognate pairs) was more valuable to Ukrainian-English bilinguals than indirect forms of discovery (e.g. reading texts replete with cognates). While focusing on cognates in isolation in an unpaced, solitary task helped those who did not receive explicit instruction to discover the meanings of several Ukrainian-English cognates, these learners, unlike the ones who had received explicit instruction, did not improve in their ability to use cognates in production.

Classroom-based research also highlights the value of helping learners to gain heightened awareness of the divergent meanings of cognates (e.g. French *anniversaire* ('anniversary' *and* 'birthday') and English *anniversary* in Horst et al.'s 2010 study, discussed above). Explicit knowledge of semantic shift is possibly even more necessary when cognates are both cross-script and semantically divergent. In Jones' (2014) study involving Japanese-English loanwords, for instance, two teaching interventions were used, the first in which only the English meanings of such words were delineated, and the second in which both the Japanese and the English ones were outlined. The contrastive approach, providing negative evidence (i.e. what the English meanings do not represent), was significantly more successful than the English-only approach (see also Daulton, 2008).

Conclusion

Examining cognate facilitation through a combination of electrophysiological and behavioural research is a very promising means of discovering the complexities of the bilingual lexicon. The implications of present and future findings for L2 pedagogy and L2 testing are profound, as they are for work on conditions such as aphasia and language attrition in bilinguals (see, for example, Costa et al., 2005). As is clear from the studies cited in this chapter, the locus of psycholinguistic work on L2 lexical acquisition and cognate facilitation has been, for the most part, in the more westerly parts of Europe and in North America (mainly on account of French and Spanish); however, new insights could be gained through studying multilingual speakers of language families outside these geographical areas. There are several research questions pertaining to cognate facilitation that have not been adequately answered as yet, of which the interaction between auditory and visual input, comparisons between the contextualised and decontextualised use of cognates in online facilitation tasks, the therapeutic use of cognates in language loss, and best practices in L2 pedagogy and assessment are but a few.

References

Amengual, M. (2012) Interlingual influence in bilingual speech: Cognate status effect in a continuum of bilingualism. *Bilingualism: Language and Cognition* 15, 517–530.
Ard, J. and Homburg, T. (1983) Verification of language transfer. In S. Gass and L. Selinker (eds) *Language Transfer in Language Learning* (pp. 157–176). Rowley, MA: Newbury House.
Beeman, W.O. (2000, August 16) Idiosyncrasies of the word 'butterfly' [Msg 11.1765]. Summary posted to http://linguistlist.org/issues/11/11-1765.html
Besson, M., Kutas, M. and van Petten, C. (1992) An event-related potential (ERP) analysis of semantic congruity and repetition effects in sentences. *Journal of Cognitive Neuroscience*. MIT Press.
Caplan-Carbin, E. (2006) Diachronic Linguistics in the Classroom: Sound Shifts and Cognate Recognition. Available: http://webgerman.com/caplan/
Carroll, S. (1992) On cognates. *Second Language Research* 8, 93–119.
Christoffels, I., Firk, C. and Schiller, N. (2007) Bilingual language control: An event-related brain potential study. *Brain Research* 1147, 192–208.
Cobb, T. (2000) One size fits all? Francophone learners and English vocabulary tests. *Canadian Modern Language Review* 57, 295–324.
Costa, A., Caramazza, A. and Sebastián-Gallés, N. (2000) The cognate facilitation effect: Implications for models of lexical access. *Journal of Experimental Psychology: Learning, Memory, and Cognition* 26, 1283–1296.
Costa, A., Santesteban, M. and Caño, A. (2005) On the facilitatory effects of cognate words in bilingual speech production. *Brain and Language* 94, 94–103.
Coxhead, A. (2000) A New Academic Word List. *TESOL Quarterly* 34 (2), 213–238.
Cristoffanini, P.M., Kirsner, K. and Milech, D. (1986) Bilingual lexical representation: The status of Spanish-English cognates. *The Quarterly Journal of Experimental Psychology* 38, 367–393.
Daulton, F. (2008) *Japan's Built in Lexicon of English-Based Words*. Clevedon, UK: Multilingual Matters.
Davis, C., Sánchez-Casas R., García-Albea J., Guasch M., Molero M. and Ferré P. (2010) Masked translation priming: Varying language experience and word type with Spanish-English bilinguals. *Bilingualism: Language and Cognition* 13, 137–155.
De Groot, A. and Keijzer, R. (2000) What is hard to learn is easy to forget: The roles of word concreteness, cognate status, and word frequency in foreign-language vocabulary learning and forgetting. *Language Learning* 50, 1–56.
De Groot, A.M.B. and Nas, G.L.J. (1991) Lexical representations of cognates and noncognates in compound bilinguals. *Journal of Memory and Language* 30, 90–123.
Dijkstra, T., Miwa, K., Brummelhuis, B., Sappelli, M. and Baayen, H. (2010) How cross-language similarity and task demands affect cognate recognition. *Journal of Memory and Language* 62, 284–301.
Dijkstra, A., Grainger, J. and van Heuven, W.J.B. (1999) Recognizing cognates and interlingual homographs: The neglected role of phonology. *Journal of Memory and Language* 41, 496–518.
Dijkstra, A., van Jaarsveld, H. and ten Brinke, S. (1998) Interlingual homograph recognition: Effects on task demands and language intermixing. *Bilingualism: Language and Cognition* 1, 51–66.
Dimitropoulou, M., Duñabeitia, J.A. and Carreiras, M. (2011) Masked translation priming effects with low proficient bilinguals. *Memory & Cognition* 39, 260–275.
Duyck, W. and Warlop, N. (2009) Translation priming between the native language and a second language. New evidence from Dutch-French bilinguals. *Experimental Psychology* 56, 173–179.

Elgort, I. (2012) Effects of L1 definitions and cognate status on test items on the vocabulary size test. *Language Testing* 30, 253–272.
Eyckmans, J. (2004) *Measuring Receptive Vocabulary Size. Reliability and Validity of the Yes/No Vocabulary Test for French-Speaking Learners of Dutch*. Utrecht: Landelijke Onderzoeksschool Taalwetenschap.
García, G.E. (1991) Factors influencing the English reading test performance of Spanish-speaking Hispanic children. *Reading Research Quarterly* 26, 371–92.
Garrison, D. (1990) Inductive Strategies for Teaching Spanish-English Cognates. *Hispania* 73 (2), 508–12.
Gerard, L.D. and Scarborough, D.L. (1989) Language-specific lexical access of homographs by bilinguals. *Journal of Experimental Psychology: Learning, Memory, and Cognition* 15, 305–315.
Gollan, T.H. and Acenas, L.A.R. (2004) What is a TOT? Cognate and translation effects on tip-of-the-tongue states in Spanish-English and Tagalog-English bilinguals. *Journal of Experimental Psychology: Learning, Memory, and Cognition* 30, 246–269.
Gollan, T.H., Forster, K.I. and Frost, R. (1997) Translation priming with different scripts: Masked priming with cognates and non-cognates in Hebrew-English bilinguals. *Journal of Experimental Psychology: Learning, Memory, and Cognition* 23, 1122–1139.
Gooskens, C. and van Bezooijen, R. (2006) Mutual comprehensibility of written Afrikaans and Dutch: Symmetrical or asymmetrical? *Literary and Linguistic Computing* 21, 543–557.
Greenhill, S.J., Blust. R. and Gray, R.D. (2008) The Austronesian Basic Vocabulary Database: From bioinformatics to lexomics. *Evolutionary Bioinformatics* 4, 271–28
Hall, C. (2002) The automatic cognate form assumption: Evidence for the parasitic model of vocabulary development. *IRAL* 40, 69–87.
Helms-Park, R. and Perhan, Z. (forthcoming) The role of explicit instruction in cross-script cognate recognition: The case of Ukrainian-speaking EAP learners. *Journal of English for Academic Purposes*.
Helms-Park, R., Petrescu, M. and Dronjic, V. (2009) Empirical evidence of cognate facilitation in established and newly designed lexical tests. Paper presented at the 2009 Conference of the American Association of Applied Linguistics, Denver, CO.
Horst, M., White, L. and Bell, P. (2010) First and second language knowledge in the language classroom. *International Journal of Bilingualism* 14 (3), 331–349.
Janhunen, J. (1998) Samoyedic. In D.M. Abondolo (ed.) *The Uralic Languages* (pp. 457–479). New York: Routledge.
Jiang, N. (2000) Lexical representation and development in a second language. *Applied Linguistics* 21, 47–77.
Jones, K. (2014) Loan Word Facilitation in the Acquisition of English Lexis by Speakers of Japanese. Master's thesis, University of Toronto.
Kelley, A. and Kohnert, K. (2012) Is there a cognate advantage for typically developing Spanish-speaking English-language learners? *Language, Speech, and Hearing Services in Schools* 43, 191–204.
Kirsner, K., Brown, H.L., Abrol, S., Chadha, A. and Sharma, N.K. (1980) Bilingualism and lexical representation. *The Quarterly Journal of Experimental Psychology* 32, 565–574.
Kondrak, G. (2003) Phonetic alignment and similarity. *Computer and the Humanities* 37, 273–291
Kroll, J.F. and Sunderman, G. (2003) Cognitive processes in second language learners and bilinguals: The development of lexical and conceptual representations. In C. Doughty and M. Long (eds) *Handbook of Second Language Acquisition*. Cambridge, MA: Blackwell Publishers.
Leacox, L. (2011) Young English Learners' Cognate Sensitivity on Picture-Word Recognition and Production. Electronic Theses, Treatises and Dissertations. Paper 5767.

Lotto, L. and de Groot, A.M.B. (1998) Effects of learning method and word type on acquiring vocabulary in an unfamiliar language. *Language Learning* 48, 31–69.
Marslen-Wilson, W. (1987) Functional parallelism in spoken word-recognition. *Cognition* 25, 71–102.
Marslen-Wilson, W. (1990) Activation, competition, and frequency in lexical access. In G.T.M. Altmann (ed.) *Cognitive Models of Speech Processing: Psycholinguistic and Computational Perspectives* (pp. 148–172). Cambridge, MA: MIT Press.
McClelland, J.L. and Elman, J.L. (1986) The TRACE model of speech perception. *Cognitive Psychology* 18, 1–86.
Midgley, K., Holcomb P. Grainger J. (2011) Effects of cognate status on word comprehension in second language learners: An ERP investigation. *Journal of Cognitive Neuroscience* 23 (7), 1634–47.
Nagy, W.E., García, G.E., Durgunoğlu, A. and Hancin-Bhatt, B. (1993) Spanish-English bilingual children's use and recognition of cognates in English reading. *Journal of Reading Behavior* 25, 241–59.
Nakayama, M., Sears, C.R., Hino, Y. and Lupker, S.J. (2013) Masked translation priming with Japanese-English bilinguals: Interactions between cognate status, target frequency and L2 proficiency. *Journal of Cognitive Psychology* 25, 949–981.
Nation, P. (1990) *Teaching and Learning Vocabulary*. New York: Newbury House.
Nichols, J.D. and Nyholm, E. (2002) *A Concise Dictionary of Modern Ojibwe* (5th ed.). Minneapolis: University of Minnesota Press.
Otwinowska-Kasztelanic, A. (2009) Raising awareness of cognate vocabulary as a strategy in teaching English to Polish adults. *Innovation in Language Learning and Teaching* 3, 131–147.
Paterson, N. and Goldrick, M. (2008) *The Pros and Cons of Cascading Activation in Bilingual Speech Production.* Paper presented at the 5th International Workshop on Language Production, Annapolis, Maryland.
Peeters, D., Dijkstra, T. and Grainger, J. (2013) The representation and processing of identical cognates by late bilinguals: RT and ERP effects. *Journal of Memory and Language* 68, 315–332.
Petrescu, M. and Helms-Park, R. (2014) Testing the Cognate Facilitation Hypothesis through an offline lexical decision task. Paper presented at the 9th International Conference on the Mental Lexicon, Niagara-on-the-Lake.
Ramat, P. (1998) The Germanic languages. In A. Giacalone Ramat and P. Ramat (eds) *The Indo-European languages* (pp. 380–414). New York: Routledge.
Ringbom, H. (1987) *The Role of First Language in Foreign Language Acquisition*. Clevedon: Multilingual Matters.
Ringe, D.A. (1992) On calculating the factor of chance in language comparison. *Transactions of the American Philosophical Society* 137, 91–109.
Roberts, P.M. and Deslauriers, L. (1999) Picture naming of cognate and non-cognate nouns in bilingual aphasia. *Journal of Communication Disorders* 32, 1–23.
Sánchez-Casas, R., Davis, C.W. and García-Albea, J.E. (1992) Bilingual lexical processing: Exploring the cognate/noncognate distinction. *European Journal of Cognitive Psychology* 4, 293–310.
Sánchez-Casas, R. and García-Albea, J.E. (2005) The representation of cognate and noncognate words in bilingual memory: Can cognate status be characterized as a special kind of morphological relation? In J.F. Kroll and A.M.B. de Groot (eds) *Handbook of Bilingualism: Psycholinguistic Approaches* (pp. 226–250). Oxford: Oxford University Press.
Scarborough, D.L., Gerard, L. and Cortese, C. (1984) Independence of lexical access in bilingual word recognition. *Journal of Verbal Learning and Verbal Behavior* 23, 84–99.
Schmitt, N. (2000) *Vocabulary in Language Teaching*. Cambridge: Cambridge University Press.

Shirai, S. (2012) Gemination in loans from English to Japanese. Master's thesis, University of Washington.
Trask, R.L. (1996) *Historical Linguistics*. London: Arnold.
Van Hell, J.G. and Dijkstra, T. (2002) Foreign language knowledge can influence native language performance in exclusively native contexts. *Psychonomic Bulletin and Review* 9, 780–789.
Voga, M. and Grainger, J. (2007) Cognate status and cross-script translation priming. *Memory & Cognition* 35, 938–952.
Warter, P. (1995) Computersimulation von Wortverstehen am Beispiel mittelniederdeutsch-skandinaviischer Sprachkontakte. In K. Braunmüller (ed.) *Niederdeutsch und die skandinavischen Sprachen II* (pp. 35–70). Heidelberg: Winter.
Warter, P. (2001) Lexical identification and decoding in Interscandinavian communication. *Arbeiten zur Mehrsprachigkeit/Working Papers in Multilingualism*, 21, 1–21.

6 Crosslinguistic Influence in the Acquisition of Spatial Prepositions in English as a Foreign Language

Rosa Alonso Alonso, Teresa Cadierno and Scott Jarvis

Introduction

Languages differ widely as to how they structure space. They differ in terms of the semantic granularity of their spatial markers (Bowerman & Choi, 2001; Wilkins & Hill, 1995) and also in terms of the semantic features and conceptual dimensions that determine their conventional use (Levinson, 1996; Pederson et al., 1998). As an illustration of both types of differences, the Spanish preposition EN covers approximately the same range of spatial relations as do the three English prepositions IN, ON and AT, whereas Dutch goes even further than English in that it distinguishes between two types of support relationships: the Dutch preposition AAN refers to spatial configurations such as a handle on a door, whereas the preposition OP refers to spatial configurations such as a book on a shelf (Bowerman, 1996). Previous research has found that the differences across languages in the expression of spatial relations constitute potential sources of difficulty for the expression of spatial relations in a second language (Ijaz, 1986; Jarvis & Odlin, 2000). The present study investigates the use of English prepositions by L2 learners from two different L1 backgrounds: Danish and Spanish. The study focuses on learners' construal of spatial configurations that are referred to by native English speakers with the prepositions IN, ON and AT. The present study also explores the extent to which learners' construal of these spatial configurations is likely to be influenced by the patterns of spatial construal that are prevalent in their L1s.

A Cognitive Linguistics Approach to Spatial Categorisation in Second Language Acquisition

As discussed by Tyler (2012a), a cognitive linguistics approach to the investigation of spatial prepositions explores the different meanings associated with prepositions, treating them as systematically motivated and grounded in human experience with the physical world. A person's choice of a preposition in a particular situation and in a particular language depends not only on the properties of the situation but also on the different elements of the situation and on how the speaker construes the relationship between them. The interplay of these factors can be seen in the differential choice of ON versus IN in the phrases 'the words on the page' and 'the words in the margin'. In the former phrase, the choice of ON reflects the fact that the paper is construed primarily as a supporting base for the words, whereas in the latter phrase, the choice of IN reflects the fact that the margin is construed as an area with a well-defined perimeter that contains the words (cf. Lee, 2001: 24–25). The choice of different prepositions in cases like this can thus be regarded as reflecting different construals. Construal, according to Langacker (1987: 487–499), is grounded in 'the relationship between a speaker (or hearer) and a situation that he conceptualizes and portrays'. Tyler (2008) similarly refers to construal as a human's ability to take different perspectives on a scene or event. This author argues that humans' embodied experience is reflected in language. Both of these definitions refer to construal as an individual-level phenomenon where, within a given language, a speaker can construe (i.e. conceptualise and express) a given phenomenon, situation or event in different ways. Tyler asserts that embodied experience occurs at the individual level but part of our environment is the language we speak and construal is reflected in language. According to Littlemore (2009), construal can also operate as a language-level phenomenon where different languages offer different conventions for construing situations and events. Crucially, the conventions for construal that exist within a particular language will affect the types of construal that are adopted and linguistically encoded by the language's individual speakers. Different languages promote different choices, and this has led Lee (2001) to assert that 'the notion of construal itself predicts that there should be some degree of conventionality (or arbitrariness) at work, since in situations that lend themselves to different construals, it is to be expected that the different languages will make different choices for their preferred coding' (27).

Bowerman (1996) similarly observed that languages make different types of categorical distinctions among spatial configurations. For instance, English uses IN to refer to a figure that is interior to a ground as in 'apple in a bowl', and uses ON to refer to a figure in contact with an outer surface, as in 'ring on a finger'. In contrast, Finnish uses the inessive case (-ssa) to refer to figures that can be either interior to a ground (e.g. 'kissa talossa' = 'cat in house') or tightly connected to its surface (e.g. 'sormus sormessa' = 'ring on finger'), and uses the adessive case (-lla) to refer to figures that are more loosely in contact with the outside surface of the ground ('kirja pöydällä' = 'book on table') (1996: 156). In other words, English uses ON to express contact regardless of whether the figure is loosely or tightly connected to the ground, whereas Finnish uses different locative cases depending on the nature of the contact: loose or close-fitting.

The fact that languages divide up and lexicalise spatial configurations and functions in different ways has also been addressed by Tyler and Evans (2003) in their Principled Polysemy Model, which provides a cognitive linguistics account of the various meanings associated with English prepositions in terms of systematically related polysemy networks. We recognise the value of this powerful model but do not rely on it in the present study because of the nature of our analysis, which focuses on learners' choice of spatial prepositions in contexts that reflect fairly prototypical meanings of IN, ON and AT. Our study is nevertheless motivated by a cognitive linguistics perspective that assumes crosslinguistic differences in the ways that speakers of different languages construe spatial configurations. We now turn to the findings of previous research regarding crosslinguistic differences and crosslinguistic influence in the expression of spatial relationships.

Crosslinguistic Differences and Crosslinguistic Influence in the Expression of Spatial Relationships

One of the misconceptions about spatial prepositions is that their use is determined solely by the spatial and geometrical configurations of the objects whose relationships they refer to (e.g. *apple in a bowl, pen on a table*). Although some prepositions in some languages (e.g. *above* in English) might refer relatively straightforwardly to geometrical configurations (but see Tyler & Evans, 2003), others are chosen more on the basis of extra-geometric information, such as location control. Location control refers to the likelihood that if the reference object moves, the located object will move with it (Coventry & Guijarro-Fuentes, 2008). The English preposition IN is chosen on the basis of both geometric (containment) and extra-geometric (location control) criteria. For example, an apple that is sitting inside a bowl is deemed by English speakers to be in the bowl because the apple is at least partially contained by the bowl and because the apple will move with the bowl if the bowl moves. An apple that is on a table underneath an upside-down bowl, on the other hand, is not in the bowl because, even though the apple is contained by the bowl, the apple will not move when the bowl moves. Studies reviewed by Coventry and Guijarro-Fuentes (2008) show that pre-linguistic infants are sensitive to both geometric and extra-geometric information in preferential looking tasks, and that it is not until infants begin acquiring their native language that their preferences become more language-specific (see also Bowerman & Choi, 2001; McDonough et al., 2003).

In the domain of second language acquisition, a study by Munnich and Landau (2010) compared Korean and Spanish learners of English on their receptive and productive performance with pictures and sentences representing various fine-grained spatial distinctions related to support (*on the table* versus *over the table*), containment (*in the bag* versus *on the bag*) and vertical displacement (e.g. *under the table* versus *over the table*). The results showed that both groups of participants performed well with prepositions denoting simple geometric relationships (e.g. *over* and *under*), but older learners (age of immersion > 13) in both groups had difficulty with the prepositions *in* and *on*. Critically, these latter prepositions are constrained by both geometric and extra-geometric factors, where '*in* entails both inclusion (geometry) and constraint of movement (function)... [whereas] *on* entails both contact (geometry) and support (function)' (55). Although the Korean-speaking and Spanish-speaking learners did not exhibit all of the same error patterns in their use of English prepositions, the authors of the study emphasised the finding that both groups were equally affected by maturational constraints (operationalised in this study as age of immersion) especially in their acquisition of the extra-geometrical entailments of L2 spatial terms.

Other studies investigating learners' development of the ability to refer to spatial relationships in a second language have suggested that this area of acquisition is guided more by universal principles than by crosslinguistic influence. In fact, this was the overall interpretation of the large-scale European Science Foundation (ESF) project dealing with the naturalistic acquisition of several European languages by native speakers of other European languages (see e.g. Perdue, 1993). Carroll and Becker (1993) provide a summary of the studies of learners' spatial reference that were included in the final report of this part of the ESF project (see Becker et al., 1988). The general finding was that, regardless of their language backgrounds and regardless of which target language they were learning, learners tended to proceed through the same stages of development regarding the spatial relationships they referred to and the linguistic means they used to do so at each stage of development. This finding is consistent with a good deal of research in the field of second language acquisition and even within the body of literature dealing with crosslinguistic influence. Numerous researchers have observed that learners tend to come to the task of acquiring a new language with a prior set of semantic predispositions that cannot be explained on the basis of learners' L1s. Such predispositions have been found to affect learners' expectations of the specific meanings and semantic ranges of target-language words (e.g. *break*; see Kellerman, 1978), even when those expected meanings are not encoded into the L1 (e.g. definiteness and referent specificity; see Huebner, 1985).

Importantly, the existence of acquisitional universals does not preclude the existence of crosslinguistic influence, and some studies have found evidence of both. For example, Schumann (1986) found that learners of English from a variety of L1 backgrounds produce similar cases of simplification (e.g. omission) and overgeneralisation of spatial prepositions. These are universal tendencies. However, the frequency of learners' omissions and the exact nature of their overgeneralisations reveal important effects of crosslinguistic influence. Sometimes the effects of crosslinguistic influence on learners' reference to spatial relationships are very clear. A study by Jarvis and Odlin (2000) found that Finnish-speaking and Swedish-speaking learners of English differ significantly in their preference for *on* versus *in*, respectively, when referring to a film scene where a man and a woman are sitting in the grass (or on the grass, depending on one's perspective) in someone's front yard. For English speakers, *in the grass* and *on the grass* are both grammatical. The choice of one versus the other among native English speakers appears to be affected by the height of the grass and possibly also by whether the grass is of uniform length or at least appears to have been cut at some point in the past. The grass in the film is of varying height and does not appear to have been cut, so the Swedish speakers' preference for *in the grass* seems quite logical from an English speaker's perspective. However, the design of the study did not make it possible to determine which specific conditions or conceptual considerations led to the different prepositional choices between the Finnish speakers and Swedish speakers. The differences in their preferences for *in* versus *on* in this context suggest that they either (a) did not share the same form-meaning mappings for these prepositions, perhaps as the result of semantic transfer; (b) did not conceptualise the scene in the same way, perhaps as the result of conceptual transfer; or (c) were guided by different sets of linguistic constraints regarding the appropriate choice of preposition (e.g. in this context, both *in* and *on* are appropriate with *grass*, but only *on* would be appropriate with *lawn*), possibly as the result of structural transfer. Critically, crosslinguistic influence (or transfer) could be the explanation behind any one of these possibilities. If semantic transfer alone were the explanation, this would mean that the Finnish speakers and Swedish speakers conceptualised the relationship between the people and the grass in the same way, but they did not share the same understanding of which preposition this meaning maps onto. If conceptual transfer were at play, this would mean that the Finnish speakers and Swedish speakers did not view the scene in the same way; even if they perceived the geometry between the people and the grass identically, they could still have differed in terms of the functional and contextual considerations that determined in their minds whether the people in the film were sitting *in* versus *on* the grass. Finally, if structural transfer were the reason for the difference, then this would mean that the Finnish speakers and Swedish speakers shared the same form-meaning mappings for *in* and *on*, and also conceptualised the scene in the same way, but were induced by a structural constraint in their native language (or other previously learnt language) to disregard meaning considerations in order to meet (what they thought was) an obligatory requirement of the target language's grammar.

Conceptual transfer in learners' spatial reference is perhaps the most intriguing of these three possibilities. Conceptual transfer in this case is essentially the notion that speakers of different languages (and thus learners from different L1 backgrounds) conceptualise and construe spatial relationships differently. The present study does not directly examine this possibility, but the Munnich and Landau (2010) study that was discussed earlier did touch on it, and a more recent study by Park and Ziegler (2014) has addressed this question even more directly while examining Korean-English bilinguals' reference to motion events that can be described with the verb + preposition combination *put in* or *put on*. The participants were given two nonverbal tasks (a triad matching task and a picture sorting task) where they were asked to indicate which pictures depicted similar versus different spatial relationships, and also to indicate how similar those relationships were. The bilinguals' performance on the two tasks showed four different patterns: (a) reliance on the L1 Korean pattern of focusing on whether the action resulted in a tight fit or loose fit between the located object and the reference object, (b) reliance on the L2 English pattern of focusing on whether the action resulted in the located object becoming contained by the reference object, (c) convergence of the L1 and L2 patterns and (d) patterns that did not resemble either the L1 or L2. L1 influence was clearly present in patterns (a) and (c), and the researchers also reported that the patterns the bilinguals showed correlated with their levels of L2 English proficiency. Those with the lowest English proficiency followed the Korean pattern, those with the highest English proficiency exhibited the English pattern and those in the middle tended to show convergence between the two systems.

The results of past studies thus show that the acquisition of the ability to construe and express spatial relationships in a second language is a complex and multifaceted process, with different factors coming into play at different stages of acquisition. Past studies have documented universal tendencies in the spatial meanings that learners refer to, the linguistic means they use to refer to these meanings and the stages they progress through, but crosslinguistic influence has also been found to affect learners' choice of spatial markers at all but the highest levels of L2 proficiency. In many cases, crosslinguistic influence is difficult to detect in this domain, but proper comparisons often reveal crosslinguistic influence even in cases where it is not directly visible (Jarvis & Odlin, 2000; Schumann, 1986). The source of crosslinguistic influence in this domain is more difficult to isolate, partly because the possible sources are manifold (e.g. structural, semantic, conceptual), and partly because of the lack of well-developed methods for disambiguating the sources. The present study is not designed to disambiguate the sources of crosslinguistic influence in learners' spatial reference, but it is designed to gauge the magnitude of crosslinguistic effects that can be found in the spatial reference of learners whose L1s are closely related versus distantly related to the L2.

The Study

The present study addresses the following research questions:

(1) How do Danish-speaking and Spanish-speaking learners of English construe spatial configurations that are typically referred to by native English speakers with the prepositions IN, ON and AT?
(2) Do Danish-speaking and Spanish-speaking learners of English differ from each other in their construal of these spatial configurations in L2 English?
(3) Do Danish-speaking and Spanish-speaking learners' spatial construals in L2 English reflect an influence of spatial construal patterns in their L1s?

The design of the study is ultimately based on Jarvis' (2000) methodological framework for investigating L1 influence, which outlines three types of evidence that should be considered in any rigorous study of L1 influence: (a) intra-L1-group homogeneity in learners' target-language behaviour, (b) inter-L1-group heterogeneity across groups of learners performing in the same target language and (c) congruity between learners' L1 and target-language behaviour. The first criterion in Jarvis' framework is only implicitly present in the design of the present study, but the second criterion is the basis for Research Question 2, and the third criterion is the basis for Research Question 3. Crucially, the methodological framework proposed by Jarvis also includes the stipulation that the effects of potentially confounding factors need to be controlled or otherwise ruled out. Such factors include between-group differences in age, cognitive maturity, target-language proficiency, type and amount of exposure to the target language, level of education and so forth. In the present study, we have attempted to recruit Danish-speaking and Spanish-speaking learners of English who were as comparable as possible in relation to these variables.

Participants

The participants in the present study include two learner groups, two L1 control groups and one native control group. The learner groups included 21 Spanish-speaking learners of L2 English from the University of Vigo whose level of English proficiency was C1 (i.e. advanced) on the Common European Framework of Reference for Languages (CEFR) scale, as well as 15 Danish-speaking learners of L2 English from the University of Southern Denmark whose level of proficiency was also C1 on the CEFR scale. The L1 control groups consisted of 20 native Spanish speakers who were first-year students at the University of Vigo, and 20 native Danish speakers at the University of Southern Denmark. The Danish participants started learning English when they were 9 years old and the Spanish subjects started learning it when they were 4 years old. The L1 control groups were not monolingual, but they were not actively studying a second or foreign language at the time of the study. The native control group included 19 native English speakers who were undergraduate students at Ohio University.

Materials and procedures

Two written tasks were used for data collection: a picture-description task and a sentence-completion task. Both tasks were taken from Murphy's (1991) *English Grammar in Use*. The picture-description task consisted of ten pictures depicting simple and commonly encountered spatial configurations, such as a label on a bottle, a car at a traffic light and a key in a door. Beneath the pictures were 13 questions beginning with the word 'where'. Three of the 10 pictures were accompanied by more than one 'where' question. For example, one of the pictures showed a door with a notice pinned to it and a key in the keyhole. The questions that accompanied this picture were 'Where's the notice?' and 'Where's the key?' The sentence-completion task consisted of 10 written sentences, each with a missing preposition that the participants were asked to supply. An example of one of the sentences is 'There were fifty rooms _____ the hotel.' The participants were given 20 minutes to complete both tasks. The target preposition for each item in both tasks was either IN, ON or AT, although native and non-native participants often provided answers that extended beyond these options. Our analysis focuses on those items where the native control group showed a strong preference for only these three prepositions.

Results

All items included in the present study were statistically analysed by means of Fisher's exact tests in order to determine whether different groups of participants exhibited significant differences in their prepositional choices. In some cases, participants did not produce a preposition at all but instead produced a simple noun or noun phrase. For instance, in an item on the picture-description task that depicts a fly on a man's arm and asks 'Where is the fly?,' some participants simply answered 'arm'. Those cases where participants produced a bare noun or simple noun phrase have been labelled as 'noun' in the following tables. However, instances representing the 'noun' category were not included in the statistical analysis.

The results obtained from the data analysis are displayed in the following tables. The tables are organised according to the three research questions and they are presented as follows: Tables 6.1 to 6.4 show the results produced by English native speakers in the use of the prepositions ON, IN and AT and the results produced by Danish speakers and Spanish learners, i.e. they compare the English native speakers' results with those produced by the two learners' groups. Table 6.5 contains the results of the Danish and Spanish learners' groups, more specifically the differences which were statistically significant in the use of the prepositions ON, IN and AT between Danish learners and Spanish learners. Finally, Tables 6.6 to 6.9 indicate the results of the two control groups, i.e. the Danish L1 speakers and the Spanish L1 speakers. Tables 6.6 and 6.7 indicate the results

Table 6.1 Spatial relationships conventionally described with ON by English native speakers. Comparison with Danish learners and Spanish learners: Percentages

Item	Task	Native English speakers		Danish learners		Spanish learners	
LABEL ON BOTTLE	PD	on	84.2	on	100	in	47.6
		noun	15.8			on	42.9
						at	4.8
						into	4.8
FLY ON ARM	PD	on	84.2	on	100	on	76.2
		noun	15.8			in	23.8
NOTICE ON DOOR	PD	on	84.2	on	100	on	47.6
		noun	15.8			at	47.6
						other	4.8
SHELF ON WALL	PD	on	94.7	on	93.3	on	76.2
		noun	5.3	upon	6.7	at	14.3
						in	9.5
SCAR ON CHEEK	SC	on	100	on	100	on	57.1
						in	33.3
						at	9.5
NAME ON DOOR	SC	on	100	on	100	on	47.6
						at	42.9
						in	9.5

Table 6.2 Spatial relationships conventionally described with IN by English native speakers. Comparison with Danish learners and Spanish learners: Percentages

Item	Task	Native English speakers		Danish learners		Spanish learners	
KEY IN DOOR	PD	in	84.2	in	100	in	57.1
		noun	15.8			other	19.0
						on	9.5
						at	9.5
						no answer	4.8
EIFFEL TOWER IN PARIS	PD	in	78.9	in	100	in	85.7
		noun	21.1			on	9.5
						at	4.8
TRAVEL IN CAR	SC	in	89.5	in	93.3	in	38.1
		to	10.5	by	6.7	on	23.8
						by	23.8
						with	14.3
ROOMS IN A HOTEL	SC	in	84.2	in	86.7	in	71.4
		at	15.8	at	13.3	at	28.6

of the Danish L1 control group for the prepositions PÅ and I respectively while Table 6.8 indicates the difference between the results obtained in the Danish control group as compared with Danish learners. No table is displayed regarding the results of the Spanish control group and the group of Spanish learners as the results are similar, therefore we focused on the cases where the Spanish control group differed from the English native speakers. Table 6.9 contains the results of the Spanish control group and its difference with English speakers.

English native speakers and Danish and Spanish learners of English

Research question 1: How do Danish-speaking and Spanish-speaking learners of English construe spatial configurations that are typically referred to by native English speakers with the prepositions IN, ON and AT?

Table 6.1 shows the items from both the picture-description (PD) task and the sentence-completion (SC) task where a clear majority of the native English speakers chose the preposition ON. Table 6.2 shows the items where native English speakers showed a clear preference for IN, and Table 6.3 shows the corresponding descriptive statistics for items where native speakers exhibited a clear preference for AT. Table 6.4 lists the items where native English speakers' preferences were divided between AT and ON. Each of these tables shows the percentages of participants in each

Table 6.3 Spatial relationships conventionally described with AT by English native speakers. Comparison with Danish learners and Spanish learners: Percentages

Item	Task	Native English speakers		Danish learners		Spanish learners	
CAR AT THE TRAFFIC LIGHTS	PD	at	73.7	at	53.3	in front of	42.9
		noun	15.8	by	40.0	at	28.6
		next to	5.3	in front of	6.7	on	9.5
		by	5.3			by	9.5
						beside	4.8
						before	4.8
MAN AT THE END OF THE QUEUE	PD	at	78.9	at	53.3	at	100
		noun	10.5	in	46.7		
		behind	5.3				
		other	5.3				
WOMAN AT THE TOP OF THE STAIRS	PD	at	78.9	at	53.3	on	47.6
		on	10.5	on	46.7	at	47.6
		noun	10.5			upstairs	4.8
CAT AT THE BOTTOM OF THE STAIRS	PD	at	73.7	at	100	at	85.7
		noun	21.1			on	4.8
		on	5.3			upstairs	4.8
						downstairs	4.8
ACCIDENT AT THE CROSSROADS	SC	at	78.9	at	60.0	in	42.9
		on	10.5	on	20.0	at	33.3
		by	10.5	by	13.3	on	23.8
				in	6.7		
BE AT YOUR SISTER'S HOUSE	SC	at	89.5	at	100	at	81.0
		in	10.5			in	14.3
						on	4.8

group who chose a particular option for referring to the target spatial relationships. Results are shown for the three groups who performed both tasks in English: the native English speakers, the Danish learners and the Spanish learners. One of the most striking and consistent results across Tables 6.1–6.4 is that the Danish learners' strongest preference for each item is usually the same as the native English speakers' top preference. The Spanish learners' top preferences less often align with those of native English speakers, and the Spanish learners also produce a greater variety of responses than either of the other two groups.

The native English speakers' preferences for the preposition ON in the items listed in Table 6.1 show that they chose ON when there was a relationship of support between a located object and a reference object construed as a two dimensional-planar surface. As noted by Herskovits (1986), the prototypical use of the English preposition ON depicts a

Table 6.4 Spatial relationships conventionally described with AT/ON by English native speakers. Comparison with Danish learners and Spanish learners: Percentages

Item	Task	Native English speakers		Danish leaners		Spanish learners	
CHILDREN AT/ON THE BEACH	PD	on	42.1	at	66.7	on	52.4
		at	42.1	on	26.7	at	23.8
		noun	15.8	at/on	6.7	at the top of	23.8
ACCIDENT AT/ON THE MOTORWAY	SC	on	78.9	on	86.7	in	38.1
		at	21.1	at	13.3	at	28.6
						on	28.6
						in/at	4.8
SHOP AT/ON THE CORNER	SC	on	57.9	at	46.7	at	42.9
		at	42.1	on	40.0	in	38.1
				at/by	13.3	on	19.0
NAME AT/ON THE TOP OF THE PAGE	SC	at	68.4	on	53.3	at	52.4
		on	31.6	at	46.7	on	47.6

scene where the located object rests on a free, horizontal upward facing surface of the reference object. In most of the scenes in Table 6.1, on the other hand, the located object rests on a vertical surface. In some of these scenes, the located object is adhered to the reference object (e.g. LABEL ON BOTTLE), whereas in others the located object is part of the reference object, as in SCAR ON CHEEK.

The Danish learner group performed very similarly to the native English speakers and showed no significant differences from the native English speakers with respect to any of the items listed in Table 6.1. The Spanish learner group, on the other hand, used a variety of prepositions for each item. Although ON was their preferred preposition for most of the items listed in Table 6.1, Fisher's exact tests showed that the differences between the native English speakers and the Spanish learners were significant for four of the six items: LABEL ON BOTTLE ($p = 0.003$), NOTICE ON DOOR ($p = 0.002$), SCAR ON CHEEK ($p = 0.001$) and NAME ON DOOR ($p < 0.001$).

The patterns of responses shown in Table 6.2 indicate that the preposition IN was used by native English speakers when the located object was contained within confining structures or boundaries of the reference object. That is, for the native English speakers, the items in Table 6.2 appear to represent relationships of containment where the reference object is construed as (a) having an interior, a boundary and an exterior (door, car), or (b) representing a container that might or might not have clearly defined boundaries (Paris). As before, the Danish learner group performed similarly to the native English speakers, showing no significant differences. Also as before, the Spanish learner group produced a range

Table 6.5 Significant differences between the Danish and Spanish learners in the use of ON, IN, AT: Percentages

Item	Task	Danish learners		Spanish learners		P
LABEL ON BOTTLE	PD	on	100	on	42.9	0.003
				in	47.6	
				at	4.8	
				into	4.8	
NOTICE ON DOOR	PD	on	100	on	47.6	0.002
				at	47.6	
				other	4.8	
CAR AT TRAFFIC LIGHTS	PD	at	53.3	in	42.9	0.012
		by	40.0	at	28.6	
		in front of	6.7	on	9.5	
				by	9.5	
				beside	4.8	
				before	4.8	
MAN AT THE END OF THE QUEUE	PD	at	53.3	at	100	0.001
		in	46.7			
NAME ON DOOR	SC	on	100	on	47.6	0.001
				at	42.9	
				in	9.5	
SCAR ON CHEEK	SC	on	100	on	57.1	0.005
				in	33.3	
				at	9.5	
TRAVEL IN CAR	SC	in	93.3	in	38.1	0.010
		by	6.7	on	23.8	
				by	23.8	
				with	14.3	
SHOP AT/ON THE CORNER	SC	at	46.7	at	42.9	0.018
		on	40.0	in	38.1	
		at/by	13.3	on	19.0	

of responses and differed significantly from the native English speakers in their reference to the TRAVEL IN CAR item ($p < .001$), and nearly significantly in their reference to the KEY IN DOOR item ($p = 0.051$)

The patterns of responses found in Table 6.3 suggest that the native English speakers used the preposition AT to convey co-location between a located object and a reference object conceptualised as a point in space. The Danish group described the scene MAN AT THE END OF THE QUEUE differently from the native speakers by showing a split preference between the prepositions AT and IN, whereas the native speakers showed a clear preference for AT. A Fisher's exact test showed that the difference between the two groups was statistically significant ($p = 0.006$), even

Table 6.6 Danish L1 control group's preferences for PÅ: Percentages

Item	Task		L1 Danish
SHELF ON WALL	PD	på	100
LABEL ON BOTTLE	PD	på	89.5
		midt på	10.5
FLY ON ARM	PD	på	100
NOTICE ON DOOR	PD	på	94.7
		overst midt på doren	5.3
WOMAN AT/ON THE TOP OF THE STAIRS	PD	overst på	94.7
		på	5.3
SCAR ON CHEEK	SC	på	100
ACCIDENT AT/ON MOTORWAY	SC	på	89.5
		på/ved	10.5
SHOP AT/ON CORNER	SC	på	89.5
		ved	5.3
		ved/på	5.3

though it is important to note that the Danish group's top preference was the same as that of the native English speakers. The Spanish learner group did not differ significantly from the native English speakers in their reference to this scene, but they did differ significantly from the native English speakers in their choice of prepositions to refer to the CAR AT THE TRAFFIC LIGHTS scene ($p = 0.007$). Whereas AT was the clear preference for English speakers referring to this scene, the Spanish learners showed a preference for saying 'in front of' (e.g. 'The car is in front of the traffic lights').

Table 6.4 lists the test items where the native English speakers showed a divided preference between AT and ON. Presumably, their split preferences reflect the fact that different individuals can construe the same spatial configurations in different ways depending, for example, on whether they choose to view the reference object as a geometric point or

Table 6.7 Danish L1 control group's preferences for I: Percentages

Item	Task		L1 Danish
KEY IN DOOR	PD	i	100
EIFFEL TOWER IN PARIS	PD	i	94.7
		midt i	5.3
MAN AT THE END OF THE QUEUE	PD	sidst i	84.2
		bagerst i	10.5
		sidst	5.3
TRAVEL IN CAR	SC	i	100

as the background for where the action takes place. As can be observed, native speakers of English can construe a spatial scene in different ways. The Danish learners also displayed divided preferences for most of these items, and in most cases their preferences were split between the same two prepositions as the native English speakers' were. The Spanish learners exhibited relatively similar preferences to the native English speakers for the CHILDREN AT/ON THE BEACH and NAME AT/ON THE TOP OF THE PAGE items. For other items, however, the Spanish learners showed an unusually high use of IN, and this resulted in significant differences between the native English speakers and Spanish learners for the following items: ACCIDENT AT/ON THE MOTORWAY ($p < 0.001$) and SHOP AT/ON THE CORNER ($p = 0.006$).

Danish learners of English and Spanish learners of English

Research question 2: Do Danish-speaking and Spanish-speaking learners of English differ from each other in their construal of these spatial configurations in L2 English?

The results presented in the preceding section focus on similarities and differences between the native English speakers on the one hand and the learner groups on the other. In order to address Research Question 2, we used Fisher's exact tests to determine whether the differences between the two learner groups were significant. For some of the items, there were no significant differences between the Danish and Spanish learners. In the present section, we will focus on those items where significant differences were found between these groups. Before presenting the differences, however, we briefly summarise the items that the two groups construed in a similar way. First, in the ROOMS AT/IN THE HOTEL item, both groups construed this spatial situation using two prepositions, IN and AT, with a strong preference for IN (86.7% and 71.4% in the Danish and Spanish learners groups respectively). For the item ACCIDENT AT/ON THE CROSSROADS, both groups used the prepositions IN, ON and AT, although in different proportions. For the item WOMAN AT/ON THE TOP OF THE STAIRS, both groups exhibited a primary preference for AT in similar proportions (53.3% and 47.6% in the Danish and Spanish groups respectively). Finally, for CHILDREN AT/ON THE BEACH, both groups chose AT and ON as their top two preferences, though in reverse proportions (AT 66.7% and ON 26.7% for the Danish learners, AT 23.8% and ON 52.4% for the Spanish learners). These are the items where the similarities between the two groups seem the strongest. We will now turn to the items where the differences between the two groups were found to be statistically significant.

As can be observed in Table 6.5, the Danish group used the preposition ON to refer to support relationships; the Spanish learners, on the other hand, produced multiple alternatives for these same items: LABEL ON BOTTLE, NOTICE ON DOOR, NAME ON DOOR and SCAR ON CHEEK. For the item TRAVEL IN CAR, the Danish group used the preposition IN almost exclusively to refer to this containment relationship, whereas the Spanish learners were once again divided between multiple alternatives. In the items where the preposition AT was involved, the Danish group was split between this preposition and one additional alternative (BY, ON or IN). The main difference between the Danish group and the Spanish group in the items CAR AT TRAFFIC LIGHTS and SHOP AT/ON THE CORNER was the Spanish group's high use of IN, where the Danish learners did not use this preposition at all. The Danish learners did use IN as a frequent alternative to AT in the item MAN AT THE END OF THE QUEUE, but in this case the Spanish speakers unanimously used AT.

Danish L1 control group and Spanish L1 control group

Research question 3: Do Danish-speaking and Spanish-speaking learners' spatial construals in L2 English reflect an influence of spatial construal patterns in their L1s?

The participants in the Danish control group, who performed both tasks in L1 Danish, produced responses that predominantly involved three prepositions: PÅ ('on'), I ('in') and VED ('at'). These prepositions have close translation equivalents in English, and it appears that the Danish control group used these prepositions in a way that corresponds with the semantic constraints of their English counterparts: PÅ appears to represent a relationship of support between a located object and a reference object similar to the use of ON, I appears to be used to mark the same types of containment relationships as the preposition IN, and VED appears to be used to convey the co-location of a located object with a reference object in a way that is very similar to the conventional use of AT. Although we know that there are a number of usage-related differences between these Danish prepositions and their English counterparts, in nearly all of the items in the two tasks we administered for the present study, the Danish prepositions PÅ, I and VED appear to have been employed for the same types of functional relations as the English prepositions ON, IN and AT, as can be observed in Tables 6.6 and 6.7. Table 6.8 lists the items where the Danish learners' prepositional choices in L2 English were different from the Danish control group's choices in L1 Danish, and Table 6.9 focuses on the items where the Spanish L1 control group differed from the native English speakers.

The items listed in Table 6.6 were overwhelmingly described by the Danish control group with the preposition PÅ. In all of these items, PÅ appears to be used to indicate a relation of support between the located object and the reference object. This is consistent with how our native English speakers used the preposition ON, as we discussed earlier.

The items in which the Danish control group overwhelmingly chose the preposition I are shown in Table 6.7. As can be observed, this preposition seems to be used to mark a relation of containment between the located object and the reference object in the same way as the preposition IN was used by our native English speakers. In the first three scenes listed in Table 6.8, the Danish control group displays the same tendencies as the native English speakers did in Table 6.2. By contrast, in the scene MAN AT THE END OF THE QUEUE, the Danish control group's high use of I (*'sidst i'* = 'last in'; *'bagerst i'* = 'back-most in') contrasts sharply with the native English speakers' strong preference for AT in the same context (compare with Table 6.3). For native English speakers, a person's position at the end of the line is evidently not construed as a containment relationship, whereas for Danish speakers it is, as was found in Danish speakers' use of both their L1 and L2 in the present study.

With regard to the use of the preposition VED, the Danish control group displayed a primary preference (78.9%) for this preposition only in the item CAR AT THE TRAFFIC LIGHTS. Their secondary choices for this item included BAG ('behind') (5.3%), FORAN ('in front of') (5.3%), PÅ ('on') (5.3%) and SKRAT FORAN ('right in front of') (5.3%). The preposition VED was also a secondary choice in CHILDREN AT/ON THE BEACH, VED (26.3%), VED/PÅ (5.3%)

Table 6.8 lists the three items where the Danish control group's prepositional choices in L1 Danish differed from the Danish learners' prepositional choices in L2 English. These are items where crosslinguistic influence does not account well for the learners' patterns of responses. For

Table 6.8 Items where the Danish L1 control group differed from the Danish learners: Percentages

Item	Task	L1 Danish		L2 English	
NAME AT/ON THE TOP OF THE PAGE	SC	på	100	on	53.3
				at	46.7
ROOMS IN/AT THE HOTEL	SC	på	84.2	in	86.7
		i/på	15.8	at	13.3
ACCIDENT AT/ON THE CROSSROADS	SC	i	36.8	at	60.0
		ved	36.8	on	20.0
		i/ved	26.3	by	13.3
				in	6.7

Table 6.9 Items where the Spanish L1 control group differed from the native English speakers: Percentages

Item	Task	L1 Spanish	
LABEL ON BOTTLE	PD	en	85
		sobre	5
		en el centro de	5
		en la parte central de	5
NOTICE ON DOOR	PD	en	85
		sobre	5
		contra	5
		en la parte de arriba de	5
CAR AT THE TRAFFIC LIGHTS	PD	en	60
		ante	25
		al lado de	10
		tras	5
WOMAN AT/ON THE TOP OF THE STAIRS	PD	al final de	55
		en	10
		al principio de	10
		sobre	5
		tras	5
		encima de	5
		en el principio de	5
		en el final de	5
ACCIDENT AT/ON THE CROSSROADS	SC	en	95
		no answer	5
ACCIDENT AT/ON THE MOTORWAY	SC	en	95
		entre	5
SCAR ON CHEEK	SC	en	80
		sobre	15
		ante	5
NAME ON DOOR	SC	en	80
		sobre	15
		ante	5

the item NAME AT/ON THE TOP OF THE PAGE, the Danish control group unanimously chose PÅ in Danish, whereas the Danish learners' choices were almost equally divided between ON and AT. For the item ROOMS IN/AT THE HOTEL, the main difference was that the control group overwhelmingly chose PÅ ('on'), whereas the learners overwhelmingly chose IN. For the item ACCIDENT AT/ON THE CROSSROADS, the control group was evenly split between I ('in') and VED ('at'), whereas the learners showed a clear preference for AT, with only one learner (6.7%) choosing IN.

We now turn to the results of the Spanish control group and compare them with the results of the Spanish learners. Importantly, as pointed out by Bull (1965), the number of spatial prepositions in Spanish is quite small, with the preposition EN covering most of the domains where AT, IN and ON are used in English. EN in Spanish is used to refer to both location and direction (cf. Whitley, 2002), with location being the more common referent. EN indicates that the located object is on-site with the reference object, but as Huerta (2009: 77) states 'it does not specifically code for contact or enclosure'. In fact, it can convey a variety of meanings, which include embeddedness, contact, containment, distance, location, proximity, the end point of a direction, and changes of state and time. The following sentences in English use three separate prepositions: 'The book is on the table,' 'The man is in the house,' 'The boy is at the bus stop,' but in Spanish all these spatial relations can be described by means of the preposition EN. As Huerta (2009) states, learners often equate the meaning of the Spanish preposition EN with a preposition that is not fully equivalent in English because they assume that the semantic boundaries of prepositions are equivalent in both languages.

For these reasons, it is perhaps not surprising that EN was the predominant prepositional choice for the L1 Spanish control group in most of the items on both tasks. As the results for the Spanish L1 control group and the group of Spanish learners are similar, in what follows, we focus only on those items where the Spanish control group's choices are incongruent with those of the native English speakers.

The items listed in Table 6.9 involve cases where the native English speakers showed a strong preference for ON or AT, and where the Spanish control group showed a similarly strong preference for EN. The only exception to this pattern is found in the item WOMAN AT/ON THE TOP OF THE STAIRS, where the Spanish control group's primary preference is the phrase AL FINAL DE ('at the end of'). Another thing that is striking about the results in Table 6.9 is the large number of secondary preferences that the Spanish control group displayed. These differences between the Spanish control group and the native English speakers seem to account quite well for the significant differences between the native English speakers and Spanish learners reported earlier: LABEL ON BOTTLE ($p = 0.003$), NOTICE ON DOOR ($p = 0.002$), NAME ON DOOR ($p < .001$), CAR AT THE TRAFFIC LIGHTS ($p = 0.007$), WOMAN AT/ON THE TOP OF THE STAIRS (p = 0.028), ACCIDENT AT/ON THE CROSSROADS ($p < .001$), ACCIDENT AT/ON THE MOTORWAY ($p = 0.001$) and SCAR ON CHEEK ($p = 0.001$). In fact, there is only one additional item beyond these eight where the Spanish learners differed significantly from the native English speakers: TRAVEL IN CAR ($p < .001$) (see Table 6.2).

In summary, the Spanish L1 control group resorted mainly to the preposition EN, using primarily one category in their L1 across items, while both the Danish L1 control group and the native English speakers relied on three separate categories that have similar semantic values across languages: I/PÅ/VED and IN/ON/AT. Consequently, the patterns of responses by the Danish L1 control group were generally quite similar to those of the native English speakers, whereas responses of the Spanish L1 control group differed from the native English speakers in a large number of cases. Importantly, the items where the native speakers differed from the L1 control groups were almost always precisely the same items where the native speakers differed significantly from the respective learners groups.

Discussion and Conclusion

Our first research question aimed at determining whether Danish and Spanish learners of L2 English would construe spatial configurations in the same way as native English speakers. Our results showed that the native English speakers used ON to convey a relationship of support between a located object and a reference object, IN to mark a relationship of containment between the two entities, and AT to represent the co-location of both entities in a specific point in space. Importantly, the native English speakers described some of the scenes with more than one preposition, perhaps reflecting the fact that certain types of spatial configurations exhibit more than one salient spatial relationship for speakers of a particular language. The Danish learners in the present study used ON for support and IN for containment in ways that were very similar to what the native English speakers did. Like the native English speakers, the Danish learners also provided multiple construals for some items. The only item where the Danish learners' responses differed significantly from those of the native English speakers was MAN AT THE END OF THE QUEUE, where the English speakers overwhelmingly chose AT and the Danish learners showed an almost equal preference for AT and IN. The Spanish learners, by contrast, did not exhibit consistent systematicity in their use of English ON for support, IN for containment or AT for a specific point in space. As a consequence, the Spanish learners also produced more prepositions than the Danish learners in a number of the items in both tasks. Overall, we found that the Danish learners differed significantly from the native English speakers in only one item, whereas the Spanish learners differed significantly from the native English speakers in nine items.

Our second question focused on whether the spatial construals of Danish and Spanish learners would differ from each other. We found eight items where the two groups differed significantly from each other (see Table 6.5); six of the eight items were among the nine items where the native English speakers differed significantly from the Spanish learners, and one of the items was the same item where the native English speakers differed significantly from the Danish learners. These results showed that the learners differed from each other mainly on the same items where the native speakers differed from the learners. In most cases where significant differences were found, the differences were between the Spanish learners on the one hand and the native English speakers and the Danish learners on the other. Again, the Danish learners' prepositional choices were very similar to those of the native English speakers, whereas the Spanish learners' choices were not. An anonymous reviewer has suggested considering the age of onset as this might have consequences for the development of L2 spatial mental categories. The reviewer has suggested that the Danish learners may not be transferring their prepositional domains but it could be the case that they learnt them better in the L2. There are differences between the two learner groups concerning the onset age of acquisition and the degree of exposure to English outside the school. Danish speakers start learning English in school later than Spanish speakers but they are exposed to extramural English to a greater extent than Spanish speakers. However, as the two groups of learners had the same degree of L2 English proficiency as measured by the Oxford placement test (C1), the results in our study seem to indicate that the different prepositional choices that Danish and Spanish learners make in L2 English reflect L1-related differences, irrespective of the age of onset or exposure to English outside the classroom.

Our third question addressed whether the learners' prepositional choices and preferences in L2 English reflect the patterns of spatial construal in their L1s. We found that there were only three items out of the total pool of 23 items where the Danish learners' responses in L2 English were not congruent with the Danish control group's responses in L1 Danish: NAME AT/ON THE TOP OF THE PAGE, ROOMS AT/IN THE HOTEL and ACCIDENT AT/ON THE CROSSROADS (see Table 6.8). We also found that there was only one item out of the total pool of 23 items where the Spanish learners' responses in L2 English were not congruent with the Spanish control group's responses in L1 Spanish: TRAVEL IN CAR. Importantly, as we said earlier, the items where the native English speakers differ significantly from the learner groups are nearly precisely the same items where the responses in L1 Danish and L1 Spanish, respectively, are incongruent with the patterns found in L1 English. These findings suggest a strong role for L1 influence in the spatial construals of advanced foreign-language learners of English. Stated in more precise terms, the different prepositional choices that Danish learners and Spanish learners make in L2 English reflect L1-related differences in their patterns of spatial construal.

It is useful to consider the specific ways in which the learners' L1s may have affected their prepositional choices in L2 English. As we indicated earlier, the only item where significant differences were found between the Danish learners and the native English speakers involved the item MAN AT THE END OF THE QUEUE, where a strong majority of the native English speakers chose AT (78.9%) and the Danish learners were almost equally divided between AT (53.3%) and IN (46.7%). In the Danish L1 control group's description of this scene, nearly all of the participants' responses included the preposition I ('in') and none of them included VED ('at'). Thus, even though L1 influence does not seem to account at all for the 53.3% of the Danish learners who construed this scene using AT, it may very well account for the 46.7% of the Danish learners who used IN. It is important to emphasise once again that the Danish learners had trouble with (i.e. produced unconventional construals in) only one item out of 23 spatial scenarios presented to them. There appear to be three inter-related reasons for this. First, like English, Danish has three prepositions that cover approximately the same range of spatial meanings as IN, ON and AT. Second, the meanings of the three Danish prepositions are relatively close translation equivalents to IN, ON and AT. Finally, the actual usage patterns of these prepositions in relation to the 23 test items presented to the participants are nearly identical between Danish and English. In short, the challenge of learning native-like conventions for construing spatial configurations in L2 English does not seem very great for Danish-speaking learners of English.

The same cannot be said for Spanish-speaking learners of English, however. As mentioned earlier, the Spanish preposition EN is a possible and often preferred option for referring to all of the types of spatial configurations dealt with in the present study. It might be tempting to say that EN carries the meanings of all three of the English prepositions IN, ON and AT, but this is not quite true. The English prepositions encode specific information about containment, support and co-location, but the Spanish preposition EN lacks these specific meanings and instead marks location more generally. The challenge for Spanish speakers is not just to learn new prepositions and to figure out which of the meanings of EN goes with each of the English prepositions, but rather to learn new meanings and distinctions that EN simply does not carry and which they might not yet have a mental category for. The Spanish learners in the present study differed from native conventions mainly in relation to spatial configurations that are typically construed with ON or AT. This is because they seem to associate Spanish EN with English IN, and this results in a good deal of positive transfer in cases where the conventional way of construing a spatial configuration in English involves the preposition IN. However, establishing IN and EN as primary counterparts also means that they tend to overuse IN in cases where ON and AT are more appropriate. This is of course not a new or surprising finding. For example, in the 1960s, Stockwell *et al.* (1965) pointed out that learners tend to have greater acquisitional difficulties in the case of splits, where learners have to move from a single category in their L1 to multiple categories in the L2 (cf. Cadierno, 2008). If anything is surprising, it is that these challenges are very difficult to overcome even for advanced learners, including the Spanish learners in the present study.

It is important to note that our Spanish learners did not have difficulties with the finer distinctions of the English prepositions on all items. For example, their construals were essentially native-like for items such as FLY ON ARM, CHILDREN AT/ON THE BEACH and MAN AT THE END OF THE QUEUE. In the following paragraphs we focus on the factors that seem to account for when their construals were and were not native-like.

With respect to spatial configurations where there is a support type of relation between the located object and reference object, it seems that the items where the Spanish learners were least likely to follow native-like conventions were those that depict a support relation on the vertical axis (NAME ON DOOR, NOTICE ON DOOR, LABEL ON BOTTLE). As can be observed, the meanings of the prepositions involve a spatial/geometric configuration between the trajector and the landmark and a functional element, as Tyler and Evans (2003) suggest, for example, when they mention that IN indicates a spatial relation in which the trajector is surrounded by a bounded landmark with a functional element of containment. Another important factor in these examples might involve physical embeddedness. Consider, for example, the differences in the Spanish learners' reference to FLY ON ARM versus SCAR ON CHEEK. In the former case, 76.2% of the Spanish learners used ON and 23.8% used IN, whereas in the latter case, only 57.1% used ON while 33.3% used IN. Different explanations can account for this result. It may be the case that the Spanish speakers have begun acquiring the prototypical meaning of ON and they know that FLY ON ARM is similar to that prototypical meaning. SCAR ON CHEEK, on the other hand, is not as similar to the prototypical meaning of ON and this seems to lead to learning difficulties on the part of the learners. Another possible explanation is that the difference may be due to a semantic prototype which is universal in nature.

At least some of the Spanish learners therefore seem to construe the relationship between a scar and a cheek as being different from the relationship between a fly and an arm, regardless of the fact that native English speakers seem to see both spatial configurations as representing a relationship of support. This explanation, if true, suggests that factors well beyond L1 influence and L2 exposure affect learners' spatial construals. Carroll and Becker (1993) refer to such factors as semantic universals – or meaning distinctions that people are naturally drawn to regardless of whether they are encoded into any of the languages they know. Distinctions between horizontal and vertical support, as well as distinctions involving degrees of physical embeddedness, might be examples of such semantic universals. This is compatible with the second possible explanation provided above.

We mentioned earlier that the Spanish learners tended to produce relatively native-like patterns on items conventionally referred to with the preposition IN. However, there was one item where an overwhelming majority of native English speakers used IN and where the Spanish learners differed significantly from the native English speakers. This was the item TRAVEL IN CAR, where 89.5% of the native English speakers used IN in the question, 'Shall we travel in your car or mine,' but where only 38.1% of the Spanish learners used IN, while 23.8% used ON, 23.8% used BY and 14.3% used WITH. The Spanish learners' diversified pattern may be related to the fact that the reference object is a car – a vehicle that moves and transports people and does not just sit still. According to Lee (2001), English speakers tend to construe cars as container-like objects but buses and trains as transporters that people are essentially attached to (i.e. supported by and not just contained in) as they are being transported. The fact that the native English speakers showed such a strong preference for IN while the Spanish learners were divided in their choices between IN, ON and BY seems to suggest that the native speakers did indeed construe the car as a container while several of the Spanish learners may have construed it as a transporter. Yet it may also be the case as Tyler (pers. comm) suggests that the trajector in this sentence: 'Shall we travel in your car or mine?' is we, referring to people, not to travel itself. As indicated by Tyler, containment can also involve support, for example, a baby in a crib is not simply surrounded by the sides and bottom of the crib but it is also supported by it. Another item where the Spanish learners differed significantly from the native English speakers was the item CAR AT THE TRAFFIC LIGHTS, which also involves a car, but this time as the located object instead of the reference object. The native English speakers showed a strong predilection (73.7%) for referring to this item with the preposition AT in a sentence such as 'The car is waiting at the traffic lights.' The Spanish learners produced a variety of prepositions, including IN FRONT OF (42.9%), AT (28.6%) and a few others. Part of the learners' problem with this item might be the fact that the reference object is not specifically the traffic lights but rather the space surrounding the traffic lights. It is this space rather than the traffic lights per se that the car co-locates with. Our data suggest that abstract construals like this involving invisible, intangible and indeterminate objects might be particularly difficult for learners to acquire.

Finally, of all the items where the native English speakers showed some degree of variability in their prepositional choices (see Tables 6.1–6.3 and especially Table 6.4), the Spanish learners differed substantially from the native English speakers on three of these. The reasons for the differences in two of these items, namely ACCIDENT AT/ON THE CROSSROADS and

ACCIDENT AT/ON THE MOTORWAY may have the same explanation given earlier for CAR AT THE TRAFFIC LIGHTS. In each of these items, the respective reference object appears to have been construed by native speakers metonymically as referring to the space surrounding the mentioned object rather than as the mentioned object itself. This seems to account for why the native English speakers used the prepositions ON, AT and BY to refer to the spatial relationship. The Spanish learners, by contrast, displayed primary preferences for IN and IN FRONT OF, suggesting that they may have construed the reference object as the mentioned object itself. In the case of the items involving the crossroads and the motorway, the Spanish learners may have construed these objects as having clearly defined boundaries that contained the located objects. The final item involving some degree of variability in the native English speakers' responses and substantial differences between the native English speakers and the Spanish learners is the item WOMAN AT/ON THE TOP OF THE STAIRS. This item appears to have a different explanation, and it is also the only item in the study where the Spanish L1 control group did not chose EN as its primary preference. The primary preference (55%) for the Spanish control group was AL FINAL DE ('at the end of'), which does not seem to account well for the Spanish learners' high use of ON (47.6% versus 47.6% for AT). In this case, we speculate that the Spanish learners' exposure to the high-frequency collocations 'on top' and 'on top of' might have attracted them to using ON with 'top'. The word 'top' was provided for them in the task.

To sum up, our results have shown that Danish, English and Spanish carry different conventions for the construal of spatial relations, but the differences between Danish and English are very small. Our results suggest that Danish-speaking learners of English appear to be drawing on similar construals to those of native English speakers, whereas Spanish-speaking learners of English differ considerably from both native English speakers and Danish learners. Following Jarvis' (2000) framework for confirming cases of L1 influence, we have found evidence of within-group similarities in learners' use of L2 prepositions, between-group differences, and similarities between the use of prepositions in both their L1 and L2. Some of the most compelling evidence for L1 influence in the present study can be seen in the fact that the items where the native English speakers' spatial construal patterns differ substantially from those of the L1 control groups are almost exactly the same items where the native English speakers show significant differences from the respective learner groups. In addition to crosslinguistic influence, we have also found evidence of other effects on learners' spatial construals. These include what might be semantic universals regarding the types of meaning distinctions that people are naturally attracted to when their language does not provide them with clear hypotheses for making sense of the language-use patterns observed in the L2. These factors also appear to include differences in how literally (versus metonymically) speakers of different languages construe the references that occur in spatial configurations. Finally, it appears that structural factors, such as collocational associations, also affect learners' and native speakers' spatial construals. Future research is needed in this area to determine when and to what extent both native speakers' and learners' spatial-reference patterns are determined by (a) how they conceptualise located objects, reference objects and the relationships between the two; (b) how they understand the meanings of spatial prepositions (or other spatial and locational markers) and (c) how much they rely on structural rules and constraints (such as collocations) rather than on meaning when choosing an appropriate preposition for a given context.

Some teaching implications can be derived from this study. The spatial configurations of English should be taught to students who are acquiring English as a second language, especially in the case of Spanish learners as they move from a single category in their L1 to multiple categories in the L2. The present study suggests the need to pursue specific studies on the pedagogical application of spatial configurations in English which focus on a usage-based/ cognitive linguistics model to instructed language learning. Traditional pedagogical approaches usually focus on memorisation as a teaching strategy where the multiple meanings associated with a given preposition are treated as arbitrary. In contrast, a cognitive linguistics approach provides students with explanations where the various meanings of a particular preposition are related in systematic ways, in terms of related meaning networks (i.e. polysemy networks), such as the studies by Tyler (2012b) and Tyler and Evans (2001, 2003). For example, Tyler (2012b) reports some empirical studies where the English prepositions *to*, *for* and *at* were taught to a group of advanced L1 Italian speakers and a group of students enrolled in major universities in Hanoi, Vietnam. Learners were presented with brief explanations of the central meaning of each preposition that was illustrated by means of diagrams followed by examples of everyday experiences where the target preposition was to be used. Following this, the extended senses of each preposition were presented by means of diagrams and subsequent sentences accompanied by pictures or cartoons that illustrated each extended use. This teacher-fronted instruction was then followed by interactive tasks where learners working in pairs were, for instance, asked to label meaning maps of the visual representations of each preposition's network. The results of these studies showed that the learners receiving the cognitive linguistics-based approach made significant gains in the use of the target prepositions after two treatment sessions. In line with Tyler and Tyler and Evans' findings, we consider that further research focusing on instruction should be conducted from a usage-based/cognitive linguistics approach.

Acknowledgements

We would like to thank Andrea Tyler for her comments on a previous draft to this paper. We also thank Iraide Ibarretxe-Antuñano for helpful discussions and ideas in the interpretation of the data. Finally we would like to thank the anonymous reviewers for their insightful comments. Any remaining mistakes are our own.

References

Becker, A., Carroll, M., and Kelly, A. (eds) (1988) *Reference to Space* (Final report to the European Science Foundation, IV). Strasbourg, Heidelberg.
Bowerman, M. (1996) The origins of children's spatial semantic categories: Cognitive versus linguistic determinants. In J. Gumperz and S. Levinson (eds) *Rethinking Linguistic Relativity* (pp. 145–176). Cambridge: Cambridge University Press
Bowerman, M. and Choi, S. (2001) Shaping meanings for language: Universal and language-specific in the acquisition of spatial semantic categories. In M. Bowerman and S.C. Levinson (eds) *Language Acquisition and Conceptual Development* (pp. 475–511). Cambridge: Cambridge University Press.
Bull, W.E. (1965) *Spanish for Teachers: Applied Linguistics*. New York: The Ronald Press Company.
Cadierno, T. (2008) Learning to talk about motion in a foreign language. In P. Robinson and N.C. Ellis (eds) *Handbook of Cognitive Linguistics and Second Language Acquisition* (pp. 239–275). New York/London: Routledge.
Carroll, M. and Becker, A. (1993) Reference to space in learner varieties. In C. Perdue (ed.) *Adult Language Acquisition: Cross-Linguistic Perspectives (Volume II: The Results)* (pp. 119–149). Cambridge: Cambridge University Press.
Coventry, K.R. and Guijarro-Fuentes, P. (2008) Spatial language learning and the functional geometric framework. In P. Robinson and N. Ellis (eds) *Handbook of Cognitive Linguistics and Second Language Acquisition* (pp. 114–138). Lawrence Erlbaum Associates: Mahwah, NJ.
Herskovits, A. (1986) *Language and Spatial Cognition. An Interdisciplinary Study of the Prepositions in English*. Cambridge: Cambridge University Press.
Huebner, T. (1985) System and variability in interlanguage syntax. *Language Learning* 35, 141–163.
Huerta, B. (2009) The Semantics of the Prepositions en, a and de: A Cognitive Approach. PhD Dissertation. Faculty of the Graduate School of the University at Buffalo, State University of New York. UMI Number: 3372152
Ijaz, I.H. (1986) Linguistic and cognitive determinants of lexical acquisition in a second language. *Language Learning* 36 (4), 401–451.
Jarvis, S. (2000) Methodological rigor in the study of transfer: Identifying L1 influence in the interlanguage lexicon. *Language Learning* 50, 245–309.
Jarvis, S. and Odlin, T. (2000) Morphological type, spatial reference, and language transfer. *Studies in Second Language Acquisition* 22 (4), 535–556.
Kellerman, E. (1978) Giving learners a break: Native language intuitions as a source of predictions about transferability. *Working Papers on Bilingualism* 15, 59–92.
Langacker, R.W. (1987) *Foundations of Cognitive Grammar*. Stanford: Stanford University Press.
Lee, D. (2001) *Cognitive Linguistics*. Oxford: Oxford University Press.

Levinson, S.C. (1996) Frames of reference and Molyneux's question: Cross-linguistic evidence. In P. Bloom, M. Peterson, L. Nadel and M. Garrett (eds) *Language and Space* (pp. 109–169). Cambridge, MA: MIT press.

Littlemore, J. (2009) *Applying Cognitive Linguistics to Second Language Learning and Teaching*. Basingstoke/New York: Palgrave Macmillan.

McDonough, L., Choi, S., and Mandler, J.M. (2003) Understanding spatial relations: flexible infants, lexical adults. *Cognitive Psychology* 46, 229–259.

Munnich, E., and Landau, B. (2010) Developmental decline in the acquisition of spatial language. *Language Learning and Development* 6, 32–59.

Murphy, R. (1991) *English Grammar in Use*. Cambridge: Cambridge University Press

Park, H.I. and Ziegler, N. (2014) Cognitive shift in the bilingual mind: Spatial concepts in Korean–English bilinguals. *Bilingualism: Language and Cognition* 17 (2), 410–430.

Pederson, E., Danzinger, E., Wilkins, D., Levinson, S., Kita, S. and Senft, G. (1998) Semantic typology and spatial conceptualization. *Language* 74, 557–589.

Perdue, C. (ed.) (1993) *Adult Language Acquisition: Cross-Linguistic Perspectives. Volume II: The results*. Cambridge: Cambridge University Press.

Schumann, J. (1986) Locative and directional expressions in basilang speech. *Language Learning* 36/3: 277–294

Stockwell, R.P., Bowen, J.D. and Martin, J.W. (1965) *The Grammatical Structures of English and Spanish*. Chicago: University of Chicago Press.

Tyler, A. and Evans, V. (2001) The relation between experience, conceptual structure and meaning: Non-temporal uses of tense and language teaching. In M. Pütz, R. Dirven and S. Niemeier (eds) *Applied Cognitive Linguistics I: Theory and Language Acquisition* (pp. 63–105). Berlin: Mouton de Gruyter.

Tyler, A. and Evans, V. (2003) *The Semantics of English Prepositions: Spatial Scenes, Embodied Meaning and Cognition*. Cambridge: Cambridge University Press.

Tyler, A. (2008) Cognitive linguistics and language learning. In P. Hogan (ed.) *Cambridge University Encyclopedia of Language Sciences*. Cambridge: Cambridge University Press.

Tyler, A. (2012a) Cognitive Linguistics and SLA. In P. Robinson (ed.) *Routledge Encyclopedia of Second Language Acquisition. London:* Routledge.

Tyler, A. (2012b) *Cognitive Linguistics and Second Language Learning*. New York/London: Routledge.

Whitley, M.S. (2002) *Spanish/English Contrasts*. Washington, D.C.: Georgetown University Press.

Wilkins, M.S. and Hill, D.P. (1995) When 'go' means 'come': Questioning the basicness of basic motion verbs. *Cognitive Linguistics* 6, 209–259.

7 Can Classroom Learners Use Statistical Learning? A New Perspective on Motion Event Construal in a Second Language

Jeanine Treffers-Daller and Xu Ziyan

Introduction

This paper[1] sets out to investigate to what extent second language learners are able to use statistical learning to restructure the ways in which they talk about motion in their second language (L2). While many researchers (Slobin, 1996; Treffers-Daller & Tidball, in press; Von Stutterheim & Nuse, 2003) have pointed out that it is very difficult for L2 learners to restructure the way in which they talk about motion, few researchers have focused on how successful learners master this difficult domain and on the cues that are available to them. One such cue could be the frequency distribution of motion verbs in the input.

According to Ellis (2002), frequency is a key determinant of second language acquisition, although frequency is of course not a sufficient condition for L2 learning to take place (Gass & Mackey, 2002). Important evidence about the role of frequency in L2 acquisition is provided by Schmitt and Dunham (1999) who show that 'moderately advanced' L2 learners are indeed aware of the frequency of words in their second language. Most recently, Treffers-Daller and Calude (2015) have shown that L2 learners make use of the frequency with which motion verbs occur in the input to master the domain of motion event construal. They claim that learners engage in what Saffran *et al.* (1996) have called statistical learning, that is, 'our ability to make use of statistical information in the environment to bootstrap language acquisition' (Rebuschat & Williams, 2012: 1). Put differently, statistical learning is a specific type of implicit learning whereby learners make use of the frequency of events present in the input to learn a language without being aware of the fact that they are doing this. The research field of statistical learning builds on the earlier work of, for example, Hasher *et al.* (1987), who showed that human beings acquire frequency information about events for a wide range of natural and experimental situations, and commit this information to memory even when they are not required to remember the events in question.

Most of the research into statistical learning has focused on L1 acquisition, while researchers in L2 acquisition have concentrated on a similar phenomenon, namely implicit learning, that is, 'the acquisition of knowledge about the underlying structure of a complex stimulus environment by a process which takes place naturally, simply and without conscious operations' (N. Ellis, 1994: 1). Clearly these two research traditions are related, as Misyak *et al.* (2012) explain, pointing out the importance of bringing about a 'synergistic fusion' between these fields. According to Saffran (2012), L2 acquisition is of particular interest for studies of statistical learning because immersion in a L2 is essentially an implicit learning experience. Statistical learning is now beginning to be explored in L2 acquisition, as is explained in Onnis (2012), who also calls for a closer integration of the paradigms of statistical learning and second language acquisition research.

While most of the research into statistical learning takes the form of artificial grammar learning in laboratory conditions which allows researchers to control for a range of factors that cannot be controlled in naturalistic settings, Saffran (2012: vi) also points to the issue of ecological validity and the importance of moving closer to studying learning 'in the wild'. Treffers-Daller and Calude (2015) were the first to apply the notion of statistical learning to the field of L2 acquisition of motion event construal, working with data collected from L2 learners outside laboratory conditions. They hypothesised that learners transfer the frequency information about words from their L1 to the L2 entry for each word, alongside semantic and syntactic information from the L1 lemma (Jiang, 2000). According to Jiang's model of lexical representation in a second language, lexical acquisition proceeds through different stages, the second of which is the L1 mediation stage where learners copy the information in the L1 lemma into the L2 entry. Many L2 learners fossilise in this stage, and do not reach the integration stage where semantic, syntactic and morphological information from the L2 is integrated into the L2 entry.

Treffers-Daller and Calude (2015) put forward that at the beginning of L2 learning, learners assume that motion verbs will occur with the same frequency in the source and the target language, but in the process of L2 acquisition they start adjusting the frequency of words in their L2 to the frequencies they hear in the input. The authors interpret this as a process of statistical learning, because the students' learning is not limited to simply copying frequencies. The English L1 learners of L2 French in their study also discover that path and manner are mapped onto linguistic structure in different ways: in French, path is most often mapped onto the main verb, and manner expressed onto a satellite, while in English, the opposite is the default pattern (Talmy, 1985, 2000). In addition, they learn the subcategorisation frames that belong to each verb.

It is possible, of course, that statistical learning and transfer of L1 information into the L2 lexical entry is facilitated in particular if the source and target language are related, as is the case with English and French. In this particular language combination there are many cognates, such as *arriver* 'to arrive' and *descendre* 'to descend', which facilitate this process of interlingual identification (Larrañaga *et al.*, 2011).We do not know to what extent transfer of frequency information can take place between a first and a second language that are typologically very different, as is the case for Chinese L1 learners of English. The current paper aims to fill the gap in our knowledge at this point by investigating to what extent intermediate and advanced Chinese L1 learners of English engage in statistical learning and adjust the frequency with which they use English verbs to the frequency in the input despite the typological differences between the languages. In addition, it is important to find out to what extent classroom learners who do not have access to large amounts of naturalistic input are sensitive to frequency of motion verbs in the input. While the advanced learners in Treffers-Daller and Calude (2015) had had extensive exposure to French during their year abroad, it is interesting to find out to what extent learners who have not been abroad for a longer period of time, but have had to rely on exposure to English in the classroom and self-study, can engage in statistical learning and adjust the frequency patterns in their L2 to those found in their input.

The paper is structured as follows. First of all, we sketch the typological differences in motion event construal in English and Chinese as well as the available evidence for transfer of L1 patterns by Chinese L1 learners of L2 English in this domain. Then we discuss how statistical learning could help L2 learners to master the domain of motion event construal. After this we formulate the research questions for this paper and describe the methodology. Subsequently we describe the results. In the discussion we discuss the findings in the light of the theories presented earlier and in the conclusion we summarise the main findings and point towards further research.

Typological Differences in Motion Event Construal Between English and Chinese

For the purpose of the present investigation we will make use of Talmy's (1985, 2000) framework of motion event construal. Talmy (1985: 60–61) defines a 'motion event' as 'a situation containing movement or the maintenance of a stationary location alike'. Talmy (2000: 26) later points out that the motion component refers specifically to the occurrence of translational motion that 'does not refer to all the types of motion that a figure could exhibit, in particular excluding "self-contained motion" like rotation, oscillation, or dilation'.

According to Talmy (1985, 2000), a motion event consists of four basic semantic components, which are motion, figure, ground and path. These basic semantic components can be identified in the following example:

Example 1

The man came out of the room.
[Figure] [Motion] [Path] [Ground]

A motion event may also include two external components, or what Talmy (2000: 25) calls 'a co-event that often has the relation of manner or of cause to it'. As is well-known, Talmy distinguishes between languages which characteristically map path onto the main verb (verb-framed languages), and languages which characteristically map path onto a satellite (satellite-framed languages). Talmy also considers the second element of a verb compound in Chinese, the resultative complement, to be a satellite.

There is still no agreement, however, regarding Talmy's (2000) dichotomy of verb-framed languages and satellite-framed languages (Beavers et al., 2010; Hendriks et al., 2008; Hendriks et al., 2009; Ibarretxe-Antuñano, 2006; Zlatev & Yangklang, 2004). Li (1993, cited in Talmy 2000: 117–118) finds support for Talmy's classification and suggests that from its classical to its contemporary form, Chinese appears to have undergone a typological shift from a path-conflation pattern to a co-event-conflation pattern. Classical Chinese was a verb-framed language, in which path verbs were used as main verbs in the representation of motion events. Through the development of a serial verb construction, these path verbs tended to occur as second-position elements following a manner/cause-conflating verb. Within the serial verb constructions, these second-position elements changed to become path satellites following a manner/cause main verb and lost their function as the path verb. (Li, 1993, 1997) also contends that the manner verb is the main verb and the path verb is the satellite. But there are some problems with this classification (Peyraube, 2006). Firstly, the Chinese satellites listed by Talmy (2000) are optional. The main verb can express the meaning very well without them. Secondly, Chinese satellites can stand alone as independent verbs, which is not possible with English satellites. Slobin (2004: 228) treats serial verb constructions in Chinese as a different case, where two or more verbs, with or without arguments, co-occur in the same clause and express the same event. Because path verbs can occur alone in Chinese, they cannot be regarded as satellites. Satellites are verb particles and affixes that do not occur alone. Slobin observes that in Chinese and other serial verb languages both path and manner receive equal weight. He proposes that it may be appropriate to have a third typological category to include serial verb languages like Thai and Chinese, which cannot be allocated to satellite-framed or verb-framed. Slobin (2004) proposes the third type, which is called 'equipollently-framed languages'. In these languages, 'both Manner and Path are expressed by "equipollent" elements', which refer to those elements 'that are equal in formal linguistic terms, and appear to be equal in force or significance' (Slobin, 2004: 228). Slobin (2006: 64) further explains *equipollently-framed* as 'a kind of framing in which both Path and Manner have roughly equal morphosyntactic status'. So he revises the definitions of verb-framed and satellite-framed by adding a third type – a trichotomy rather than Talmy's (1985, 2000) dichotomy typology.

Slobin points out two caveats concerning this revised typology. One is to place 'languages on a cline of Manner salience[2], rather than placing them into dichotomised or trichotomized typologies' (Slobin, 2004: 228). Manner salience is the level of attention paid to manner in describing events. Another is that 'typological characterizations often reflect tendencies rather than absolute differences between languages' (Berman & Slobin, 1994: 118). Interestingly, some researchers (Huang & Tanangkingsing, 2005) propose a four-way typology based on Talmy's two-way typology. The vertical axis represents path salience and the horizontal axis represents manner salience. Chinese is considered to have the highest Manner salience compared with six Western Austronesian languages: Saisiyat, Malay, Tagalog, Tsou, Cebuano and Squliq. Croft *et al.* (2010) elaborated Talmy's typological classification as verb framing, satellite framing, double framing and symmetrical framing. Double framing refers to the construction in which 'the path or framing expression is expressed twice, once as a detached satellite and once as part of the verb' (Croft *et al.*, 2010: 8). There are three symmetric strategies, which are coordination, serialisation and compounding. Beavers *et al.* (2008) point out that some languages may show both satellite-framed patterns and verb-framed patterns or even equipollent-framed patterns. They also emphasise that pragmatic situations may influence the choice of typological patterns – a verb-framed language may prefer satellite-framed patterns in certain pragmatic situations.

In the process of L1 acquisition, the specific way in which the components of a motion event are mapped onto linguistic forms in a child's L1 become entrenched and it is very difficult to learn a new way of talking about motion (Carroll & Von Stutterheim, 2003; Choi & Bowerman, 1991), although not all researchers agree on the importance of the influence of the L1 on the L2 in this domain. Some researchers (Hendriks *et al.*, 2008; Inagaki, 2001, 2002; Treffers-Daller & Tidball, in press) studying second language learners' acquisition of motion event expressions provide evidence in favour of crosslinguistic influence (CLI), while other researchers report opposite results (Cadierno & Ruiz, 2006; Navarro & Nicoladis, 2005).

While according to Ho and Platt (1993), convergence between the different languages spoken by multilinguals from Singapore may lead to the transfer of serial verb constructions from Chinese into Singaporean English, we assume that this will not happen in classroom settings among Chinese L1 learners of English, because the positive evidence in the input in textbooks and classroom language will enable L2 learners to discover the basic rules of mapping of manner and path on to linguistic forms in English. While in English manner is typically encoded in the main verb, Chinese speakers prefer to use serial verb constructions with manner verbs, with the word in the first slot expressing manner and the word in the second slot expressing path, as in Example 2, where the serial verb construction 跑进 *pao3jin4* 'run enter' expresses the notion path and manner in Chinese.

Example 2

一个抢劫犯跑进银行.
Yi1 ge4 qiang3jie2fan4 pao3jin4 yin2hang2.
one -CL robber run enter bank
'A robber runs into the bank.'

Because of the typological differences between the languages, learning to map the different components of a motion event onto a linguistic form in English as a L2 is not easy. According to Yu (1996) negative transfer can arise because of these typological differences. The author notes that to say, for instance that *'(the ball) crashed through the window into the room'*, Chinese EFL learners use *'smash/crash the window into the room'* without the preposition *'through'*. In the Chinese translation equivalent for *'smash into the room'*, given in Example 3, there is no directional complement after the verb 破 *po4* 'break'.

Example 3

破窗而入
po4 chuang1 er2 ru4
break window and enter
'(The ball) crashed through the window into the room.'

The author seeks the source of this error in transfer from Chinese. While this may be the case, a comparison with a group of L2 learners of English with a different L1 would be needed to find out whether the phenomenon in question is indeed due to L1 transfer or to other factors (Jarvis, 2000).

Transfer may also be more subtle in that the frequency with which a word is used increases or decreases under the influence of the frequency in the L1. This type of transfer is sometimes called *indirect transfer* (Silva-Corvalán, 1994) or *covert transfer* (Mougeon *et al.*, 2005). Mougeon *et al.* define covert transfer as a marked increase in the frequency of a feature under the influence of another language where the feature is very frequent. While Silva-Corvalán and Mougeon *et al.* discussed indirect or covert transfer in the context of contact between speaker groups which have a long-standing tradition of language contact, we assume that it can also play a role in L2 acquisition.

Covert transfer is particularly interesting for the current study which focuses on the frequency with which L2 learners use motion verbs. While L2 learners might, on the one hand, be trying to adjust to the L2 frequencies of motion verbs, they might, on the other hand, be influenced by the frequencies with which motion verbs occur in their L1. In other words, we hypothesise that the frequencies of motion verbs in the L2 and the frequencies of translation equivalents of these verbs in the L1 function as push and pull factors in the acquisition of motion event construal in a L2.

In the current paper we aim to find out to what extent covert transfer from the L1 can indeed explain the frequencies with which learners use motion verbs in the L2. We assume that L2 learners start using motion verbs with the same frequency as in their L1 (covert transfer), but adjust these frequencies in the course of L2 learning to the frequencies in the L2 input. With increasing amounts of input, they should be more successful at approaching the L2 target, if indeed they are able to use the input for statistical learning, which is the topic of the next section.

Statistical Learning and Motion Event Construal in a Second Language

Statistical learning is, basically, the discovery of patterns in the input (Romberg & Saffran, 2010), and in the context of language learning, such information can be used to further language development. One of the key mechanisms involved in statistical learning is entrenchment. Brooks and Tomasello (1999) argue that hearing a particular form or construction very frequently in a particular construction will lead to this form or construction becoming entrenched or strengthened in the learner's mind. Other researchers (Boyd & Goldberg, 2011; Goldberg, 2006) have demonstrated that learners can use statistical cues in the input 'to infer constraints specifying how a word *cannot* be used by considering how it *is* used in their input' (Boyd *et al.*, 2012: 1). Learners can do this by making use of another mechanism of statistical learning, called pre-emption or blocking. Thus, for example, learners can discover that using intransitive verbs such as *disappear* transitively as in *He disappeared him* is not allowed when they notice the occurrence of the periphrastic causative in the input (*He made him disappear*). This information can provide indirect negative evidence to learners that the transitive form **He disappeared him* is not grammatical in English, and should be blocked.

Treffers-Daller and Calude (2015) show that frequency information in the input provides an important cue to learners on how to restructure their L2 grammar in the domain of motion event construal. They assume that English L1 learners of French L2 start from the assumption that the verb *marcher* 'to march' is used as frequently in French as in English, but with increased exposure to French they notice that this verb and other manner verbs are not used as frequently and they start replacing these with path verbs, such as *partir* 'to leave'. Thus, the frequency with which advanced learners of French used motion verbs was found to be more closely aligned to the frequency patterns found among native speakers of French. Advanced learners of French did not only adjust the frequency with which they use motion verbs to that of native speakers, but also used the verbs with the appropriate subcategorisation frames: advanced learners know, for example, that French *entrer* subcategorises for a prepositional phrase headed by *dans* 'into'. Thus, Treffers-Daller and Calude conclude that the learners acquire not only the verbs but also the patterns in which they occur, and these replace the L1 patterns (structures of *entrer* without the prepositional phrase) which were frequently found among intermediate learners. For further information about the transfer of subcategorisation information, see Adjémian (1983).

Statistical learning thus helps learners to discover that path is generally conflated in the main verb in French, whilst manner is expressed optionally in a satellite (see above for details). As a result of statistical learning, L2 verb-framed patterns become entrenched and replace L1-based satellite-framed patterns. However, learners are not able to acquire the boundary crossing constraint (Aske, 1989; Slobin & Hoiting, 1994) because of the absence of direct negative evidence (explicit corrections) and the paucity of indirect negative evidence (see Treffers-Daller & Calude, in press, for further details).

It is possible that the advanced learners in Treffers-Daller and Calude's study could make use of statistical learning because they had been exposed to French during their year abroad. It is unclear whether classroom learners who have much less access to the target language are able to do the same. In addition, it is possible that the existence of cognates (such as *entrer* 'enter' and *arriver* 'arrive') between French and English facilitates learning of new motion event patterns. The typological differences between Chinese and English described above may make it more difficult for learners to replace L1 patterns with L2 patterns. The current paper seeks to clarify to what extent Chinese L1 learners of L2 English (who have only had access to English in the classroom and through private study) are able to make use of statistical learning and adjust the frequency with which they use motion verbs in their L2, despite the typological distance and the absence of cognates between both languages.

Hypotheses of the Current Study

We assumed that if Chinese L1 learners of L2 English are able to make use of statistical learning, they will use English verbs with frequencies that approach those of native speakers (the pull factor). A comparison of intermediate and advanced level learners will therefore reveal that the advanced learners are more closely aligned with the frequencies with which motion verbs occur in the input than the intermediate-level learners. In addition, the advanced learners should be better at using the constructions in which these verbs occur because they learn the subcategorisation frames with the verbs. Thus, the advanced learners will, for example, be better at using the appropriate preposition in combination with manner-or-path verbs (e.g. *rush into the lake* rather than *rush in the lake* and *arrive at the beach* rather than *arrive the beach*).

As explained above, learners may also be influenced by the frequencies of the L1 translation equivalents (the push factor) and transfer the frequency with which they use verbs in their L1 to their L2. We assumed this to be the case particularly with intermediate-level learners.

Methods

Informants

All the Chinese EFL learners were students at Beijing Institute of Technology (BIT) There were 30 L1 Chinese learners of L2 English with intermediate English proficiency (the IC group) and 30 Chinese learners with high English proficiency (the HC group). The L1 of all subjects was Mandarin. The subjects in the intermediate English level group were non-English major first year students in BIT. The HC were English major fourth year students in the School of Foreign Languages in BIT.[3] Since the English major group had obtained much more input in English, we can infer that they had a higher proficiency in English than the non-English majors. Setting additional language tests was impossible due to time constraints. No Chinese EFL learners in these groups had ever lived or stayed in English-speaking countries. A group of 29 native speakers of English from the University of the West of England, Bristol formed the control group (the NSE group).

There were equal numbers of male and female participants in the IC group and the NSE group, but in the HC group there were more female subjects (23) than male subjects (seven) because in many countries there are more female students enrolled on language degrees (McNabb et al., 2002).

Materials

The frequency of motion verbs in this data base was compared to that of a corpus of learner language elicited with the help of two frog stories, namely *Frog, where are you?* and *Frog goes to dinner* (Mayer, 1969), and two short cartoon stories, which do not have a title, but will be called *the dog story* and *the bank story*, and were written by Plauen (1952). The stories were counterbalanced across the groups and the languages: 15 intermediate and 15 advanced learners told *Frog where are you?* and *the dog story* in English, and *Frog goes to dinner* and *the bank story* in Chinese. The remaining intermediate and advanced students (15 in each group) told the same stories but the languages were reversed. None of the students told the same story in English as well as Chinese to avoid translation effects. The frog stories have been used in many motion event studies in many languages including English and Chinese, following the work of Berman and Slobin (1994) and Plauen's stories have been used for various other studies of motion event construal (Daller et al., 2011; Treffers-Daller & Tidball, in press).[4]

The source of information about the frequency of motion verbs in the English input was obtained from the oral data on the CELEX database which is available under the N-watch programme (http://www.pc.rhul.ac.uk/staff/c.davis/Utilities/). This database is built on the basis of the 1991 version of the COBUILD corpus. The database contains 17.9 million tokens and 1 million of these are from oral data (Baayen et al., 1995). The latter were used for the current analysis.

As we were interested in finding out to what extent learners transfer the frequencies of verbs in their L1 to their L2, we also obtained the frequency of occurrence of the Chinese motion verbs from the ZhTenTen11 corpus (11 billion words) which can be accessed through the Sketchengine database (http://www.sketchengine.co.uk/). There were no frequency data available for spoken Chinese, so we used the written frequencies from this database. In order to be able to investigate the impact of L1 frequencies on the L2, we had to map English verbs onto their Chinese translation equivalents, which was of course very difficult, as there is not always a one-to-one correspondence between words from two languages. In the case of Chinese and English, this was particularly challenging, not only because it was often difficult to find verbs which expressed exactly the same meaning, but also because some verbs were used with different meanings in the English data set and these corresponded to different translation equivalents in Chinese. Finally, some English verbs do not correspond to a single Chinese word but are best translated as a serial verb construction (see the literature review for further details). We used the KWAL command in CLAN to look up which meanings were the intended ones in our data set, and searched the verb whose meaning was most closely related to this meaning in the Sketchengine corpus.[5]

Procedure

The subjects were asked to tell stories based on the picture book and the stories were tape-recorded for future transcriptions. Each subject was presented with a task explanation written in English to ensure every student obtained exactly the same instructions.[6] In the instruction, the participants were informed that they were going to tell stories based on picture books and cartoons and that these would be tape-recorded. The subjects were asked to tell the stories in as much detail as possible. The data were collected in a one-to-one setting in China and the United Kingdom. The data from native English speakers were collected either in a one-to-one setting with one of the researchers or in the booths of the interpreting laboratory where they recorded themselves after they had read the written task explanation.

Transcriptions

The stories were first tape-recorded and then transcribed by the second author. To ensure accuracy, all these transcriptions were checked by three other native or fluent speakers of English. Then the data were transformed into CHAT format, the transcription and coding format developed by MacWhinney (2000). This made it possible to analyse the data further with the help of CLAN, a package of analysis programs, developed by MacWhinney (2000), which is freely available on the internet (http://childes.psy.cmu.edu/).

The mean length of the stories was 1030 characters for the Chinese stories, 734 for advanced level L2 learners, 600 words for intermediate-level Chinese EFL levels and 1344 words for native English speakers.

Data analysis

In total, 71 English motion verbs were used by the two learner groups and the native speaker group, across the four stories.[7] We created a file with all motion verbs for English and a similar one for Chinese and searched all motion verbs in the data using the FREQ command with the list of motion verbs as an included file. The KWAL command was used to check the contexts in which the verbs were used, to verify the meaning to enable us to establish which forms were suitable translation equivalents of the English verbs in the Chinese data set and to establish whether the verb was used to describe translational movement. As illustrated in Examples

4–6, a detailed analysis of individual constructions was needed to check these issues. The phrase *turned towards some musicians* in Example 4 does not indicate translational meaning (in the context), as the figure remains in the same place in the act of turning and does not move to another location. Examples 5 and 6, on the other hand, do express translational motion in the given context. Even though the word *stuck* and its Chinese equivalent 塞*sai1* do not indicate motion per se, *getting stuck* and 塞进*sai1jin4* 'stuck enter' qualify as motion verbs. For further details of the analysis of translational movement in Chinese, see Chen and Guo (2009).

Example 4

As they sit down to look at their menus, the frog jumps out of the boy's pocket, *turns towards* some musicians. (NSE 315)

Example 5

He leapt high into the air and *ended up getting stuck* in a saxophone. (NS 318)

Example 6

小男孩口袋中的青蛙突然跳了出来,塞进了萨克斯手的萨克斯里. (NSC 202)
Xiao3 nan2hai2 kou3dai4 zhong1 de0 qing1wa1 tu1ran2 tiao4 le0 chu1 lai2,
small boy pocket in NOM frog suddenly jump PFV exit come <u>*sai 1jin4*</u> *le0 sa4ke4si1shou3 de0 sa4ke4si1 li3.*
<u>stuck enter</u> PEV saxophonist GEN saxophone in
'The frog in the boy's pocket suddenly jumped out and got stuck in the saxophone of the saxophonist.'

The frequency with which they were used by all groups, with corresponding frequency information about the Chinese translation equivalents used by native speakers of Chinese who told the same stories, were entered into a spreadsheet. Finally, we entered the frequency data about the English and the Chinese motion verbs from the two databases into the spreadsheet, to enable us to investigate the effect of the frequency in the input on learners' use of English motion verbs.

Because the data were categorical (count) and not normally distributed, we used non-parametric tests to compute correlations between variables. After having investigated the correlations between the frequencies of the learner data, the native speaker data and the corpus data we built a GLM with Poisson Distribution for each of our learner groups, which allowed us to investigate the impact of different predictor variables on the frequency with which the two learner groups use English motion verbs.

Results

In this section, we first report the correlations between the frequencies with which the two learner groups and the native speakers of English use the motion verbs, and the frequencies with which native speakers of Chinese use these verbs to tell the same stories. Then we use a Poisson regression to find out which variables are the best predictors of the students' use of motion verbs, and finally we present a frequency analysis of individual motion types. As explained in the Method section, we have also calculated the correlations between these data and the frequencies with which all verbs occur in the input to learners. These figures were obtained from the CELEX database and the Chinese ZhTenTen11 corpus, which provided the frequencies of Chinese words.

Correlations between frequencies of motion verbs

Table 7.1 gives an overview of the correlations between the different data sets. For this table we used the relative frequency of the motion verbs in the learner data and the native speaker data, that is, the number of motion verbs divided by the total number of words used by the speakers, multiplied by 10. For the data from the CELEX and the ZhTenTen11 corpora we used the frequency of each verb per million words in the corpus. First of all, we need to note that the correlations between the learner groups and the native speaker groups are relatively high, which is partly due to the fact that all participants told the same stories, which resulted in the participants choosing similar words to verbalise the events. But the same event can be narrated in very different ways, so there is only a partial overlap between the words chosen by participants. There are also mid-strength correlations with verb frequencies from the English CELEX database, which are unrelated to the data from our project, so the similarity in content between the stories cannot fully explain the results.

Table 7.1 Spearman correlations between the relative frequency of motion verbs in the learner data, Chinese native speaker data and corpus data

	HC	NSE	CELEX	NSC	ZhT
IC	0.773**	0.577**	0.566**	0.522**	0.422**
HC		0.567**	0.467**	0.408**	0.467**
NSE			0.546**	0.318**	0.337**
CELEX				0.413**	0.600**
NSC					0.523**

IC: intermediate-level learners of English; HC: higher level learners of English; NSE: native speakers of English; CELEX: frequency of English motion verbs in the CELEX database; NSC: native speakers of Chinese; ZhT: frequency of Chinese motion verbs in the ZhTenTen11corpus; ** $p < 0.001$.

The strongest correlations ($r_s = 0.773$) can be found between the datasets from the two learner groups[8], which is understandable as these two groups are most closely related in terms of language backgrounds. Both learner groups correlate slightly less strongly with the native speakers of English who told the same stories ($r_s = 0.58$ for the IC group and 0.57 for the HC group). The correlations with the CELEX database are of approximately the same magnitude, although it is a little surprising that the IC group frequencies correlate slightly more strongly with the CELEX data ($r_s = 0.57$) than HC group frequencies ($r_s = 0.47$). Both learner groups also correlate fairly strongly with the NSC group. It is interesting that the IC correlate more strongly with the Chinese data than the HC ($r_s = .052$ for the IC group and 0.41 for the HC group). The frequencies in both learner groups are also related to the ZhT database ($r_s = 0.42$ for the IC group and 0.47 for the HC group). This could indicate that the frequency with which learners use English verbs is also influenced by their frequency of use in Chinese. The fact that there is a mid-strength correlation ($r_s = 0.55$) between English native speaker data and the CELEX data indicates that verbs that are frequent in the larger database are also chosen frequently by the English native speakers to tell the stories. Finally, the existence of correlations between frequencies across the two large databases for Chinese and English ($r_s = 0.60$) is probably due to the fact that some verbs with a low degree of semantic specificity (e.g. *arrive*, *jump* and *walk*) are frequent in both languages, whilst verbs which express a high degree of semantic specificity (e.g. *creep* and *swoop*) are less frequent in each language. Further discussion about the spatial scale or granularity in the encoding of motion in language can be found in Vulchanova and Van der Zee (2012).

Predicting the frequency with which L2 learners use motion verbs

As our data were count data, the most appropriate model to be used was a GLM Poisson loglinear model. This model is particularly useful for low-frequency count variables when many of the counts are zero (Nussbaum *et al.*, 2008), which is the case with the motion verbs under study because some occur with high frequency and are used by almost all participants (e.g. *jump*) while others are used by only one participant (e.g. *hoik*). The raw frequencies of motion verbs used by the HC group were the dependent variable, and four variables were used as predictors: the frequency of motion verbs used by native speakers who tell the same stories (NSE), the frequency of motion verbs in the CELEX database (CELEX), the frequency of motion verbs used by Chinese native speakers who told the same stories (NSC) and the frequency of motion verbs in the ZhTenTen11 (ZhT). We checked for multicollinearity but found the correlations between predictor variables did not exceed the limits specified in Field (2013) because tolerance values were not below 0.1 and VIF values did not exceed 10^9. While this produced an overall statistically significant model, ZhT was found not to

Table 7.2 GLM Poisson model for the HC group with three predictor variables

Parameter	β	SE	Wald Chi square	p	Exp(β)
(Intercept)	0.344	0.1005	11.679	0.001	1.410
NSE	0.026	0.0008	973.972	< 0.000	1.026
CELEX	0.005	0.0008	38.344	< 0.001	1.005
NSC	0.002	0.0003	48.404	< 0.001	1.002

Table 7.3 GLM Poisson model for the IC group with four predictor variables

Parameter	β	SE	Wald Chi square	P	Exp(β)
(Intercept)	0.246	0.1038	5.618	0.018	1.279
NSE	0.022	0.0012	310.406	< 0.001	1.022
NSC	0.007	0.0008	84.503	< 0.001	1.007
CELEX	0.004	0.0008	25.632	< 0.001	1.004
ZhT	−0.002	0.0004	35.635	< 0.001	0.998

be a significant predictor in this model and we decided to remove it. This way we obtained a significant model (χ^2 (3) = 1034.6, $p < .001$) with three significant predictors, of which the NSE was the strongest, followed by CELEX and NSC (see Table 7.2). The latter two have very small but still highly significant effects on the frequency with which higher level learners use English motion verbs.

We then repeated the process with the frequency of motion verbs used by the IC group as the dependent variable. We started by including all four predictor variables in the model, which was found to be significant (χ^2 (4) = 1142.58, $p < 0.001$). The results can be found in Table 7.3.

While the model is very similar to that for the HC group, there is a minor difference between both models in that the frequency of verbs in the ZhT corpus has a marginal negative effect on the frequency with which English verbs are used by the IC group. In other words, the more frequently a verb occurs in the Chinese corpus, the *less* frequently its translation equivalent occurs in the English learner data from the IC group. This is difficult to interpret, and as the effect is marginal, it is probably best left out. If we do leave it out, the model becomes virtually identical to that of the HC group (see Table 7.4). We also tested whether there was an effect of group (IC versus HC) on the frequency with which motion verbs were used, but the group factor turned out not to be significant, as could be expected on the basis of the two separate Poisson regressions we computed for each group.[10]

The frequency of individual motion verbs in the learners' language

We now turn to differences between the groups in their use of motion types. Out of the 71 motion types found in the data, the IC group used 20 types, the HC group used 27 types and the NSE group 67

Table 7.4 Poisson model for the IC group with three predictor variables

Parameter	β	SE	Wald Chi square	P	Exp(β)
Intercept	0.238	0.1058	5.057	0.025	1.269
NSE	0.27	0.0008	1025.319	< 0.001	1.025
CELEX	0.004	0.0008	20.907	< 0.001	1.002
NSC	0.003	0.0003	112.847	< 0.001	1.003

types. We found that there were significant differences in the numbers of types used by the IC and the NSE groups ($\chi^2(1) = 68.05, p < 0.001$) and between the HC and the NSE groups ($\chi^2(1) = 52.78, p < 0.001$), but the differences between the two learner groups were not significant. Out of the 71 motion types, 42 were used exclusively by native speakers. Many of these were manner verbs with a high degree of semantic specificity such as *barge, cower, creep* and *lunge*, which learners from both groups did not actively know. There were also a few differences between the two learner groups: *drop* and *float* were used only by the IC group but not by the HC group, while *chase, dash, enter, flee, land, leap, slip, sneak* and *tumble* were only used by the HC group and not by the IC group.

More information about differences between the groups can be obtained by comparing the relative frequencies of individual motion verbs as used by different groups. Figure 7.1 shows that the IC group tends to make more use of manner-of-motion verbs with a low degree of semantic specificity, such as *jump* and *climb*, than the HC or the NSE groups while the opposite is true for manner-of-motion verbs with a higher degree of semantic specificity, such as *leap* and *sneak*[11]. The same contrast can be observed for path verbs.

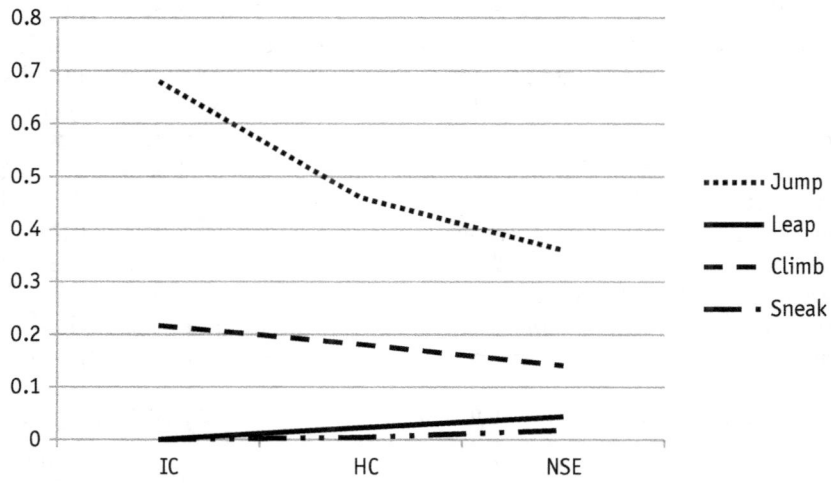

Figure 7.1 Frequency trajectory of individual manner-of-motion verbs

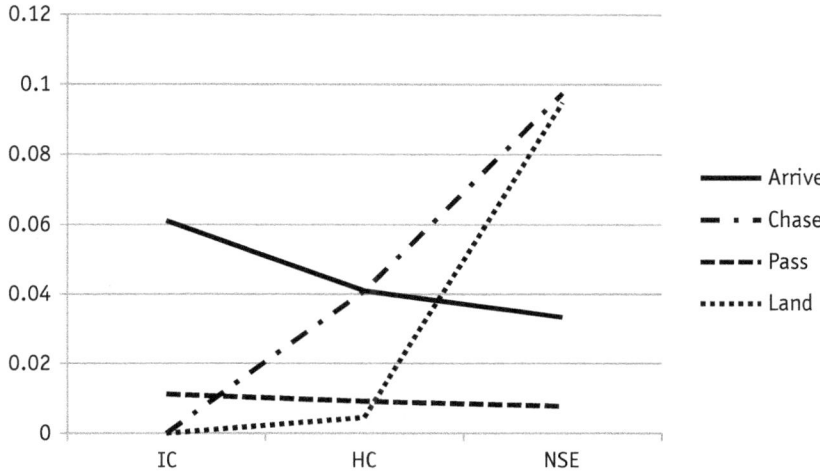

Figure 7.2 Frequency trajectory of individual path verbs

In Figure 7.2 we can see that path verbs with a low degree of semantic specificity, such as *arrive* and *pass*, occur most frequently among the IC group while path verbs with a high degree of semantic specificity, such as *chase*[12] and *land*, are used more frequently by the HC and the NSE groups. For some of these verbs, for example *arrive* and *pass*, an explanation of these facts can be sought in the very high frequency with which the translation equivalents are used in Chinese.

Finally, we found that there is some evidence that learners in the HC group were better at using the appropriate subcategorisation frame belonging to verbs. In the IC group, three learners used *arrive* without a prepositional phrase (*arrive the restaurant*) while none of the learners in the HC group omitted *at*. However, the choice between a simple and a compound preposition (e.g. *in* versus *into*) in combination with *jump* was problematic for nine learners in the IC group and seven learners in the HC group, which shows there were no real differences between the two groups with respect to the use of the constructions involving this verb. The fact that *jump* can be combined with a wide range of different prepositions is probably the reason why acquiring target-like constructions with *jump* is more difficult than target-like expressions with *arrive*, which is always used with the preposition *at*.

Discussion

In this paper we attempted to find out to what extent L1 Chinese learners of L2 English can make use of statistical learning to restructure the domain of motion event cognition. The study makes an important contribution to our understanding of statistical learning in that it is one of the first studies into this type of learning in a classroom setting, which is closer to situations in the wild than studies which are based on learning of artificial grammars in a laboratory context. While there is a wealth of studies pointing out how difficult it is to restructure motion event cognition, few studies have tried to investigate to what extent frequency information in the input provides a clue to learners as to how they need to restructure their grammars. We agree with Ellis (2002) that frequency is a key determinant in L2 acquisition, and hypothesised that learners would be influenced by the frequency of motion verbs in the input in learning how to talk about motion. At the same time, we expected that learners would be influenced by the frequencies of the translation equivalents of these motion verbs in their L1 if it is indeed the case that learners transfer the frequency information about words from their L1 to their L2, alongside semantic and syntactic information from the L1 lemma (Jiang, 2000). In other words, learners find themselves between the push and pull factors of the frequencies of motion verbs in their L1 and their L2. We expected that with increased exposure to English, learners would be able to align themselves with the frequencies of motion verbs in the input, as was shown to be the case in Treffers-Daller and Calude (2015) who studied English L1 learners of French L2. While one of the groups in the latter study consisted of learners who had been to France on a year abroad, and had therefore had extensive exposure to the target language, the current study focused on classroom learners who had never been to an English-speaking country. The current study also differs from that of Treffers-Daller and Calude because the L1 and the L2 of the learners are typologically very different, which could make it more difficult to transfer information from the L1 to the L2 or to use statistical learning.

We obtained the frequency with which learners use motion verbs in English from stories told by intermediate learners (IC) and advanced learners (HC) of English whose L1 was Chinese and compared this with frequency data from native speakers of English (NSE) and frequency data from native speakers of Chinese (NSC) who told the same stories. In addition, a large corpus of English (CELEX) was used to provide information about the frequency of motion verbs in English and a corpus of Chinese was used to establish how frequent each verb was in the learners' L1. Of course we are aware that the frequency with which verbs are found in corpora does not necessarily reflect the frequency with which they are found in the input to second language learners, in particular, if the input largely consists of classroom language (see Roemer, 2004 for a discussion). In the absence of information about the frequency of the verbs under study here in the input to classroom learners, the evidence from the corpora mentioned above provides an important source of information for the current study.

We found that there were mid-strength correlations between the learners' and the native speakers' frequencies, as well as between the learners' frequencies and those in the CELEX database. In addition, there were mid-strength correlations across languages between the data from the NSE and the NSC groups, which could be interpreted as evidence for the push and pull factors from the two languages. We do want to treat this result with some caution, because there were also mid-strength correlations across languages between the frequencies of verbs in the CELEX and the ZhTenTen11 databases. These are probably due to the fact that verbs with a low degree of semantic specificity (such as *leave* and *walk*) are frequent in both languages, while verbs with a high degree of semantic specificity (such as *drift* and *sneak*) are infrequent in both languages. We had not anticipated there would be relatively strong correlations between both databases, as this makes it more difficult to disambiguate between the push and the pull factors (the source and the target languages).

Some evidence for the fact that learners do indeed adjust the frequency of the verbs they use to that of native speakers in their environment was obtained from a comparison of individual verbs in the stories of the native speakers on the one hand and the intermediate and advanced learners of English on the other hand. We have shown that verbs with a low degree of semantic specificity, such as *arrive* and *jump*, were used more frequently by the IC group than by the HC and the NSE groups, while verbs with a higher degree of semantic specificity, such as *chase* and *sneak* were used more frequently by the advanced group. In other words, the intermediate learners relied more on high frequency verbs with a low degree of semantic specificity while the advanced learners relied less on those and had acquired some low-frequency verbs with a high degree of semantic specificity. Some of the verbs which were highly frequent in the ZhTenTen11 database (e.g. *arrive*) but not in the CELEX database were clearly used more frequently by the intermediate learners than by the advanced learners. For these verbs there is some evidence for a push effect of the L1 (that is, covert transfer).

A Poisson regression was carried out to study the effect of different predictor variables (the frequency of motion verbs used by the NSE, NSC and the two databases) on the informants' use of motion verbs in English. For both learner groups very similar models emerged which showed that the frequency of use by the NSE group had the strongest effect, while small but significant effects were also found for CELEX and the NSC (in that order). We interpret these findings to mean that the two learner groups aligned themselves more closely with the frequency of motion verbs in their L2 than with the frequency of the verbs in their L1, and that statistical learning of motion verbs did indeed take place. The regression model provided little evidence for covert transfer from the L1, although covert transfer could have contributed to the high frequency with which *arrive* and *pass* were used by intermediate learners, as explained above.

It was somewhat surprising that the regression models for the two groups of learners were virtually the same, because we expected the advanced learners to be more strongly aligned with the native speakers than the intermediate learners. The absence of significant differences between both learner groups could be due to the fact that neither of the two groups had been to English-speaking countries. It is possible, therefore, that the difference between the two groups is less important than the difference between the intermediate and the advanced learners in Treffers-Daller and Calude (2015). The advanced learners in the latter study had been to the country of the target language during their year abroad, and had therefore had far more extensive exposure to the L2 than the Chinese L1 learners of English in the current study. It is likely that the informants in Treffers-Daller and Calude (2015) were better able to approach the frequencies with which native speakers use motion verbs than those in the current study. In addition, the typological distance between English and Chinese may have contributed to the difficulty for Chinese L1 learners of English to master the domain of motion event cognition, as English motion event constructions do not always map easily onto Chinese translation equivalents, which often involve serial verb constructions. Finally, the fact that there is a difference between the frequency of the verbs in the corpora and the frequency of these verbs in the actual input to learners could be an issue. Further information about frequencies in the actual input to learners could shed new light on how the input to learners affects their ability to use target-like motion event expressions. The learners in both studies were to a certain extent able to learn the subcategorisation frames belonging to the verbs in question. The advanced learners in the current study were clearly better at using the preposition *at* with *arrive*, for example, which some intermediate-level learners omitted. This indicates the advanced learners do more than copy the frequencies with which native speakers use motion verbs. They are also able to integrate L2 lemma information into the entry for an L2 word, which according to Jiang (2000) is indicative of learners moving away from the L1 mediation stage towards the L2 integration stage in building up an L2 vocabulary.

Conclusion

In conclusion, this study has shown that classroom learners can adjust the frequency with which they use L2 verbs to that of native speakers of the target language, but they are less successful at doing this than L2 learners who had been exposed to the target language during a year abroad. In addition to the absence of a year abroad, the typological differences between the source and target language could have played a role in the different outcomes of both studies: it is probably more difficult to map meaning onto form in a new way when the source and target language are typologically very different from each other. We interpret the adjustment of the frequency of motion verbs to the target language as a process of statistical learning because learners make use of statistical information in the input to discover patterns in the L2, and learn new ways to map meaning (e.g. manner and path) onto linguistic forms (e.g. verbs and satellites). Put differently, as a result of statistical learning, L2-based motion event patterns become entrenched and replace L1-based patterns. Although we do not think that analysing frequency patterns in the input is sufficient for learners to completely restructure their grammars in the domain of motion event cognition, as discussed in Treffers-Daller and Calude (2015), it is likely that the frequency distribution of motion verbs provides learners with an important cue about the ways in which meaning is mapped onto form in their L2. This cue has so far not been investigated in great detail in research on motion event cognition. We are aware that frequency information constitutes only one piece of the puzzle: learners will need to use it together with other sources of information. When learners start using frequency information and how they use this information in combination with other cues such as saliency and transparency in the L2 acquisition of this particular domain could not be addressed in this study, but these are obviously important issues that need to be investigated in follow-up studies. In addition, more studies are needed investigating the ways in which structures involving motion verbs can be taught as there are virtually no studies of the teachability of motion event construal, apart from the work by Antonijević and Berthaud (2012). Further studies in this domain are needed to help teachers evaluate what information learners can obtain from the input and what needs to be taught explicitly.

In future research of the statistical learning of motion event construal, it would be interesting to focus more on the trade-off between the push and the pull factors in learning to talk about motion in a second language. In the current study it was difficult to disentangle the role of frequency in the L1 from frequency in the L2 because there were mid-strength correlations between the frequency of verbs in both languages. A study of the trade-off between both factors is probably best done with an experimental design in which the motion verbs under study clearly differ in frequency in the source and the target language. However, studies of statistical learning 'in the wild' will still be needed if we want to examine links between learning in the lab and real-world language outcomes (Romberg & Saffran, 2010). In particular, studies in which the degree of exposure to the target language is systematically manipulated are likely to shed new light on whether or not L2 learners in different contexts can make use of statistical learning and what the role of statistical learning is by comparison with other factors which impact on the learnability of these constructions.

Notes

(1) We are very grateful to Rosa Alonso for inviting us to contribute to this volume and to two reviewers for detailed comments on a previous version of the chapter.

(2) Slobin (2006: 70) has made assessments of manner salience across languages from various aspects of language use, such as ease of lexical access, imagery and understanding of manner verbs, conversational use, child language acquisition, use in elicited oral narratives, use in creative fiction, translation of creative fiction, metaphoric extensions of manner verbs, etc.

(3) In our experience the classification in English majors and non-English majors is valid because it is based on the national tests that most university students in China take to get a Bachelor's degree. All English majors in BIT are required to pass the Test of English Major Band 4 (TEM4) after two years' study in university and to pass the Test of English Major Band 8 (TEM8) in the fourth year. Non-English majors are required to pass the College English Test Band 4 (CET4) after one year's study in BIT and they can take the College English Test Band 6 (CET6) subsequently. The national tests for English majors and non-English majors are different tests in content and difficulty. The CET6 is roughly equivalent in difficulty to the TEM4. That is, when the data was collected, the intermediate-level Chinese EFL learners were not qualified to take the CET4 because they were level two students. They can only take the national test after they have finished level four English study in BIT. In contrast, all the high-level Chinese EFL learners had finished the TEM8, which is far more difficult than the TEM4/CET6. Unfortunately, the teachers/students did not allow us to access the results of those tests.

(4) Although the stories are clearly rooted in Western culture, this did not constitute a barrier for the Chinese students who were asked to tell the story. None of the students complained that the story was incomprehensible or inappropriate in any way.

(5) We are very grateful to Yixin Wang for her help in compiling the correspondences between the English and the Chinese translation equivalents.

(6) Although the fact that the task explanation was given in English might have helped to put the learners in an English mode, we consider this effect is negligible in the current study because the recordings were made in a Chinese-speaking environment. Effects of the language mode and of the language of instruction are potentially measurable in reaction time studies but there is little evidence that these effects are noticeable in the frequency with which subjects choose Manner-or-Path verbs in narrative tasks.

(7) We decided to exclude the deictic verb *go* from the analysis because it is used frequently in constructions that are not motion events (e.g. *everything goes wrong*). It was beyond the scope of the current paper to make a detailed analysis of the 400 tokens of this verb to establish whether they were used in a motion event or not. Because we had excluded one of the key deictic motion verbs, we decided to exclude the other deictic verb *come* too. In addition, we excluded the caused motion verb *take* (and phrasal verb combinations such as *take off, take out,* etc.), which learners frequently used in non-target-like ways to express movement towards the speaker.

(8) We checked whether the strength of these correlations could be due to the fact that learners use fewer motion verb types, so that there are many zeros in the columns for the learners. A large number of zeros in the columns for the two learner groups could have inflated the correlation coefficients. Running the correlation once more only the verbs for which there was at least one token in

either group (n = 18) led however to an increase in the strength of the correlation (r_s = 0.876, p < 0.001), so we did not assume the large number of zeros did artificially inflate the figures.
(9) As specified in Field (2013: 795), the SPSS interface does not offer the possibility to check for multicollinearity as part of logistic regression analysis, so we obtained these figures by running a linear regression using the same outcome and predictor variables.
(10) As one reviewer has pointed out, it is possible that differences between both groups would have been found if a different task had been used.
(11) Some of the verbs were not used by the IC group. It was not possible to compute a chi-square because the expected frequencies for the IC group were below 5.
(12) *Chase* is a special case because path as well as manner are conflated in this verb according to Özçalışkan and Slobin (2000).

References

Adjémian, C. (1983) The transferability of lexical properties. In S.M. Gass and L. Selinker (eds) *Language Transfer in Language Learning* (1st edn), (pp. 250–268). Rowley: Newbury Home.
Antonijević, S. and Berthaud, S. (2012) L2 Acquisition of verbal constructions: Expressing motion in L2 French and English. In M. Bouveret and D. Legallois (eds) *Constructions in French* (pp. 155–174). Amsterdam: John Benjamins.
Aske, J. (1989) Path predicates in English and Spanish: A closer look. *Berkeley Linguistic Society Papers* 14, 1–14.
Baayen, R.H., Piepenbrock, R. and Van Rijn, H. (1995) The CELEX database: Linguistic Data Consortium, University of Pennsylvania, Philadelphia.
Beavers, J., Levin, B. and Wei Tham, S. (2010) The typology of motion expressions revisited. *Journal of Linguistics* 46 (2), 331–377.
Berman, R.A. and Slobin, D.I. (1994) *Relating Events in Narrative: A Crosslinguistic Developmental Study*: Psychology Press.
Boyd, J.K., Ackerman, F. and Kutas, M. (2012) Adult Learners Use Both Entrenchment and Preemption to Infer Grammatical Constraints. Paper presented at the 2012 IEEE International Conference on Development and Learning and Epigenetic Robotics (ICDL).
Boyd, J.K. and Goldberg, A.E. (2011) Learning what not to say: The role of statistical preemption and categorization in adjective production. *Language* 87 (1), 55–83.
Brooks, P.J. and Tomasello, M. (1999) Young children learn to produce passives with nonce verbs. *Developmental Psychology* 35 (1), 29.
Cadierno, T. and Ruiz, L. (2006) Motion events in Spanish L2 acquisition. *Annual Review of Cognitive Linguistics* 4 (1), 183–216.
Carroll, M. and Von Stutterheim, C. (2003) Typology and information organisation: Perspective taking and language-specific effects in the construal of events. In A. Ramat (ed.) *Typology and Second Language Acquisition* (pp. 365–402). Berlin: De Gruyter.
Chen, L. and Guo, J. (2009) Motion events in Chinese novels: Evidence for an equipollently-framed language. *Journal of Pragmatics* 41 (9), 1749–1766.
Choi, S. and Bowerman, M. (1991) Learning to express motion events in English and Korean: The influence of language-specific lexicalization patterns. *Cognition* 41 (1), 83–121.
Croft, W., Barðdal, J., Hollmann, W., Sotirova, V. and Taoka, C. (2010) Revising Talmy's typological classification of complex event constructions. In H. Boas (ed.) *Contrastive Studies in Construction Grammar* (pp. 201–35). Amsterdam: Benjamins.

Daller, M.H., Treffers-Daller, J. and Furman, R. (2011) Transfer of conceptualization patterns in bilinguals: The construal of motion events in Turkish and German. *Bilingualism: Language and Cognition* 14 (1), 95–119.

Ellis, N. (1994) Implicit and explicit language learning: An overview. *Implicit and Explicit Learning of Languages*, 1–31.

Ellis, N.C. (2002) Frequency effects in language processing. *Studies in Second Language Acquisition* 24 (2), 143–188.

Field, A. (2013) *Discovering Statistics Using IBM SPSS Statistics*. Los Angeles: Sage.

Gass, S.M. and Mackey, A. (2002) Frequency effects and second language acquisition. *Studies in Second Language Acquisition* 24 (2), 249–260.

Goldberg, A.E. (2006) *Constructions at Work: The Nature of Generalization in Language*. Oxford: Oxford University Press.

Hasher, L., Zacks, R.T., Rose, K.C. and Sanft, H. (1987) Truly incidental encoding of frequency information. *American Journal of Psychology* 100, 69–91.

Hendriks, H., Hickmann, H. and Demagny, A.C. (2008) How adult English learners of French express caused motion: A comparison with English and French natives. *Acquisition et Interaction en Langue Étrangère* 27, 15–41.

Hendriks, H., Ji, Y. and Hickmann, M. (2009) Typological issues regarding the expression of caused motion: Chinese, English and French. In M. Brala-Vukanoviü and L. Gruiü- Grmuša (eds) *Space and Time in Language and Literature* (pp. 22–38). Cambridge: Cambridge University Press.

Ho, M.L. and Platt, J.T. (1993) *Dynamics of a Contact Continuum: Singaporean English*: Clarendon Press Oxford.

Huang, S.F. and Tanangkingsing, M. (2005) Reference to motion events in six western Austronesian languages: Toward a semantic typology. *Oceanic Linguistics* 44 (2), 307–340.

Ibarretxe-Antuñano, I. (2006) Leonard Talmy. A windowing onto conceptual structure and language: Part 2: Language and cognition: Past and future. *Annual Review of Cognitive Linguistics* 4 (1), 253–268.

Inagaki, S. (2001) Motion verbs with goal PPs in the L2 acquisition of English and Japanese. *Studies in Second Language Acquisition* 23 (2), 153–170.

Inagaki, S. (2002) Japanese learners' acquisition of English manner-of-motion verbs with locational/directional PPs. *Second Language Research* 18 (1), 3–27.

Jarvis, S. (2000) Methodological rigor in the study of transfer: Identifying L1 influence in them interlanguage lexicon. *Language Learning* 50 (2), 245–309.

Jiang, N. (2000) Lexical representation and development in a second language. *Applied Linguistics* 21 (1), 47–77.

Larrañaga, P., Treffers-Daller, J., Tidball, F. and Ortega, M.c.G. (2011) L1 transfer in the acquisition of manner and path in Spanish by native speakers of English. *International Journal of Bilingualism*, 1367006911405577.

Li, F. (1993) *A Diachronic Study of V-V Compounds in Chinese*. (Doctoral dissertation) State University of New York at Buffalo, Buffalo.

Li, F. (1997) Crosslinguistic lexicalization patterns: diachronic evidence from verb-complement compounds in Chinese. *Sprachtypologie und Universalienforschung,* 50 (3), 229–252.

MacWhinney, B. (2000) The CHILDES project: Tools for analyzing talk: Volume I: Transcription format and programs, volume II: The database. *Computational Linguistics* 26 (4), 657–657.

McNabb, R., Pal, S. and Sloane, P. (2002).Gender differences in educational attainment: the case of university students in England and Wales. *Economica* 69, 481–503.

Mayer, M. (1969) *Frog, Where Are You?* New York: Dial books for young readers.

Misyak, J.B., Goldstein, M.H. and Christiansen, M.H. (2012) Statistical-sequential learning in development. In P. Rebuschat and J.N. Williams (eds) *Statistical Learning and Language Acquisition* (pp. 13–54). Berlin: Walter de Gruyter.

Mougeon, R., Nadasdi, T. and Rehner, K. (2005) Contact-induced linguistic innovations on the continuum of language use: The case of French in Ontario. *Bilingualism: Language and Cognition* 8 (2), 99–115.

Navarro, S. and Nicoladis, E. (2005) *Describing Motion Events in Adult L2 Spanish Narratives.* Paper presented at the Selected Proceedings of the 6th Conference on the Acquisition of Spanish and Portuguese as First and Second Languages.

Nussbaum, E.M., Elsadat, S. and Khago, A. (2008) 21 Best Practices in Analyzing Count Data Poisson Regression. Best practices in quantitative methods. In J. Osborne (ed.) *Best Practices in Quantitative Methods* (pp. 306–324). Thousand Oaks, CA: SAGE.

Onnis, L. (2012) The potential contribution of statistical learning to second language acquisition. In P. Rebuschat and J.N. Williams (eds) *Statistical Learning and Language Acquisition* (pp. 203–236). Berlin: Mouton de Gruyter.

Özçalışkan, Ş. and Slobin, D.I. (2000) Climb Up vs. Ascend Climbing: Lexicalization choices in Expressing Motion Events with Manner and Path Components. Paper presented at the Proceedings of the 24th Annual Boston University Conference on Language Development.

Peyraube, A. (2006) Motion events in Chinese. In H. Hickman and S. Robert (eds) *Space in Languages: Linguistic Systems and Cognitive Categories* (Vol. 66, pp. 121–135). Amsterdam: Benjamins.

Plauen, E.O. (1952) *Vater und Sohn*. Ravensburg: Ravensburger Taschenbuch.

Rebuschat, P. and Williams, J.N. (2012) Introduction: Statistical learning and language acquisition. In P. Rebuschat and J.N. Williams (eds) *Statistical Learning and Language Acquisition* (pp. 1–12). Berlin: Walter de Gruyter.

Roemer, U. (2004). Comparing real and ideal language learner input: The use of an EFL textbook corpus in corpus linguistics and language teaching. In G. Aston, S. Bernardini and D. Stewart (eds) *Corpora and Language Learners* (pp. 151–168). Amsterdam: John Benjamins.

Romberg, A.R. and Saffran, J.R. (2010) Statistical learning and language acquisition. *Wiley Interdisciplinary Reviews: Cognitive Science* 1 (6), 906–914.

Saffran, J.R. (2012) Preface. In P. Rebuschat and J.N. Williams (eds) *Statistical Learning and Language Acquisition* (pp. v–vi). Berlin: Walter de Gruyter.

Saffran, J.R., Aslin, R.N. and Newport, E.L. (1996) Statistical learning by 8-month-old infants. *Science* 274 (5294), 1926–1928.

Schmitt, N. and Dunham, B. (1999) Exploring native and non-native intuitions of word frequency. *Second Language Research* 15 (4), 389–411.

Silva-Corvalán, C. (1994) *Language Contact and Change: Spanish in Los Angeles*. New York: Oxford University Press.

Slobin, D. (1996) From 'thought and language' to 'thinking for speaking'. In J.J. Gumperz and S.C. Levinson (eds) *Rethinking linguistic relativity* (pp. 70–96). Cambridge: Cambridge University Press.

Slobin, D. (2004) The many ways to search for a frog. *Relating Events in Narrative. Vol, 2*, 219–257.

Slobin, D. (2006) What makes manner of motion salient? Explorations in linguistic typology, discourse, and cognition. In H.H.M. Hickman (ed.) *Space in Languages: Linguistic Systems and Cognitive Categories* (Vol. 66, pp. 59–81). Amsterdam/Philadelphia: John Benjamins.

Slobin, D. and Hoiting, N. (1994) Reference to movement in spoken and signed languages: typological considerations. *Proceedings of the Berkeley Linguistics Society* 20, 487–505.

Talmy, L. (1985) Lexicalization patterns: Semantic structure in lexical forms. *Language Typology and Syntactic Description* 3, 57–149.

Talmy, L. (2000) Toward a cognitive semantics, Vol. II: Typology and process in concept structuring. *Language, Speech, and Communication*. Cambridge, MA: The MIT Press.

Treffers-Daller, J. and Calude, A.S. (2015) The role of statistical learning in the acquisition of motion event construal in a second language. *International Journal of Bilingual Education and Bilingualism* 18 (5), 602–623.

Treffers-Daller, J. and Tidball, F. (2016) Can L2 learners learn new ways to conceptualise events? Evidence from motion event construal among English-speaking learners of French. In P. Guijarro-Fuentes, K. Schmitz and N. Müller (eds) *The Acquisition of French in Multilingual Contexts* (pp. 145–184). Bristol: Multilingual Matters.

Von Stutterheim, C. and Nuse, R. (2003) Processes of conceptualization in language production: language-specific perspectives and event construal. *Linguistics* 41 (5), 851–882.

Vulchanova, M. and Van der Zee, E. (eds) (2012) *Motion Encoding in Language and Space*. Oxford: Oxford Scholarship.

Yu, L. (1996) The role of L1 in the acquisition of motion verbs in English by Chinese and Japanese learners. *Canadian Modern Language Review* 53 (1), 191–218.

Zlatev, J. and Yangklang, P. (2004) A third way to travel. In S. Strömqvist and L. Verhoeven (eds) *Relating Events in Narrative: Typological and Contextual Perspectives* (pp. 191–218). Mahwah, NJ: Lawrence Erlbaum Associates.

8 L1-Fraught Difficulty: The Case of L2 Acquisition of English Articles by Slavic Speakers

Monika Ekiert and ZhaoHong Han

Introduction

L2 research has long grappled with the vexed question of why some grammatical structures are more difficult than others to acquire (see e.g. DeKeyser, 2005). A solid understanding thereof is particularly craved for second language instruction, the efficacy of which derives essentially from finding the best match between the targeted unit of acquisition and the best intervention (e.g. explicit or implicit).

Although extant research has shed much light on the question, empirical research is still lacking and, consequently, the general understanding remains vague. The purpose of our study was to take an in-depth look at the question by closing in on a notoriously hard-to-acquire subsystem of English, the articles (see e.g. Garcia Mayo & Hawkins, 2009), and tellingly, in speakers of Slavic languages (Polish, Russian and Ukrainian), languages devoid of articles.

In the sections that follow, we will first provide the research background. Then we will present the study and discuss the findings and implications for future research.

Theoretical Background

L2 difficulty

The concept of 'difficulty' is elusive, to say the least (cf. DeKeyser, 2005; Han & Lew, 2012), and therefore not easy to operationalise in empirical studies. For example, in their meta-analysis of research on the interaction between instruction and type of grammatical structure, Spada and Tomita (2010), in determining easy versus difficult structures, refer to an array of variables gleaned from the literature, including developmental stages, L1/L2 difference, form-meaning relation, learnability, teachers' perception of learner difficulty, structural complexity and typological markedness, but eventually settle on structural complexity only. Using 'the number of linguistic transformations' as a criterion, Spada and Tomita arrive at a taxonomy encompassing simple structures (derived by one transformational rule), such as articles, and complex structures (requiring two or more transformations), such as relative clauses. Finding no interaction between the type of grammatical structure and the type of instruction, Spada and Tomita express misgivings about operationalising 'difficulty' in terms of formal complexity (cf. Han & Lew, 2012). In particular, they question their treatment of articles as 'simple features', which flies in the face of every teacher's observation that 'articles in English pose persistent problems for second/foreign learners even at very advanced levels' (289; cf. Spada & Tomita, 2010), hypothesising, in hindsight, that psycholinguistic criteria would have been better suited for the focus of their meta-analysis (cf. Han & Lew, 2012).

Tying 'difficulty' to formal complexity has more or less been a standard practice in SLA research. Nevertheless, that has come under scrutiny in recent years. Larsen-Freeman (2010), among others, cogently argues that a usage-based perspective may better elucidate the nature of acquisitional difficulty, especially as it pertains to grammatical morphemes and functors such as articles, rebuking the traditional conception that the latter 'bear little semantic weight' (224; cf. Han, 2008, 2009, 2011).

Similarly, DeKeyser (2005) offers a pathway to understanding the construct of difficulty by performing a componential analysis of the construct, teasing out various elements associated respectively with form, meaning and form-meaning connections. It follows that difficulty may arise from form complexity (i.e. the number of choices involved in picking the right morpheme and the number of choices in positioning the morpheme in the right place), meaning complexity (i.e. novelty or abstractness) or complexity of form-meaning mapping (i.e. transparency of the relationship between form and meaning). Accordingly, articles in English are considered to lie in the realm of meaning complexity (cf. N. Ellis, 2008). One thing to note about this framework for our purposes is that form-meaning complexity is tied to the target language and never to the L1. As such, it projects a TL-centric view on SLA (Larsen-Freeman, 2006) over an IL-orientated view, one we chose to pursue in our study.

From our perspective, a key weakness of the TL-centric approach stems from the conception that it is the target language complexity that is primarily responsible for learning difficulty, which overlooks the fact that L2 learners come to the learning setting with a full-blown formal, semantic and conceptual system. The construct 'interlanguage' (Selinker, 1972) is precisely intended to capture that fact. Interlanguage is a system in its own right with its own syntax, semantics, pragmatics and so forth. The system is neither like the first language nor completely like the target language. Its semantic deviance from the target language, for one, can be caused by the L2 learner failing to recognise the form-meaning relations in the target language, or more profoundly, their underlying thought patterns. Fundamentally, linguistic differences are reflections of thought differences (von Humboldt, 1836). Odlin (2005), citing von Humboldt, notes that second language acquisition is 'the only way an individual may escape from the conceptual world of the native language. Yet the escape is ... never completely successful' (7). Odlin hints at the recalcitrant nature of crosslinguistic conceptual influence.

In their study of grammatical morpheme acquisition, Jiang, Novokshanova, Masuda and Wang (2011) attribute the acquisitional difficulty to crosslinguistic contrast between the L1 and the TL, specifically, to two factors: the absence of the morpheme in the L1 and the lack of concept the morpheme encodes. In their words, the acquisition of such a morpheme would require 'much more learning', as its 'related meaning is not grammaticalized in the learner's L1, which means that the related meaning is not part of the routinely activated meanings in the learner's mind' (959).

It would seem, then, that a consideration of L2 difficulty in the study of crosslinguistic influence would be inadequate without taking into account the fact that a given L1 predisposes its speakers to conceptualise and articulate their experience in a unique way (Kellerman, 1995). In the present study, we hoped to shed light on the interaction between the L1-specific conceptual system and that of the target language.

Form-meaning mappings of English articles and crosslinguistic differences

The study of the English article system traditionally concerns itself mostly with the surface forms, *a/an* and *the*, differentially labelled indefinite and definite articles. Contemporary accounts, in general, reject the binary analysis in favour of a semantic approach, whereby the article system is treated as a superordinate expression of the abstract concept of definiteness, with subordinate expressions of more concrete concepts such as *specificity* and *familiarity* (Bickerton, 1981; Chesterman, 1991; J. Hawkins, 1978, 1991, 2004; Lyons, 1999; Prince, 1981).

Specificity, according to Fodor and Sag (1982), relates to the 'speaker's ability to identify the referent' (356). A specific expression has a unique referent in the real world (as in *A dog bit me*, henceforth 'referential *a*'), whereas a nonspecific expression applies to any token of its type in the real world (as in *John is a plumber*, henceforth 'nonreferential *a*'). In the present study, we investigated two uses of *a*: the referential and the nonreferential. Lyons (1999) contrasts two indefinite phrases in direct object positions in the following sentences: *John bought a car* and *John didn't buy a car*. He notes that they differ, in that while neither involves a referent identifiable to the hearer, the first refers to something specific (and familiar to the speaker), but the second does not. Familiarity with the referent, by earlier accounts, is a perspective taken by the speaker. However, contemporary accounts put premium on the hearer's perspective (Lyons, 1999). By and large, shared knowledge between the speaker and the hearer is considered key to correct use of referential expressions in English.

Shared knowledge, typically inferred either from previous discourse or from the situation surrounding an utterance, is the centrepiece of J. Hawkins' (1978) location theory, where locability is deemed somewhat akin to the more traditional concept of familiarity. More specifically, locability refers to both the speaker's and the hearer's ability to locate a referent in a shared set, which determines the use (or not) of the definite article *the*. This theory was adapted for use in Liu and Gleason's (2002) L2 investigation of four nongeneric uses of the definite article *the*. Inspired both by the location theory and its L2 application, the present study set out to examine three scenarios of *the* usage: (1) the textual or anaphoric, where *the* is used with a noun that has been previously referred to or is related to a previously mentioned noun (e.g. *Fred bought a car on Monday. On Wednesday, he crashed the car*); (2) the structural or cataphoric, where *the* is used with a first-mention noun that has a modifier (e.g. *The shade on this lamp is really ugly*); and (3) the situational, where *the* is used when the referent of a first-mention noun can be sensed directly or indirectly by the interlocutors, or where the referent is known to members of a local community, such as the only dog in a family or the only zoo in a local community (e.g. *At the zoo, I saw several tigers*).

Recent corpus studies (e.g. Yoo, 2009) have reported that contrary to the general belief, the textual (or anaphoric) uses of *the* are, in actuality, not as common in conversation, newspaper or academic prose as the situational or structural (cataphoric) uses of *the*. Even if it is just from a surface point of view, the textual versus inferential use of *the* – one tied to an explicit referent and the other to an implicit referent – can potentially be a source of confusion, and hence difficulty, for L2 learners.

According to J. Hawkins (1978), the explicit use of the referential *the* is discourse-motivated, whereas the implicit use is situation-motivated. They form two distinct classes of referential definites (cf. Lyons, 1999). The former, subsuming both textual and structural uses, stand apart from situational uses, the latter, in that the context within which the referent is to be found is linguistic (i.e. the discourse) as opposed to situational or extralinguistic, where the recovery of the referent calls for use of encyclopedic knowledge or knowledge of the immediate or wider social environment.

The uses of articles discussed here are above sentence level. They are grounded in the content of the discourse space in question, comprised of a set of elements and the relations held among them (Radden & Dirven, 2007). Following cognitive-linguistic accounts, to characterise the use of articles in discourse, one needs to construct the current discourse space, a mental space which is evoked, created and modified by the addition of new elements and relations. These elements and relations are construed as being shared or otherwise by the speaker and the hearer. In English, the speaker must ensure that the hearer can identify the things being spoken of – otherwise, miscommunication may arise.

Unlike English, languages without articles – such as the ones of concern in the present study – use other devices, most of them pragmatic, to ensure referent identifiability. Allan (1986) notes that definiteness is not a necessary property of noun phrases in, for example, Polish[1], in which the phrase *Potknąłem się o psa* can mean either *I tripped over a dog* or *I tripped over the dog*. Lyons (1999) observes that the conception of definiteness as a grammatical category is based largely on how articles work in languages like English, only to be extended to other languages, including those without articles. Consequently, work on definiteness in non-article languages is sparse and seemingly random, nested mostly in translation research. What can be gleaned from that body of work is that in non-article languages, definiteness is often left to be inferred in a variety of ways. A question, therefore, arises: Do other types of structures convey the definiteness expressed by articles?

Translation studies have shown that word order, verbal aspect (perfective versus imperfective verbal forms), case marking, lexical items (especially the word *one*) and deictic categories such as demonstratives and possessives of Slavic languages are often used to convey definite and indefinite meanings. However, none of these devices encode the indefinite/definite contrast consistently or reliably.

Articles, when interpreted in a narrow sense, give additional and unique semantic content to the interpretation of the referent, which does not seem to be true of other determiners. For example, as far as demonstratives, possessives and quantifier equivalents are concerned, Trenkic's (2002) corpus analysis shows that in non-article Slavic languages, demonstratives, possessives and quantifiers are translation equivalents of English demonstratives, possessives, and quantifiers, but not of the articles *the* and *a*. Therefore, she suggests that in making crosslinguistic comparisons, instead of looking for equivalents, one should simply register the fact that while definiteness is conventionally encoded via use of articles in English, in non-article Slavic languages the concept is expressed 'conversationally', aided by relevant context and the interlocutors' general knowledge of the world. In a similar vein, Tabakowska (1993), from the point of view of professional translation, argues that the 'context of situation' should be considered decisive for the definite/indefinite contrast in non-article Slavic languages. She defines the 'context of situation' in writing as the interaction of all constituents of the text, emphasising the subjective character of the definite/indefinite interpretation.

Analysing the translations of an extract of a Polish literary text by two bilinguals, Tabakowska (1993) found that definiteness in the original Polish text was mediated through scene construal, attention, selection, figure/ground organisation, viewpoint or perspective, and through levels of specificity and/or schematicity of reference. In the English rendition, on the other hand, this myriad of devices resulted in corresponding changes in the use of articles. Moreover, in the original Polish text, the indefinite and definite distinction did not effectuate into any grammatical change, certainly not in any systematic way. In her search for a coherent answer to the question, 'Where, then, do the bilingual participants get the idea of definiteness when rendering the same text in English?,' Tabakowska wound up emphasising the subjective character of the process of referent identifiability. The following example illustrates what occurred in translation:

Source sentence: ...*odkładasz więc niedoczytaną gazetę*
(you) put aside   so   unfinished-Acc   paper-Acc

English translation 1 (E1): *you fold <u>a</u> newspaper that you never finish reading*

English translation 2 (E2): *you put aside <u>the</u> unfinished newspaper*

(794)

Regarding the discrepancy between the two renditions, Tabakowska explained that E2 conformed to the English rule that an entity mentioned earlier (*newspaper*) requires definite determination. In contrast, E1 seemed to 'break the rule', though conceptually consistent with the original Polish text. In other words, the narrator of the translated text was conceptualised as someone who folded a different paper on each occasion, and the nonreferential *a* denoted a typical representative of the given class, in this case. Tabakowska concluded that the two translations were in stark opposition when it came to the definite/indefinite distinction, and the Polish text did not offer any grammatical clues that might resolve this discrepancy.

Relating these concerns to advanced L2 learner writing, Tabakowska (1993) argued that what the teacher may consider an article error is often only 'an interpretational difference which merely reflects the possibility of alternative views on reality' (785). The communicative intentions of the speaker allow the addressee of, for example, a Polish stretch of discourse more conceptual freedom in text interpretation. It follows that establishing the definiteness status of referents in meaningful communication is an interactional process. Trenkic (2002) points out that the task of a speaker in languages with grammatical definiteness (i.e. with a system of articles), such as English, is in many aspects similar to the task of a hearer in languages without articles, such as the Slavic languages in question. Both have to determine the definiteness status of a referent: 'the former [the speaker in English] in order to adequately mark it grammatically, the latter [the hearer in a Slavic language] in order to adequately interpret the message' (124). This is key to understanding the difficulty facing L2 learners of English from non-article Slavic L1 backgrounds.

L2 research has taken a particular interest in articles, especially among speakers of non-article languages. Although differences in theoretical orientations and methodological choices prevent straightforward comparisons, the studies converge on the finding that crosslinguistic influence figures prominently in the acquisitional difficulty observed. Jarvis (2012) notes that cases where the TL has a feature that does not exist in the L1 may offer a rare opportunity to gain insight into the most fascinating – subtle, complex and unpredicted – aspects of L1 influence. These cases are likely to provide evidence of indirect L1 effects where 'learners' use of TL features often goes well beyond any possible L1 model, but nevertheless exhibits L1-group-specific patterns' (8).

The present study considered how the characteristics of the target language, English, and those of the source languages, such as Polish, interact and what consequences there are for the acquisition of English articles by speakers of non-article Slavic languages, exploring, in particular, what is (or is not) difficult. The linguistic targets of the study, as mentioned earlier, were three uses of *the* – the textual or anaphoric use (e.g. *Fred bought a car on Monday. On Wednesday, he crashed the car*); the structural or cataphoric use (e.g. *The shade on this lamp is really ugly*); and the situational use (e.g. *At the zoo, I saw several tigers*) – and two uses of *a*: the referential (e.g. *An earthquake broke out and a siren rips out through the night*) and the nonreferential (e.g. *He is a teacher*).

The following were the guiding questions:

(1) Do various uses of English articles present differential difficulty for L2 learners whose Slavic L1s – Polish, Russian and Ukrainian – do not employ articles?
(2) If so, what is the nature of the difficulty?

Method

The study adopted a mixed-methods design, with quantitative and qualitative research approaches to data collection and analysis.

Participants

Sixty-five adult ESL learners participated in the study. At the time of data collection, they were enrolled in high intermediate and advanced English classes in a community language programme in the United States, having taken the programme's placement test, a theme-based assessment that measures communicative language ability. They were all speakers of a Slavic language: Polish (n=42), Russian (n=11) or Ukrainian (n=12). The three Slavic languages are typologically similar, all without articles and all employing similar devices for referent identification. All participants had completed high school and most of them were college-educated in their native countries.

Baseline data were collected in both English and Polish, but they will not be reported in this account (see, however, Ekiert, 2010).

Instruments

Three written tasks, controlling for genre, were designed to elicit narrative production, and are briefly described below.

Video retelling

The participants had one viewing of a silent, five-minute clip of the sitcom 'Frasier', in which a man waiting for his date in an upscale apartment decided to iron his pants and a series of disastrous events ensued. The viewing was uninterrupted, following Jarvis (2002), who observes that interrupting the story stimulus can have an effect on participants' use of articles, and the participants were allowed to take notes. After that, they were asked to produce a written narrative of the events that took place in the apartment. The task was untimed and, on average, took 30 minutes to complete.

Missing word

This task used a 273-word narrative adapted from an Aesop's fable. Missing from the text were 38 target items: 4 items of nonreferential *a*; 8 items of referential *a*; 20 items of textual *the*; 2 items of situational *the*; and 4 items of structural *the*. In addition, there were 10 other missing items serving as distractors. Following a suggestion from Liu and Gleason (2002), no blanks were given for the missing items, for fear that it might compel learners to fill every blank, and, therefore, compromise the validity of the data. The task was untimed and, on average, took 20 minutes to complete.

Translation

For this task, the participants translated a cartoon-based, 227-word narrative from the participant's L1 into English, the target language. The story was about a man and a woman dining out in a restaurant. Again, the task was untimed and, on average, took 30 minutes to complete.

In addition to the three written tasks, the participants were administered an immediate stimulated recall task, using the worksheets they completed on the missing word task, and they were allowed to explain their answers in their L1.

Procedures

The video retelling and missing word tasks were administered to all 65 participants, and the translation and stimulated recall tasks to 15 Polish-speaking participants, the largest L1 sub-group in the study. The task sequence for the sub-group was (a) video retelling, (b) translation, (c) missing word and (d) stimulated recall.

Data coding and analyses

Two experienced raters independently coded the data from the video retelling, missing word and translation tasks, identifying any unnecessary use of articles as well as inserting any that were missing yet obligatory. Each obligatory and non-obligatory incidence was coded for type (referential or nonreferential uses of *a*; anaphoric, cataphoric or situational *the*).

Target-like use (TLU; Pica, 1983) scores were then computed for the five article types. The TLU formula takes into account both obligatory and non-obligatory contexts, producing scores that reflect the participants' command of the distributional properties of the target structure.

To determine the difficulty status of the article types, the TLU scores were fed into many-facet Rasch measurement analysis (hereafter 'Rasch'). Rasch analysis has been widely used in educational measurement and L2 testing research over the past four decades (cf. McNamara & Knoch, 2012). In the present context, it helped to establish target-item difficulty and did so in a task-independent and participant-independent way, by virtue of it being a sample-independent model of measurement. It also helped to capture the ways in which the task type and learner proficiency variables contributed to difficulty in article use.

While the data from the three written tasks were analysed quantitatively, the stimulated recall data were analysed qualitatively, using Butler's (2002) taxonomy. As is typical of qualitative data analysis, the data were inspected iteratively until saturation, in order to identify common themes from the recalls, with sufficient confidence. Consequently, three such themes were established vis-à-vis reasons for article use: (a) textuality (first and subsequent marking of the referents), (b) specificity and (c) perspective-taking.

Results

Descriptive statistics

Table 8.1 gives the descriptive statistics of the participants' TLU scores from the video retelling, missing word and translation tasks. With the exception of the pre-designed missing word task, not all target article

Table 8.1 Descriptive statistics for target-like use (TLU) scores for articles by task

Article Use	Task	TLU Mean	SD
referential *a*	video retelling (n = 65)	35.50	29.30
	missing word (n = 65)	34.38	25.42
	translation (n = 15)	36.46	23.38
nonreferential *a*	video retelling (n = 38)	29.39	40.20
	missing word (n = 65)	50.14	33.94
	translation (n = 15)	61.13	33.73
textual *the*	video retelling (n = 65)	61.87	28.15
	missing word (n = 65)	47.94	32.02
	translation (n = 15)	84.86	13.65
situational *the*	video retelling (n = 65)	60.30	24.18
	missing word (n = 65)	14.49	18.22
	translation (n = 15)	35.60	21.93
structural *the*	video retelling (n = 48)	70.35	36.67
	missing word (n = 65)	27.35	27.09
	translation (n = 14)	57.35	26.70

Note. The maximum total score was 100 points

types were mandated in the other two tasks, as reflected in the unequal n-values in Table 8.1. As shown, the highest TLU scores were obtained from the textual *the* uses (i.e. anaphoric mentions of known referents as in *I bought a book yesterday. The book was on sale*): M = 47.94 for the missing word task, M = 61.87 for the video retelling task and M = 84.86 for the translation task. In contrast, the mean TLU scores were the lowest for referential *a* (i.e. first mention of a specific referent as in *I brought a gift for you*): M=34.38 for the missing word task, M = 35.5 for the video retelling, and M = 36.46 for the translation. On average, the mean TLU scores were lowest on the missing word task. Since estimates of difficulty may not be detected by 'a naked eye' (Bond & Fox, 2007), results from the Rasch measurement are presented next.

Facets of difficulty

A graphic display of the Rasch results is given in Figure 8.1. The first column contains the logit scale. The logit scale is a true equal-interval scale, unlike a scale based on raw scores in which the distances between intervals may not be equal. The second column shows the participants' TLU scores. Each ID number denotes one participant. The participants are ordered from the highest performer, placed at the top of the column, to the lowest performer, at the bottom of the column. This column reveals less-than-two-logit variation in the participants' scores (from -0.93 to 0.90 logits), suggesting considerable homogeneity with respect to the participants' ability to use English articles. This finding is expected, given the relatively advanced proficiency of the participants. The third column illustrates the scope of difficulty among the five target uses of articles. The distribution of the scores displays a continuum of difficulty: the article uses appearing higher in the column are shown to be more difficult than those appearing lower in the column (ranging from -0.33 to 0.32). The fourth column shows task as a facet, where the task appearing in the higher position corresponds to greater difficulty and that appearing in the lower position to lesser difficulty. Thus, the missing word task at 0.57 logits was more difficult than the translation task at 0.08 logits and, in turn, the video retelling task at 0.01 logits. This

```
+---------+------------------------------------+-----------------------+------------------+---------+
| Logit   | High scoring participants          | Hard article uses     | Hard tasks       | Scale   |
|---------+------------------------------------+-----------------------+------------------+---------+
|         |                                    |                       |                  |  (5)    |
|   1   + |                                    +                       +                  +         |
|         |  1   63                            |                       |                  |         |
|         | 21   23                            |                       |                  |         |
|         | 10                                 |                       |                  |   4     |
|         | 25   38                            |                       |                  |         |
|         | 42                                 |                       | missing word     |         |
|         | 37                                 |                       |                  |---------|
|         | 58    9                            |                       |                  |         |
|         | 60                                 |                       |                  |         |
|         | 64   29  31  52  11  20  36        | referential a         |                  |         |
|         | 22   62                            |                       |                  |   3     |
|         | 44   19  41  45                    | situational the       |                  |         |
|         |  2    3                            |                       |                  |         |
|         | 55    7       49  27               |                       | translation      |         |
|         | 56                                 |                       |                  |---------|
|  *  0   |*28   18  24                        |*                      |* movie description|*       |
|         | 59   51  15                        |                       |                  |         |
|         | 17   30  61  50                    | nonreferential a      |                  |         |
|         | 33   34                            | structural the        |                  |   2     |
|         | 14   39                            |                       |                  |         |
|         | 65                                 |                       |                  |         |
|         | 13                                 | textual the           |                  |         |
|         | 16    5  26  35  40                |                       |                  |---------|
|         | 47                                 |                       |                  |         |
|         | 32   48  57                        |                       |                  |         |
|         | 43                                 |                       |                  |         |
|         |  6                                 |                       |                  |         |
|         | 12   46  53                        |                       |                  |         |
|         |  4    8                            |                       |                  |   1     |
|         | 54                                 |                       |                  |         |
|  -1   + |                                    +                       +                  +         |
|         |                                    |                       |                  |  (0)    |
|---------+------------------------------------+-----------------------+------------------+---------+
| Logit   | Low scoring participants           | Easy article uses     | Easy tasks       | Scale   |
+---------+------------------------------------+-----------------------+------------------+---------+
```

Note. The first column displays the logit scale. The second column presents the distribution of the participants' TLU scores in the production tasks. Each number corresponds to the participant's ID and the numbers in bold indicate the group of 15 participants who took the translation task and participated in recall sessions. The third column represents the variation in difficulty among the article uses. The fourth column compares the difficulty of the three production tasks. The fifth column graphically depicts the rating scale.

Figure 8.1 Facets summary for article use on three production tasks

order of difficulty is consistent with our expectation, since it mirrors our intended degree of task demand for managing the form-meaning relations of articles. Finally, the fifth column shows the scale used to score participants' performance on the tasks, where the TLU scores were collapsed to form a six-point scale.

A summary of the Rasch results for article type difficulty appears in Table 8.2. As shown, the difficulty estimates ranged between −0.33 logits for textual *the*, the easiest type, and 0.32 logits for referential *a*, the most difficult type. The article uses tended to cluster in a relatively narrow band with a spread of little more than half a logit (0.65) for difficulty measures. The relatively large separation index (3.83) suggests that the analysis was reliably separating different article uses into distinctly different levels of difficulty. The separation index (G) was used to determine the number of statistically distinct difficulty strata by using the formula (4G+1)/3 (Myford & Wolfe, 2003). The index yielded the value of 5.17 specifying five statistically distinct levels of difficulty, suggesting that five distinct meanings were encoded by the two surface forms, *a* and *the*. The reliability of separation, analogous to Cronbach's alpha, was high at 0.94 (with the possible values ranging from 0 to 1), indicating, again, that the article uses targeted in this study were reliably different in terms of difficulty. The chi-square of 67.2 (df = 4) was significant at $p < .001$, providing further confirmation that it was more difficult for the participants to use the referential *a* and situational *the* than it was to use the nonreferential *a* and structural *the*, which were, in turn, more difficult than the textual *the*.

The infit statistics, which indicate the extent to which the observations fit the modelled expectations of predictability with the expected value of

Table 8.2 Summary statistics for the article facet (n = 65)

Article uses	Measure logit	Model error	Infit mean square
referential *a*	0.32	0.07	0.74
situational *the*	0.22	0.07	0.81
nonreferential *a*	−0.09	0.07	1.31
structural *the*	−0.11	0.07	0.96
textual *the*	−0.33	0.06	1.11
Mean	0.00	0.07	0.99
SD	0.26	0.00	0.23
Separation	3.86		
Reliability of Separation	0.94		
Chi-square (df)	67.2 (4)		
Significance	0.00		

1, show the infit mean-square mean to be 0.99 (SD = 0.23) for the article facet (i.e. type of article), with no misfitting elements of the facet. In other words, no values outside the range of 0.53–1.45 were found. This signifies that none of the article uses measured in the study functioned in a redundant manner.

Recall

The stimulated recall data revealed that the participants had different reasons for supplying (or not) articles in the missing word task. The emergent themes in the participants' retrospection are discussed below in conjunction with their production data.

Textuality

The excerpt and recall comments by Participant 13 (P13) provide a representative sample of the stimulated recalls.

Excerpt 1:

> (i) <u>Very tired man</u>, <u>a</u> donkey, and <u>a</u> dog were traveling. <u>Man</u> was <u>a</u> salesman from nearby village returning home after week-long stay in town. (ii) <u>Man</u> decided to take <u>a</u> break, and he fell asleep under <u>a</u> tree by side of country road he was traveling on. <u>The</u> donkey wandered out into field, feeding on some grass. Dog followed. As soon as animals were some distance away from (iii) <u>the man</u>, dog said quietly to donkey: 'You're having <u>a</u> nice lunch, but I'm quite hungry. (P13)

Recall on Excerpt 1:

> (i) No word would fit here. In English, one always needs these prepositions [sic]. But if there is an adjective in front of the noun, then I think you don't need these. (P13)
> (ii) Sounds good as is. (P13)
> (iii) We know who this is, so you can use the definite – the man who's the owner of the dog and the donkey. (P13)

As shown in Excerpt 1, the participant omitted articles in the first mention of the referent *man* (introduced in the text with a pre-modifier *very tired*) as well as in the two subsequent mentions of the same referent. However, he inserted *the* with the third mention of *man* which he took to be a known referent during recall (see [iii]). When asked if anything could be inserted in one of the two bare previous mentions of the same referent, P13 replied that it sounded better when the word *man* was bare (ii).

A text analysis of word order provided some insight into this pattern of article use. In theory, definiteness marking is associated with topic marking and newness of information, linked to referent unidentifiability (and, by some, with indefiniteness). Givenness, on the other hand, is associated with referent identifiability (hence, definiteness). In (i) of Excerpt 1, the two referents missing the definite article *the* both appeared in sentence-initial position, indicating given information. In contrast, the referent signalled by *the* occurred in sentence-final position, typically reserved for new information. And it appears that the article *the* was used by the participant to signal the referent *man* only when the latter occupied a sentence-final position, a position typically reserved for new information in discourse. Functionally, it served to disambiguate the reference to the already mentioned person – in the previous sentences, the definiteness of the reference was already afforded by the sentence position of the two nouns. Pragmatically, the additional marking of *man* for identifiability may have seemed redundant to the participant, because the referent status of the bare noun vis-à-vis definiteness had already been established through word order. However, word order in Slavic L1s is neither a consistent nor a reliable means of establishing the definiteness status of a referent in a sentence. Accordingly, the target-like introduction of *a donkey* and the subsequent reference to *the donkey* in the same stretch of discourse should be of little surprise, although this interpretation invites caution in the absence of corresponding L1 data.

According to their recall comments, L1 Polish participants tended to evaluate noun reference in terms of its discursive status. They seemed to follow their own 'first mention-subsequent mention' rule. As a result, they produced the less-preferred use of the indefinite *a* with first-mention nouns that had post-modifiers, as in Excerpt 2.

Excerpt 2:

> He fell asleep under the tree by this side of (i) <u>a</u> country road he was traveling on. (P1)

Recall on Excerpt 2:

> (i) I inserted *a* because it is mentioned in the story for the first time (P1)

P1's recall justified his use of *a* in Excerpt 2. For him, *a* was needed (i) to signal the first mention of the referent *road* in the story. Interestingly, the recall also reveals that in choosing to use *a*, he had ignored the structural information in the post-modifying position, *he was traveling on*. Overall, it is worth noting that in the context provided by Excerpt 2, only half of the participants used an article: four participants used the indefinite *a*, four used the definite *the*, and the remaining participants used neither, leaving the noun phrase *country road* bare.

In contrast, elsewhere the structural use of *the* was adopted by a majority of the recall participants, as shown in Excerpt 3.

Excerpt 3:
   I could reach into (i) *the pack that you're carrying.*

For Excerpt 3, four participants opted for *a,* based on the first-mention criterion (as this was indeed the first mention of the object in the story), another five chose *the,* based on multiple criteria which will be discussed later, and one participant inserted the demonstrative *that*. The remaining three participants, who used nothing, suggested possible use of articles in that context, when probed about the possibility of any word insertion.

A closer look at the elements surrounding the two noun phrases in Excerpt 2 versus Excerpt 3 reveals that in the former, the noun has a pre-modifier (i.e. *country road*), but the noun in the latter does not (i.e. *pack*). It is possible that the pre-modification of a noun may have influenced some participants' use of articles.

The recall data further suggest that the participants were most conflicted when encountering pre-modified noun phrases in the first-mention versus subsequent-mention referential environments. An example is given in Excerpt 4.

Excerpt 4:
   (i) *Very tired man, (ii) a donkey, and (iii) a dog were traveling.* (P55, P65)

Recall on Excerpt 4:
   (i) Nothing is needed here – this man is very specific for the narrator (P55)
   (i) No, I wouldn't insert anything. This is a defined, specific, tired man traveling with a donkey and a dog. Maybe *the* would fit. (P65)

Data from the missing word task show that five recall participants omitted *a* with a first-mention referent appearing in a pre-modified noun phrase (i), but inserted articles with the next two first-mention referents, (ii) and (iii). When asked about the possibility of inserting anything in front of the phrase *very tired man* – the first mention of the referent in discourse, two participants (P55 and P65) commented that the referent was already identifiable in this context and therefore, no article was necessary. This is reminiscent of a similar comment from P13 on Excerpt 1 (i), that because there is an adjective in front of the noun, no article is required.

Specificity

The recall data shed interesting light on the unique understanding of specificity by many participants. For example, in Excerpt 5, P28 commented that he inserted *the*, because the noun, *wolf*, refers to only one animal, even though it is its first mention.

Excerpt 5:

Suddenly, (i) *the wolf sprang out from behind the bush.* (P28)

Recall on Excerpt 5:
(i) *The* is needed because there is one wolf that springs here, a specific one (P28)

Consistent with this 'rule', in Excerpt 6 *a* was used, because the object encoded by the noun was perceived to be nonspecific.

Excerpt 6:

I could reach into (i) *a pack that you're carrying.* (P17, P37)

Recall on Excerpt 6:
(i) I thought this is first mention; a nonspecific pack; what pack? we don't know (P17)
(i) I intended to say 'some pack', mentioned for the first time (P37)

In analysing the recall data, it became increasingly clear that the participants' use of articles was driven also by their interpretation of the content of the story, along with their assumptions about specificity and familiarity of the referents rather than by the TL discursive context and conventions.

Excerpt 7 further illustrates how speaker assumptions motivate the use (or not) of articles.

Excerpt 7:

Very tired man, (i) *a donkey, and* (ii) *a dog were traveling. Man was a salesman from nearby village returning home after a week-long stay in a town. Man decided to take a break, and he fell asleep under a tree by the side of the country road he was traveling on. Donkey wandered out into field, feeding on some grass. Dog followed. As soon as animals were some distance away from the man, dog said quietly to donkey: 'You're having nice lunch, but I'm quite hungry. I'm* (iii) *the dog and I don't eat grass. If you would only lie down for moment or two, I could reach into a pack that you're carrying and see what our master has brought this time. I promise not to touch any meat, but maybe I could have bone, if there is one in* (iv) the *pack.'* (P60)

Recall on Excerpt 7:

    (i) I thought I don't know which one specifically it was; my assumption is that I don't know. (P60)
    (ii) Same thoughts. This is a problem for me. When I speak of something for the first time and assume that the person I speak to doesn't specifically know anything about that something, I then use *a*. But if we speak of something and that person knows, and I know, then *the* is appropriate. (P60)
    (iii) The dog speaks of himself, so it should use *the*. (P60)
    (iv) The donkey doesn't see it, but, he should feel it, right? So it's *the*. (P60)

Thus, for participant P60, *specificity* and *referent orientation* were important considerations when using articles. They worked in tandem, as illustrated by her comment on *a donkey* (i), invoking the notion of specificity and speaker perspective – 'I don't know which one specifically it was; my assumption is that I don't know.' Referring to *a dog* (ii), P60 continued to cite the lack of specificity of the referent as a factor, but brought in a hearer perspective as well – 'When I speak of something for the first time and assume that the person I speak to doesn't specifically know anything about that something, I then use *a*.' Her comments on the last two uses of *the* (iii) further exhibit perspective-taking when referring to articles in English: she again took a speaker-orientated perspective, interestingly, that of an animal character in the story – 'The dog speaks of himself, so it should use "the."' Similarly, on her use of *the* in *if there is one in the pack* (iv), she adopted the perspective of another animal character in the story – 'The donkey doesn't see it, but, he should feel it, right, so it's "*the*"'. In sum, P60's use of articles appears to have been driven by her assumptions about specificity and familiarity as well as a shift in perspectives. As a result, the meanings conveyed by the forms adopted were fluid rather than static.

Perspective

In their recalls, several participants used the pronoun *we*, as in 'we don't know this character yet', 'we haven't heard of this before', or 'we're familiar with this character' (P65, P13, P16 and P17). For these participants, the speaker's perspective clearly outweighed the hearer's (see also P28's comment on Excerpt 5).

As noted above, the taking of a perspective sometimes underwent a shift from the storyteller to a character in the story. This is further exemplified in Excerpt 8.

Excerpt 8:

...returning home after week-long stay in (i) *the town... he fell asleep under* (ii) *the tree by side of* (iii) *the country road he was traveling on.* (P28)

Recall on Excerpt 8:

(i) I thought *the* because he's coming back from a specific place: he visited a specific town. (P 28)
(ii) Not sure, but there was one specific tree in the picture, so *the*. (P28)
(iii) I intended to say that this is a specific road; this man is in a specific situation. (P28)

P28's comments on the three instances of *the* in Excerpt 8 reveal that he had placed himself in the shoes of a character in the story, so to speak, picturing himself coming back from a particular town he had visited and was familiar with, traveling on a particular road that he knew he was on, and lying down under a particular tree.

Similarly, another recall participant, P55, assumed the stance of one of the animal characters in the story when inserting the target-like *the*, as shown in his recall regarding Excerpt 9.

Excerpt 9:

I could reach into (i) *the pack that you're carrying.* (P55)

Recall on Excerpt 9:

(i) The dog has a specific pack in mind – hence *the*. (P55)

Excerpt 9 shows again that perspective-taking not only played into the participants' use of English articles, but it was also driven by their own interpretation of the story. Yet, what was glaringly absent was a consideration of the hearer or reader, which is required of target-like use of articles.

Discussion and Conclusion

The present study investigated the acquisition of English articles among L2 learners with an L1 Slavic language background, with a view to identifying aspects of the article usage that present particular difficulty. Multiple functional types of *a* and *the* use were therefore examined, both quantitatively and qualitatively. Rasch analysis of learners' production data from three tasks – video retelling, missing word insertion and translation – has revealed that the three types of *the* and two types of *a* in question posed unequal challenges to the participants, with the referential use of *a* and the situational use of *the* being the most, and textual use of *the* least, difficult.

Although the referential *a* and the situational *the* concern two different morphemes, they share a discourse orientation as well as a semantic component. First of all, they both mark first-mention of specific referents (cf. Chaudron & Parker [1990] on the relative difficulty of identifying new referents in discourse). They differ, however, in hearer/reader familiarity with the referent: the assumed unfamiliarity requiring an indefinite description and the assumed familiarity a definite description. What appeared to be particularly problematic for the participants of this study was the use of these constructions in discourse where there was a dynamic interplay between assuming what was known to the hearer and deciding what form to use, at least in the case of first-mention referents.

Rasch analysis has shown that textual uses of *the*, which correspond to the subsequent mentions of the referents in discourse, appeared to be the easiest for the study participants. This finding indirectly speaks to the conceptualisation of hearer knowledge as lying at the centre of difficulty with English articles: once the referent's status in discourse in terms of hearer knowledge was established, the learners were more at ease with using the definite article *the*. This echoes Tarone and Parrish's (1988) finding of high accuracy levels in article use involving subsequent mentions of persons and objects on the narrative task they employed. Tarone and Parrish attributed this to the nature of the task, noting the task demand for clear anaphoric tracking of referents. Without excluding the task influence, the present study, however, offered a complementary explanation for these findings, narrowing the area of difficulty down to the highly abstract, dynamic and context-dependent nature of determining what was known to the hearer, or hearer knowledge, in short.

Data from the stimulated recall task in the present study further shed light on the source of difficulty. It appears that learners' grammar was influenced by what Givón (1985) refers to as the *pragmatic mode* of narration, in which the interlocutors fill in large quantities of linguistically uncoded information from the context. In the present case, this mode was reflected in the learners' 'extra' considerations based more on their idiosyncratic interpretation of the content of the story than on its discursive context (see e.g. comment by P28 on Excerpt 28).

Importantly, such a pragmatic mode of L2 production is rooted in the L1. In article-lacking Slavic languages, referential interpretations are based on world knowledge and contextual and pragmatic considerations, thus drawing much from extralinguistic information. When establishing the definiteness status of a referent, the speaker of a non-article Slavic language is not obligated to mark it grammatically for the hearer. As Trenkic (2002) observes, the way objects are referred to mirrors the state of knowledge of the speaker only. Thus, although referential expressions in article-lacking Slavic languages do convey the meaning of specificity, they are motivated solely by the speaker's or writer's own perspective, the hearer's/reader's perspective largely absent from the equation. Findings of this nature show subtle, complex, and even unpredictable influence of the L1 on L2 use, which cannot be undone without the learner revising his or her existing conceptual knowledge.

One interesting finding that is worth underscoring here is that the learner's perspective in article use was not stable; rather, it shifted from one to another within the confines of the speaker and/or the story characters. A case in point is P60's recall comment, cited earlier, in Excerpt 7, that 'The dog speaks of himself, so it should use *the*,' and similarly, the intriguing use of 'we' in a comment by P13 in Excerpt 1, that 'We know who this is, so you can use the definite. When we began this story we didn't know who this was about, but as we move along, we already know.'

The shift in perspective is arguably traceable to L1 influence as well. When probed on her thinking concerning the use of *a* in the first-mention, specific context, P60 said that 'I don't know which one specifically it was; my assumption is that I don't know,' which suggests the speaker-only perspective she was taking when applying the indefinite article *a*. In general, the L1-Polish participants considered speaker-orientated identifiability sufficient for reference tracking in English. This predilection is consistent with their L1 system of reference, which represents the state of knowledge of the speaker only. A similar observation was reported in Butler (2002) on L1 Japanese learners' difficulty in determining the circumstances that would make a reference identifiable to the hearer. Butler noticed in her participants what she termed an 'excessive introduction of extralinguistic knowledge into [their] readings of the text or some similar misinterpretation of the text' (472). Though recognising crosslinguistic influence as a factor, she ultimately ascribed the major cause of difficulty in interpreting *definiteness* to the learners' inaccurate determination of noun countability.

The acquisition of English articles by L2 learners whose L1s do not utilise article-like forms requires not only the learning of a new form, but also of a new grammaticalised meaning. On the challenge confronting the learning of an 'incongruent morpheme', Jiang *et al.* (2011) wrote that 'the learner has to learn to automatically activate and represent a meaning that is not routinely activated in L1 processing in the absence of a related lexical item' (959). Granted, the learner, in our view, has to restructure his conceptual system, as what is ultimately at stake is whether the learner can acquire the perspective-taking specific to the target language. Absent conceptual restructuring, the difficulty is likely to persist, as shown in the longitudinal case study by Han (2010) involving Chinese, a non-article language, as the source language and English as the target language.

A number of directions can be taken from here on to substantiate the findings from the present study, but three in particular: first, the study sample can be expanded to include other language groups for finer-grained crosslinguistic contrasts. Doing so would allow for a more precise approximation of acquisitional difficulty and improve the generalisability of the findings of the present study beyond the population of L1 Slavic speakers. Second, for the current study, it was deemed important that the genre did not become a source of variability in article use, and, as a result, only the narrative genre was used for data elicitation. But future research should consider broadening the scope of genre and data types to allow for a fuller understanding of article use in L2 English, especially of whether genre, like task type, is a factor. Last but not least, longitudinal research, whether case study or cross-sectional study, is essential to uncovering and understanding the developmental dynamics of article use by L2 learners from non-article L1 backgrounds.

A further avenue of exploration is that of the effectiveness of pedagogical intervention. There has been a sizable body of research on the effectiveness of instruction in English article acquisition (cf. Bitchener, 2008), yet the results have been limited and inconclusive. Notably, few of these studies have taken upon themselves to perform a finer-grained analysis of the complexity of the article system as a point of departure and to investigate the nature of acquisitional difficulty accordingly. Equally, in most of the extant studies, pedagogical intervention has not been devised in accordance with the differential complexity within the article system. Until such a deeper conceptualisation of L2 acquisition is pursued as a basis for instruction, any pedagogical intervention is expected to remain shallow, if not counter-productive.

Note

(1) For consistency of presentation and ease of explication, the examples used here for illustrative purposes were drawn exclusively from Polish. This is a plausible approach, in light of the fact that their equivalents in Russian and Ukrainian differ only lexically, not syntactically or morphologically.

Acknowledgements

This research was supported in part by a grant from the Office of Policy and Research at Teachers College, Columbia University. We are grateful to Kristen di Gennaro and Philip K. Choong for their assistance in data coding, and to the editor and the reviewers for their constructive comments on an earlier version of this chapter. Any inaccuracies that remain are our own.

References

Allan, K. (1986) *Linguistic Meaning*. London: Routledge and Kegan Paul.
Bickerton, D. (1981) *Roots of Language*. Ann Arbor, MI: Karoma Publishers.
Bitchener, J. (2008). Evidence in support of written corrective feedback. *Journal of Second Language Writing* 17, 1–17.
Bond, T. and Fox, C. (2007) *Applying the Rasch Model: Fundamental Measurement in the Human Sciences* (2nd edn). Mahwah, NJ: Lawrence Erlbaum.
Butler, Y. (2002) Second language learners' theories on the use of English article: An analysis of the metalinguistic knowledge used by Japanese students in acquiring the English article system. *Studies in Second Language Acquisition* 24, 451–480.
Chaudron, C. and Parker, K. (1990) Discourse markedness and structural markedness: The acquisition of English noun phrases. *Studies in Second Language Acquisition* 12, 43–63.
Chesterman, A. (1991) *On Definiteness: A Study with Special References to English and Finnish*. New York: Cambridge University Press.
DeKeyser, R. (2005) What makes learning second-language grammar difficult? A review of issues. *Language Learning* 55, 1–25.
Ekiert, M. (2010) Investigating articles as expressions of definiteness in L2 English of Slavic speakers. Unpublished doctoral dissertation, Teachers College, Columbia University, New York.
Ellis, N. (2008) Usage-based and form-focused language acquisition: The associative learning of constructions, learned attention, and the limited L2 state. In P. Robinson and N. Ellis (eds) *Handbook of Cognitive Linguistics and Second Language Acquisition* (pp. 372–405). New York: Routledge.
Ellis, R. (2001) Grammar teaching – practice or consciousness-raising? In J. Richards and W. Renandya (eds) *Methodology in Language Teaching* (pp. 167–174). Cambridge: Cambridge University Press.
Fodor, J. and Sag, I. (1982) Referential and quantificational indefinites. *Linguistics and Philosophy* 5, 355–398.
Garcia Mayo, M. and Hawkins, R. (2009) *Second Language Acquisition of Articles: Empirical Findings and Theoretical Implications*. Amsterdam: John Benjamins.
Givon, T. (1985) Function, structure, and language acquisition. In D. Slobin (ed.) *The Crosslinguistic Study of Language Acquisition* (pp. 1005–1028). Hillsdale, NJ: Erlbaum.
Han, Z-H. (2008) On the role of meaning in focus on form. In Z-H. Han (ed.) *Understanding Second Language Process* (pp. 45–79). Clevedon: Multilingual Matters.
Han, Z-H. (2009) Interlanguage and fossilization: Towards and analytic model. In V. Cook (ed.) *Handbook of Contemporary Applied Linguistics* (pp. 137–162). London: Continuum.
Han, Z-H. (2010) Grammatical morpheme inadequacy as a function of linguistic relativity: A longitudinal study. In Z.H. Han and T. Cadierno (eds) *Linguistic Relativity in SLA: Thinking for Speaking* (pp. 154–182). Bristol: Multilingual Matters.
Han, Z-H. (2011) Fossilization – A classic concern of SLA research. In S. Gass and A. Mackey (eds) *The Routledge Handbook of Second Language Acquisition* (pp. 476–490). New York: Routledge.
Han, Z-H. and Lew, W.M. (2012) Acquisitional complexity: What defies complete acquisition in SLA. In B. Szmrecsanyi and B. Kortmann (eds) *Linguistic Complexity in Interlanguage Varieties, L2 Varieties, and Contact Languages* (pp. 192–217). Berlin: Walter de Gruyter.
Hawkins, J. (1978) *Definiteness and Indefiniteness*. London: Croom Helm.
Hawkins, J. (1991) On (in)definite articles: Implicatures and (un)grammaticality prediction. *Journal of Linguistics* 27, 405–422.

Hawkins, J. (2004) *Efficiency and Complexity in Grammars*. Oxford: Oxford University Press.
Jarvis, S. (2002) Topic continuity in L2 English article use. *Studies in Second Language Acquisition* 24, 387–418.
Jarvis, S. (2012) The detection-based approach: An overview. In S. Jarvis and S. Crossley (eds) *Approaching Language Transfer Through Text Classification: Explorations in the Detection-based Approach* (pp. 1–33). Bristol: Multilingual Matters.
Jiang, N., Novokshanova, E., Masuda, K. and Wang, X. (2011) Morphological congruency and the acquisition of L2 morphemes. *Language Learning* 61, 940–967.
Kellerman, E. (1995) Crosslinguistic influence: Transfer to nowhere. *Annual Review of Applied Linguistics* 15, 125–150.
Larsen-Freeman, D. (2006) The emergence of complexity, fluency, and accuracy in the oral and written production of five Chinese learners of English. *Applied Linguistics* 27, 590–619.
Larsen-Freeman, D. (2010) Not so fast: A discussion of L2 morpheme processing and acquisition. *Language Learning* 60, 221–230.
Liu, D. and Gleason, J. (2002) Acquisition of the article *the* by nonnative speakers of English: An analysis of four nongeneric uses. *Studies in Second Language Acquisition* 24, 1–26.
Lyons, C. (1999) *Definiteness*. Cambridge: Cambridge University Press.
McNamara, T. and Knoch, U. (2012) The Rasch wars: The emergence of Rasch measurement in language testing. *Language Testing* 29, 555–576.
Myford, C. and Wolfe, E. (2003) Detecting and measuring rater effects using many-facet Rasch measurement: Part I. *Journal of Applied Measurement* 4, 386–422.
Odlin, T. (2005) Crosslinguistic influence and conceptual transfer: What are the concepts? *Annual Review of Applied Linguistics* 25, 3–25.
Pica, T. (1983) Methods of morpheme quantification: Their effect on the interpretation of second language data. *Studies in Second Language Acquisition* 6, 69–78.
Prince, E. (1981) On the inferencing of indefinite this NPs. In A. Joshi, B. Webber and I. Sag (eds) *Elements of Discourse Understanding* (pp. 231–250). Cambridge: Cambridge University Press.
Radden, G. and Dirven, R. (2007) *Cognitive English Grammar*. Amsterdam: John Benjamins.
Selinker, L. (1972) Interlanguage. *International Review of Applied Linguistics* 10, 209–231.
Spada, N. and Tomita, Y. (2010) Interactions between type of instruction and type of language feature: A meta-analysis. *Language Learning* 60, 263–308.
Tabakowska, E. (1993) Articles in translation: An exercise in cognitive linguistics. In R. Geiger and B. Rudzka-Ostyn (eds) *Conceptualizations and Mental Processing in Language* (pp. 785–800). Berlin: Mouton de Gruyter.
Tarone, E. and Parrish, B. (1988) Task-related variation in interlanguage: The case of articles. *Language Learning* 38, 21–43.
Trenkic, D. (2002) Establishing the definiteness status of referents in dialogue (in languages with and without articles). *University of Cambridge Working Papers in English and Applied Linguistics* 7, 107–131.
Von Humboldt, W. (1836/1999) In M. Losonsky (ed.) *On Language: On the Diversity of Human Language Construction and Its Influence on the Mental Development of the Human Species* (P. Heath, trans.). Cambridge: Cambridge University Press.
Yoo, I. (2009) The English definite article: What ESL/EFL grammars say and what corpus findings show. *Journal of English for Academic Purposes* 8, 267–278.

Appendix 1: Aesop's Fable for the Missing Word Task

A very tired man, a donkey, and a dog were traveling. The man was a salesman from a nearby village returning home after a week-long stay in town. The man decided to take a break, and fell asleep under a tree by the side of the country road he was traveling on.

The donkey wandered out into the field, feeding on some grass. The dog followed. As soon as the animals were some distance away from the man, the dog said quietly to the donkey: 'You're having a nice lunch, but I'm quite hungry. I'm a dog and I don't eat grass. If you would only lie down for a moment or two, I could reach into the pack that you're carrying and see what our master has brought this time. I promise not to touch any meat, but maybe I could have a bone, if there is one in the pack.'

Surprisingly, the donkey was not interested in helping the hungry dog. In general, a/the grey Balkan donkey is happy to help out others in need. However, in this story, the donkey was indifferent to the needs of his friend. It said, 'You'll have to wait until the master wakes up. He'll give you some food.' Suddenly, a wolf sprang out from behind the bush and grabbed the donkey by the neck. 'Help! Help!' cried the terrified donkey to the dog.

The dog, however, would not move. Generally speaking, the/a German long-haired dog is not a vindictive animal. But, the dog in this story likes his revenge. 'You'll have to wait until the master wakes up. He'll help you,' said the dog.

Appendix 2: Translation Task

In Polish

Wczoraj wieczorem byłam na przemiłej kolacji z koleżanką z Chicago. Poprosiła mnie, żebym zaproponowała restaurację, a ponieważ jest kucharzem, więc zrobiłam wszystko, żeby znaleźć bardzo eleganckie miejsce w centrum. Świetnie się bawiłyśmy plotkując, popijając wino i podgryzając zakąski. Mojej koleżance najbardziej smakował marynowany śledź. Generalnie woli śledzia bałtyckiego, mniejszego i mniej tłustego od atlantyckiego. Tym razem jednak oceniła przystawkę ze śledzia atlantyckiego bardzo wysoko. Właśnie miałam poprosić ją o podanie soli, kiedy naszą uwagę zwrócił głośno zachowujący się mężczyzna przy stoliku obok.

Mężczyzna siedział z piękną kobietą, która rozkoszowała się kolacją i winem. Nagle mężczyzna wskazującym palcem prawej ręki pokazał swej partnerce coś co pływało w jego talerzu. Krzyknął do kobiety, że to chyba mucha. Nie ukrywając swego wzburzenia zawołał kelnera. Wywiązała się między nimi nieprzyjemna wymiana zdań. Kelner próbował coś tłumaczyć, był zestresowany, a facet krzyczał coraz głośniej. *Wymachując palcem przed nosem kelnera zaczął rozwodzić się nad higieną w tej restauracji. W tym momencie już wszyscy goście byli zaabsorbowani całą sytuacją.* Kelner w końcu nie wytrzymał, rzucił *fartuch, odwrócił się i* ruszył do wyjścia. To doprowadziło mężczyznę do takiej furii, że podniósł się z krzesła i odtąd krzyczał za wychodzącym kelnerem na stojąco. W tym momencie nie wytrzymała także kobieta, która wcześniej próbowała uspokoić awanturującego się mężczyznę. Wstała od stołu i wyszła, zostawiając swojego towarzysza samego nad talerzem. Mężczyzna siedział kompletnie oniemiały, z otwartymi ustami.

In English

Last night I was having a lovely dinner with a friend from out of town who's a chef in Chicago. She asked me to choose a restaurant, so I made a point of selecting a very chic place downtown that might impress her. We were having a really nice time chatting, drinking wine, and nibbling at our appetizers. My friend's favourite appetiser was the pickled herring. The restaurant served Atlantic herring which, to some, is too greasy and strong tasting. The Atlantic herring, which come from saltier waters, tend to grow larger. The Baltic herring, which she prefers, are smaller than the common herring found in the North Atlantic, and contain less fat. She was very pleased to find the pickled Atlantic herring delicious.

I was about to ask my friend to pass the salt when our attention was shifted to a loud and rude man sitting at the table next to us. The rude man was dining with a beautiful woman. She appeared to be enjoying her meal and the wine they were drinking, but he had the most annoyed expression on his face. Out of nowhere, the man got very upset and started pointing with his index finger at the bowl of dip sitting on the table. I tried to see what he was pointing at and saw that a small fly had gotten stuck in the dip. Very loudly and rudely he called over a young waiter to complain. At this point, all the patrons were disturbed by the scene he was making. He reprimanded the waiter, standing up to yell even louder at the poor young man. The waiter, who looked like he could be an actor, appeared very upset by the man's actions; he couldn't take being yelled at anymore. He threw off his apron, walked out, and quit his job on the spot. After this happened the rude man's companion had had enough. She got up and left the table, leaving him to finish the dinner alone. The man, with his mouth open, looked totally shocked and just sat there. I don't know why he was surprised – he had acted terribly.

9 Learning Grammatical Gender in a Second Language Changes Categorisation of Inanimate Objects: Replications and New Evidence from English Learners of L2 French

Panos Athanosopoulos and
Bastien Boutonnet

Introduction

Despite the substantial progress in the investigation of the linguistic relativity hypothesis (the idea that the language we speak affects the way we think, Whorf, 1956) in many strands of cognitive science (for reviews see Casasanto, 2008; Regier & Kay, 2009; among others), only a limited number of second language acquisition (SLA) studies have directly examined whether L2 learning can affect categorisation patterns in adults (see e.g. Pavlenko, 2011, 2014). Recent studies have shown shifts in mental representation of L2 users in different domains such as time (Miles et al., 2011), colour (Athanasopoulos et al., 2010), grammatical number (Athanasopoulos, 2006; Cook et al., 2006) and grammatical gender (Boroditsky et al., 2003).

Using the by now well-established research paradigm of the voice attribution technique (VAT) asking participants to assign a male or female voice to inanimate objects (Sera et al., 1994) to reveal the effects of grammatical gender on object categorisation, and adopting the longitudinal approach employed recently by Kurinski and Sera (2011) to study voice attribution patterns in adult English learners of L2 Spanish, the current paper conducts an investigation of the effects of second language acquisition of grammatical gender on object classification patterns of adult English learners of L2 French. Since French has but English lacks grammatical gender on common nouns, we ask whether acquisition of this category will change the way English learners of L2 French perceive objects that correspond to masculine and feminine nouns in French. We revisit Kurinski and Sera's (2011) design to address two crucial issues arising from their study that require further exploration.

Firstly, Spanish might not be the ideal language to test effects of grammatical gender on voice attributions because its grammatical gender system might be more aligned with other conceptual cues. Indeed, it has been observed that the masculine/feminine grammatical distinction in Spanish corresponds closely to the conceptual artificial/natural distinction. That is, nouns with masculine grammatical gender tend to have referents that denote artificial objects, and vice versa for nouns with feminine grammatical gender (Sera *et al.*, 1994; Sera *et al.*, 2002). The demonstrated changes in voice attribution patterns reported by Kurinski and Sera (2011) show that learning Spanish grammatical gender may boost a pre-existing bias reported for speakers of English as a first language (see discussion of the natural/artificial distinction in Sera *et al.*, 1994; Sera *et al.*, 2002). This finding in itself constitutes strong evidence in favour of linguistic relativity, but it leaves open the question of the extent to which learning novel grammatical categories may lead to changes in categorisation when those categories do not already map onto pre-existing conceptual biases, such as the natural/artificial distinction.

Secondly, Kurinski and Sera (2011) used the same object stimuli in each of the testing sessions in their longitudinal design. Learners must have acquired the correct gender of the noun in order to apply the corresponding Spanish-gender compatible voice in the VAT, but it is currently unknown how much the task itself, rather than exposure to the L2 per se in the classroom and elsewhere, facilitated the observed shift in voice attribution patterns due to repeatedly exposing learners to the same stimuli. Kurinski and Sera (2011) acknowledge this limitation in their study, but state that if different object stimuli had been used each time, the researchers would not have been able to infer whether the changes observed over time were due to learning or to the fact that different items were used. However, one could explicitly test for the effect of repeated testing by including previously seen items with items seen for the first time. This is precisely what we did in this study. If performance in the VAT is primarily driven by exposure to specific experimental items repeatedly used in the task, then French gender-compatible voice attributions in these items should increase over time, relative to new items seen for the first time.

Background to the Study

Most of the world's languages express gender and a large subset of them has included gender as a *formal* system, which is often referred to as *grammatical gender* (Corbett, 1991). Gender as a formal system translates into the assignment of all nouns (including nouns for inanimate objects) into two, three or more classes. The most common classes (genders) in Indo-European languages are *masculine, feminine* and *neuter*. Gender assignment (i.e. which words belong to which class) is generally recognised to be fairly arbitrary. Indeed, crosslinguistic evidence seems to support such an idea since the gender of both animate and inanimate objects is often contradictory even between languages as close as French, Spanish or Italian (Foundalis, 2002). While most of the time, nouns for living beings follow the biological sex of the entity, there is no direct evidence on which to base the assignment of gender to inanimate objects such as toasters, tables and cups. Because inanimate objects carry no obvious perceptual characteristics that could immediately reveal their grammatical gender in a particular language, it appears that in this domain stronger language effects are found when the use of language is explicitly promoted in the task, such as when participants are asked to classify inanimate objects as 'more male like' or 'more female like' when no other cues are given as a basis of classification.

One such task is the voice attribution task, pioneered by Sera *et al.* (1994) and used in a number of highly influential studies since then. Sera *et al.* (1994) asked children and adult monolingual speakers of Spanish and English to assign voices to pictures of inanimate objects. The results showed that Spanish-speakers' voice-assignments were highly consistent with the grammatical gender of the objects. Conversely, the English speakers' voice-assignment exhibited the artificial/natural distinction whereby they assigned mostly a male voice to artificial (man-made) objects (e.g. a car, a table) and a female voice to natural (i.e. naturally occurring) objects (e.g. a strawberry, a cloud). In a subsequent study, Sera *et al.* (2002) elicited data using the same voice-assignment task from children and adults speakers of French, German, Spanish and English. The results confirmed and extended the same patterns from the Spanish to French speakers but not to the German-speaking participants, a finding attributed to the fact that in contrast to Spanish and French, German has a three-way grammatical gender classification system (including neuter).

Acquisition of grammatical gender in an L2 is notoriously difficult and even advanced L2 learners may show persistent errors, both at the grammatical and lexical level (Dewaele & Véronique, 2001). More recently, studies have begun to investigate effects of L2 acquisition of grammatical gender on voice attribution patterns, following Sera and colleagues' paradigm. Forbes *et al.* (2008) elicited data from French- and Spanish-English bilinguals on a voice attribution task and while both language groups were influenced by the grammatical gender of their languages, the group of French speakers differed more from the English monolinguals. This confirms previous evidence reported by Sera *et al.*

(1994) where it has been suggested that Spanish gender assignment might be consistent with other conceptual cues which English speakers rely on when performing the tasks (e.g. artificial versus natural, size, use, function, etc.).

The most recent study to date on grammatical gender and object categorisation in bilinguals was carried out by Kurinski and Sera (2011) and used a longitudinal design that followed a more simple case of bilingualism: adult English classroom learners of L2 Spanish. The data was elicited using the voice attribution paradigm combined with a naming task (to measure the acquisition of grammatical gender), and participants were tested once before they had received any Spanish instruction and three times throughout the rest of the academic year. Their results showed no significant changes in voice attribution patterns after 10 weeks of instruction, but such changes were found only after 20 weeks of L2 instruction, as indexed by a significant increase in L2 learners' voice attribution patterns that were consistent with Spanish grammatical gender.

Aims of the Study

The current study implements a voice attribution task in a longitudinal design following the progression of three groups of English L1 learners of French L2. As argued in the introduction, French is ideally suited to test effects of L2 learning on cognition because the implementation of grammatical gender in the nominal system of that language does not correspond closely to the conceptual natural/artificial distinction, in contrast to Spanish (Sera *et al.*, 1994). Additionally, we aim to shed light on the possible facilitating role of the categorisation task itself (in this case, the VAT) in cognitive restructuring by using 'new' stimuli (i.e. objects encountered for the first time in the experiment) and 'old' stimuli (objects encountered in previous experimental sessions) in each of the testing sessions.

Method

Participants

Sixteen English monolinguals (age range: 18–24; 6 female, 10 male), 17 French monolinguals (age range: 19–26; 6 female, 11 male) and 49 English learners of French (referred to as L2 French henceforth) took part in the study. The group of L2 French were English L1 undergraduate students doing a French degree at Bangor University. These 49 participants were divided into three groups according to their level of study as follows: 1st years ($n = 15$, age range: 18–25; 13 female, 5 male), 2nd years ($n = 16$, age range: 18–24; 8 female, 8 male) and 4th years ($n = 18$, age range: 21–23; 13 female, 5 male). At the time of testing, the group of 4th years all had spent a minimum of 6 months in a French-speaking country.[1] The group of English monolinguals were undergraduate Linguistics students at Bangor University. While the majority of them self-reported that they were absolute monolinguals, some reported having had experience of another language in high school, although all of them admitted that knowledge in those languages is now minimal or non-existent. None of the English monolinguals had spent more than two consecutive weeks in any of the countries where those languages are spoken, with the exception of Wales. The two participants who reported having limited knowledge of Welsh were just taking a few hours a week of conversational Welsh in which no explicit reference to grammatical rules or grammatical gender could have been discussed. The French monolinguals, who were tested in France, all had some knowledge of English due to the nature of the educational curriculum in France. However, they all reported having limited knowledge of the language, almost never using it and not having spent more than two weeks in an English-speaking country.

Voice attribution task

Materials

A total of 60 black and white line drawings of everyday objects along with four control items with natural gender (male and female characters) were used as stimuli. This ensured that we could evaluate whether participants had understood the task and treat their data accordingly. All pictures were selected after consultation with the French language instructors to ensure that the learners had been exposed to the nouns representing the objects at some point in their 1st year classes. The pictures were then divided into three sets of 20 pictures so that participants would be exposed to 20 new pictures which were added to the 'old' stimuli in every testing session. Thus, at Time 2, participants received 40 pictures, comprised of the 20 they had received at Time 1, plus 20 new ones; and at Time 3 participants received the 40 items they had received in Time 2, plus 20 new ones. This will allow us to directly assess the potential facilitating role of repeated exposure to the same stimuli in the voice attribution task. Each set was composed of ten pictures of naturally occurring items (e.g. hand, tomato, see appendix for a complete list of stimuli) and 10 pictures of artificial (man-made) objects (e.g. house, basket). This division between artificial and natural was made in order to avoid a bias in the results (see Sera *et al.*, 1994) and to follow Kurinski and Sera's (2011) design as closely as possible. However, no analysis comparing the attribution to voices between artificial and natural items is reported in this paper. The control groups (English and French monolinguals) only received a subset of 40 pictures which corresponds to the intermediary session at Time 2 for the experimental groups. Stimuli were randomised and presented using the Keynote application running on an Apple MacBook. Most pictures were taken from the International Picture Naming Project (IPNP) (Szekely *et al.*, 2004) or from clipart databases when items could not be found in the former. All pictures were scaled to fit within a 540 pixels square using Adobe Photoshop CS3 software.

Procedure

In this task, participants were asked to assign a male or female voice to pictured objects. All 81 participants were handed an answer booklet with a questionnaire in order to assess their language background and biographical details. Once the questionnaire was filled in, they were asked to read the task's instructions on the screen. The groups of English controls and L2 French all received the instructions in English while the group of French controls had a translated version of the following instructions:

> We are thinking of making a new movie in which some everyday objects come to life, sing and dance. You will see a series of pictures of these objects and will need to determine whether each item should have a man's/boy's voice or a woman's/girl's voice.
>
> If you decide that an object should have a female voice please circle 'F' in the column named 'VOICE' on your answer sheet. If you decide that it should have a male voice, then circle 'M'.
>
> Please make sure that picture numbers correspond to the numbers on your answer sheet.

The groups of learners were tested in a classroom in Bangor University and stimuli were presented on a white projector screen, linked to an Apple MacBook laptop. Participants were asked not to discuss their answers with others and the rooms were arranged so that the possibility of a participant looking at another's responses was minimal. Most of the participants in the control groups were tested in a similar environment but some had to be tested individually. In this case, the participants were tested in a quiet room in Bangor University and the stimuli were presented from an Apple MacBook laptop's screen. In each trial, a 500ms fixation cross preceded a 5000ms target picture which was followed by a 2000ms blank screen. Given that Kurinski and Sera (2011) did not find any effects after 10 weeks of instruction, this was considered a viable starting point for implementing the VAT to the 1st year learners and the rest of the learner groups. Thus, all learner groups were first tested approximately 10 weeks into the first semester of that year's study, and then subsequently tested two more times into the academic year. The interval between the 3 testing sessions was of a minimum of 8 weeks and no more than 11.

Language task

Participants
Only the group of L2 French was subjected to this task.

Materials
In this task the same 64 pictures as in the voice attribution task were used. Each session therefore received the same set of 20 new pictures as in the previous task. Only the order in which the pictures appeared on the screen was changed between the tasks.

Procedure
This task followed the voice attribution task and was administered after a short break. Participants were asked to turn to the next page of their answer booklet and were presented with the following instructions:

> This time, can you please name the object presented on this image as well as its indefinite article (un/une).
> For example, if you see a picture of a dog, write 'un chien' in the column
> 'ARTICLE + NOUN'.
> If you see a picture of a girl, then write 'une fille'.
> You don't have to worry too much about the spelling. If you are not sure how to spell a word its [sic] better to answer something than leaving a blank.

Even though asking for the indefinite article might be considered a less intuitive choice, the phenomenon of elision in French forced us to do so. Indeed, when the vowel of the definite article (*le*, masculine or *la*, feminine) is the same as the vowel of the following noun, the article switches to l' – its vowel gets elided. For example, the word *escargot* requires the masculine definite article *le*, which would result in the succession of two identical vowels (*le escargot). In that case, the only grammatical option is to delete the *e* of the definite article: *l'escargot*. This phenomenon would therefore prevent us from checking whether participants really knew the grammatical gender of those words. As in the previous task, the participants were tested in a classroom in Bangor University and stimuli were presented on a white projector screen linked to an Apple MacBook running the presentation application Keynote.

Result

Voice attribution task

The task required participants to choose between two answers (male or female voice). Correct answers received the mark of 1 and the sum was converted into percentages. In this task an answer was deemed correct when the voice given by the participant was consistent with the grammatical gender of the item in French. For instance, if the item *house* was given a female voice, the answer was scored 1 because the word *maison* has feminine gender in French.

Between-group differences across Time

Figure 9.1 shows the mean scores of the different groups of participants across all three testing times. Figure 9.1 shows a clear distinction between the performance of the two monolingual groups, with the group of French monolinguals highly consistent with French grammatical gender and the group of English monolinguals around 50%. A one-way ANOVA with the results of Time 1 as a dependent variable factored by language group revealed a significant effect of group ($F(4, 77) = 21.461, p < 0.001$) and post-hoc tests revealed that the difference was situated between the groups of English native speakers (monolinguals and L2 learners) and French monolinguals

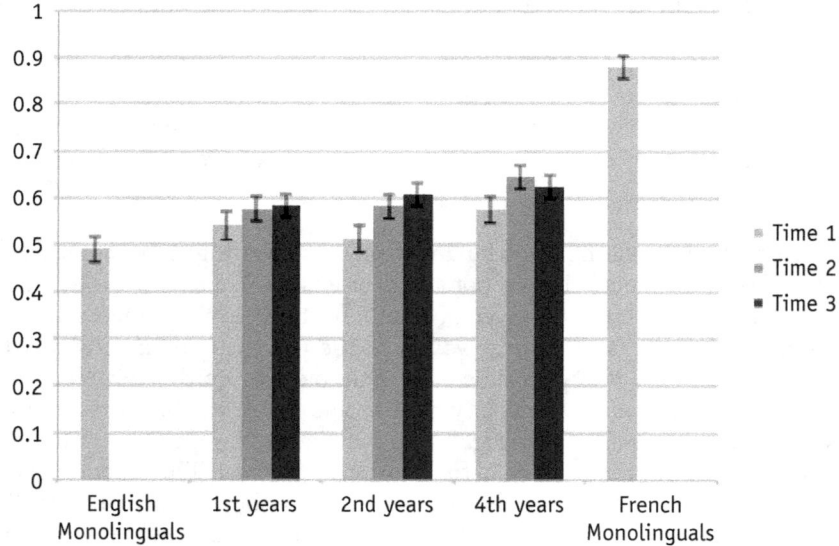

Figure 9.1 Chart of participants' mean proportion of voice attributions (and standard errors on error bars) which were consistent with French grammatical gender for all three testing times

(Bonferroni, $p < 0.001$). Two separate one-way ANOVAs with the VAT patterns of Time 2 and then Time 3 as dependent variables factored by Language Group were carried out to compare the performance of all groups to the English and French monolingual reference points. Unsurprisingly, both ANOVAs revealed a significant effect of group (Time 2: $F (4, 77) = 19.496, p < 0.001$; Time 3: $F (4, 77) = 15.287, p < 0.001$). In addition to the significant difference between French and English monolinguals established at Time 1, post-hoc tests revealed a significant difference in both Time 2 and 3 between the group of 1st years and the French monolinguals (Bonferroni, $p < 0.05$), between the 2nd years and the French monolinguals (Bonferroni, $p < 0.05$), and between the 4th years and the French and English monolinguals (Bonferroni, $p < 0.05$).

Tests against chance level

We additionally explored the behaviour of all learner groups against chance levels. While the groups of English monolinguals, 1st years and 2nd years did not differ significantly from chance at Time 1 ($t (15) = -0.351, p > 0.05$; $t (14) = 1.666, p > 0.05$; $t (15) = 0.430, p > 0.05$ respectively) the group of 4th years did ($t (17) = 2.684, p < 0.05$). At Time 2 and 3 all groups of learners differed significantly from chance therefore performing significantly above 50% (Time 2: 1st years, $t (14) = 4.688, p > 0.001$; 2nd years, $t (15) = 2.431, p > 0.05$; 4th years, $t (17) = 6.026, p > 0.001$; Time 3: 1st years $t (14) = 3.854, p > 0.05$; 2nd years, $t (15) = 3.993, p > 0.05$; 4th years, $t (17) = 5.153, p > 0.001$).

Time as a within-subject factor

The longitudinal design of the study allowed us to measure the performance of the experimental groups (L2 French) three times in the course of the academic year. In order to explore the influence of time on the groups' performance a mixed ANOVA with Time as a within-subject factor and Language Group as a between-subject factor was carried out. The ANOVA revealed a significant main effect of Time ($F (2, 92) = 3.886, p < 0.05$). Post-hoc tests reveal a significant difference between Time 1 and Time 3 (Bonferroni, $p < 0.05$) overall. There was no significant interaction of Time × Language Group ($F (4, 92) = 1.118, p > 0.05$), which suggests that all groups exhibited the same evolution.

Old versus New items, an exploration into potential effects of repeated exposure to stimuli

One of the issues we outlined earlier with Kurinski and Sera's (2011) study was that the same stimuli were used for all testing sessions. The experimental design used here allowed us to separately examine performance on items which participants were exposed to in previous

Old items

As presented in Table 9.1, the performance of all groups on the twenty oldest items (i.e. the items introduced in the first testing session) increases through time. A 3 × 3 ANOVA, with Time as a within-subject factor and Language Group as a between-subject factor reveals a main effect of Time ($F(2, 92) = 16.201$, $p < 0.001$). Post-hoc t-tests locate a significant difference between Time 3 and Time 1; and between Time 3 and Time 2 (*Bonferroni*, $p < 0.05$) in all groups, but no significant difference between Time 2 and Time 1 in any group.

New items

As presented in Table 9.2, the performance of all groups on the new items for every session seems to follow an inverted U-curve, whereby participants perform higher at Time 2 but almost identically at Time 1 and 3. A similar 3 × 3 ANOVA (Time as a within-subject factor and Language Group as a between-subject factor) also reveals a (smaller) main effect of Time ($F(2, 92) = 6.122$, $p < 0.05$), with a significant difference between Time 2 and Time 1 as well as between Time 2 and Time 3 in all groups. (*Bonferroni post-hoc t-tests*, $p < 0.05$).

Exploration of the performance at T3

To investigate further the potential effect of repeated exposure to the same stimuli, planned-comparisons paired t-tests were carried out on the performance of all groups at Time 3. Table 9.3 summarises the means of the performance on the items first seen at Time 1, Time 2 and Time 3, averaged across all groups of learners. The t-tests revealed a significant difference between the objects seen at T1 and T2 ($t(48) = 2.358$, $p < 0.05$), as well as between T2 and T3 ($t(48) = 4.140$, $p < 0.001$) and T1 and T3 ($t(48) = 7.194$, $p < 0.001$). This points out to a gradual significant decrease in performance modulated by the degree of newness. Namely, the older the item, the more compatible with French grammatical gender leaners' voice attributions for that item tend to be. This analysis provides the strongest evidence that L2 learners gradually increased their French

Table 9.1 Participants' mean performance (and standard errors) on the 20 oldest items in the voice-attribution task

	OLD_T1	OLD_T2	OLD_T3
1st Years	0.541 (0.037)	0.564 (0.035)	0.650 (0.046)
2nd Years	0.504 (0.035)	0.550 (0.034)	0.688 (0.044)
4th Years	0.574 (0.029)	0.650 (0.028)	0.694 (0.037)

Table 9.2 Participants' mean performance (and standard errors) on the 20 newest items for every session in the voice-attribution task

	NEW_T1	NEW_T2	NEW_T3
1st Years	0.541 (0.037)	0.623 (0.044)	0.514 (0.039)
2nd Years	0.504 (0.035)	0.579 (0.042)	0.513 (0.037)
4th Years	0.574 (0.029)	0.635 (0.035)	0.535 (0.031)

gender-compatible voice attributions as a function of repeated exposure to the same stimuli.

Naming task

Correct answers received a mark of 1. In this task, because we wanted to check whether the participants knew the *gender* of the object an answer was deemed correct if the participant provided the right determiner.

Figure 9.2 shows the mean scores of the groups of learners across all three testing times (different shades of grey). While there is no striking difference between the three groups, we can see that their performance decreases through time. In a similar way to the VA task, a mixed ANOVA with Time as a within-subject factor and Language Group as a between-subject factor was carried out. The ANOVA revealed a significant main effect of Time ($F(2, 92) = 14.282$, $p < 0.001$) and post-hoc Bonferroni t-tests reveal that the difference is situated between Time 1 and Time 3 for all groups ($p < 0.05$). There was no significant relation of Time × Language Group ($F(4, 92) = 0.509$, $p > 0.05$), which suggests that all groups exhibited the same progression.

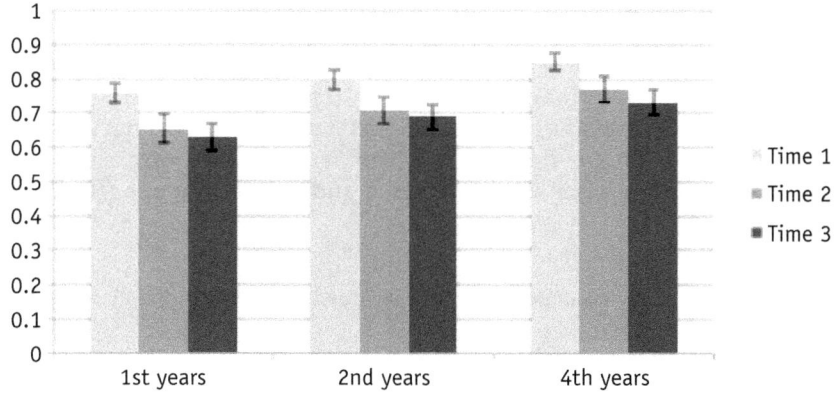

Figure 9.2 Chart of participants' mean proportion of article + noun (and standard errors on error bars) which was consistent with French grammatical gender for all three testing times

Table 9.3 Participants' mean performance at Time 3 on items first seen at Time 1, Time 2 and Time 3

T1 Items	T2 Items	T3 Items
0.68 (0.0192)	0.62 (0.024)	0.52 (0.0198)

Old versus New items, an exploration into potential effects of repeated exposure to stimuli

Like the results from the VAT, the experimental design allowed for a comparison between old and new items since 20 new items were added every testing time and two subsequent analyses were performed.

Old items

As summarised in Table 9.4, the 20 first and oldest items (i.e. the ones participants were most familiar with) were extracted from the data. From these results we can see that through time the performance on the naming task seems to increase. A similar ANOVA to the general analysis above (Time as within-subject factor and Language Group as a between-subject factor) also revealed a main effect of time (F (2, 92) = 6.609, $p < 0.05$) and post-hoc tests located a significant difference between Time 3 and Time 1; and between Time 3 and Time 2 (*Bonferroni*, $p < 0.05$) in all groups, but no significant difference between Time 2 and Time 1 in any group. Thus, like in the VA task, clear effects of repeated exposure to the same stimuli can be observed in the naming behaviour of the learners at Time 3. The 'older' the item, the more successful learners are at retrieving its correct grammatical gender in French.

New items

Table 9.5 summarises participants' mean performance on exclusively new items (i.e. the 20 new items added to each session). The means, contrary to the performance on the old items, decrease through time. The same ANOVA was carried out and revealed a main effect of time (F (2, 92) = 32.061, $p < 0.001$). Post-hoc tests point out a significant difference between Time 1 and Times 2 and 3 in all groups (*Bonferroni*, $p < 0.001$).

Table 9.4 Participants' mean performance (and standard errors) on the 20 oldest items in the naming task

	OLD_T1	OLD_T2	OLD_T3
1st Years	0.777 (0.034)	0.787 (0.037)	0.891 (0.036)
2nd Years	0.779 (0.033)	0.754 (0.036)	0.812 (0.035)
4th Years	0.850 (0.028)	0.832 (0.030)	0.871 (0.029)

Table 9.5 Participants' mean performance (and standard errors) on the newest 20 items for every session in the naming task

	NEW_T1	NEW_T2	NEW_T3
1st Years	0.777 (0.034)	0.591 (0.060)	0.445 (0.078)
2nd Years	0.779 (0.033)	0.608 (0.057)	0.529 (0.075)
4th Years	0.850 (0.028)	0.668 (0.048)	0.606 (0.063)

Probing the relationship between the VAT and naming patterns

Obviously, for VAT patters to change towards the French monolingual pattern, L2 learners must know the grammatical gender of the relevant items. In other words, there should be a positive correlation between performance in the VAT and performance in the naming task. Furthermore, and perhaps more interestingly, if repeated exposure to stimuli across testing sessions promotes learning of grammatical gender of the relevant stimuli, then the positive correlation between VAT and naming patterns should strengthen over time. This is precisely what our correlational analyses showed. Collapsing all learner groups into one group for these analyses, we found that at Time 1, VAT patterns were significantly correlated with naming patterns, $r = 0.308$, $p < 0.02$. At Time 2, this correlation was stronger, $r = 0.474$, $p < 0.001$, while Time 3 yielded the strongest correlation, $r = 0.661$, $p < 0.0001$.

Discussion

There is an increasing body of evidence suggesting that bilingual individuals whose languages differ in their grammatical and/or lexical categories seem to differ from monolingual speakers of their L1 and shift towards speakers of their L2 to different degrees in their cognitive representation of those categories. The present study was conducted to address the role of adult second language learning in object categorisation. The specific question we asked was whether, and to what degree, an L2 grammatical category like gender influences speakers of an L1 which lacks obligatory grammatical gender in its nominal system.

We sought to address two main issues with Kurinski and Sera's (2011) approach. Firstly, the L2 Spanish speakers studied in Kurinski and Sera (2011) are learning a second language where the masculine/feminine distinction in its nominal system corresponds very closely to the conceptual natural/artificial distinction. We addressed this issue by examining another L2, namely French, where the grammatical distinction between masculine and feminine items does not correspond closely to a pre-existing semantic distinction (such as the natural/artificial distinction, Sera *et al.*, 1994). The results from the global analysis showed that there was a clear difference between the French and English monolinguals where the French speakers' voice attributions were highly consistent with French gender while the group of English monolinguals performed at chance. These results lend solid support to results reported in Kurinski and Sera (2011) and in previous studies on a number of different languages (e.g. Boroditsky et al., 2003; Flaherty, 2001; Forbes et al., 2008; Sera et al., 1994, 2002) which show an influence of grammatical gender marking on voice attributions.

Regarding the groups of instructed learners, the results from the t-tests against chance reveal that the advanced learners (4th years) performed significantly above chance from Time 1 onwards and at Time 2 and 3 all groups of learners showed a similar pattern in their voice attributions. Additionally, while the groups of 1st and 2nd years did not differ significantly from English monolinguals at any point, significant differences between the groups of 4th years and English monolinguals became apparent from Time 2 onwards. Again, these results confirm previous findings by Sera and colleagues (Sera et al., 1994; Sera et al., 2002; Kurinski & Sera, 2011). The longitudinal design of the study allowed us to track the effect of grammatical gender along with language learning in order to assess how linked they may be. From this analysis we can see that L2 learners' performance on the VAT seems to be progressively more influenced by French grammatical gender, especially at Time 3. Namely, English learners of French are starting to categorise objects more as male or female in line with French gender. This finding corroborates Kurinski and Sera's (2011) main claim that learning a second language as an adult can affect one's categorisation of objects.

The second issue that we addressed relates to how these categorisation changes come about in L2 learners. The design of the present study allowed us to investigate a potential effect of repeated exposure to the same stimuli by adding new stimuli for every session while retaining old, and therefore previously seen, items. Firstly, looking at the performance on old items only, a significant increase in performance in Time 3 relative to Time 1 was revealed. Secondly, the series of statistical tests carried at Time 3, comparing the performance between all three degrees of novelty, revealed a significant increase in performance according to the degree of novelty where the older the items were, the better the performance. Thirdly, correlational analyses revealed a positive correlation between VAT and naming patterns, which strengthens with each testing session. Taken together, these three pieces of converging evidence suggest that the source of the differences in VAT performance in this and in Kurinski and Sera's (2011) study is likely rooted in the repeated exposure to the same stimuli across the different testing sessions.

The scores from the naming task further revealed that the decrease in overall performance can be attributed to the possibility that L2 learners had not yet acquired the grammatical gender of a substantial proportion of the new items in each session, and this could explain the gradual decrease in performance in this task across the 3 testing sessions. Although the nouns used had been selected to ensure that they did not include items likely to be unfamiliar to the learners since the learners had been exposed to them during their studies (see Materials section), our results suggest that introducing the nouns in the classroom does not automatically entail that learners will successfully acquire the relevant grammatical gender properties of each noun. Be that as it may, the analysis on the old items in the naming task mirrored the pattern found in the VAT task for old items. Specifically, naming performance for old items was significantly better at Time 3 than at Time 1 (see results), indicating that repeated exposure to the same items across the 3 testing sessions can yield improvements in L2 grammatical gender acquisition.

Interestingly, the cross-sectional comparison against chance revealed that the group of 4th years were already performing significantly above chance at Time 1. It is impossible that this difference is due to an effect of repeated exposure to previously seen stimuli and might therefore be due to the fact that this group of learners is the most advanced and have all spent at least six months in a French-speaking country. Thus, while the main driving factor behind cognitive changes in L2 learners here and in Kurinski and Sera's (2011) study may have been the use of the same items across testing sessions, we also find some evidence that overall proficiency and expertise in the L2 may also exert some influence on the degree to which cognitive patterns shift towards the L2, a finding that is consistent with most studies on bilingual cognition in grammatical domains like number and gender (see Pavlenko, 2014 for an overview of findings across different domains).

Conclusion

Together, the experiments carried out in this study demonstrate the following:

(a) Native language affects VAT patterns, both in a language where the grammatical gender system is similar to the conceptual gender system (Spanish), and in a language that is more arbitrary in terms of its relationship to the conceptual gender distinctions.
(b) It is possible for a second language to alter VAT patterns in adult L2 classroom learners, and this effect can be found in beginners as well as more experienced learners.
(c) One of the major underlying causes of this cognitive restructuring is repeated testing with the same stimuli – exposure to previously seen items seems to reinforce VAT patterns consistent with the L2.

Pavlenko (1999; see also 2005, and Jarvis & Pavlenko, 2008) proposed seven possible outcomes for conceptual representation in bilinguals whose languages exhibit contrasting conceptual representations: (1) conceptual coexistence, (2) L1 conceptual transfer, (3) internalisation of new conceptual representations, (4) conceptual shift, (5) conceptual convergence, (6) conceptual restructuring (or reverse transfer) and (7) conceptual attrition. All of these outcomes come under the umbrella of conceptual change, which refers to the interaction of language-specific concepts in the mind of the bilingual person. For the current paper, two of those processes are most relevant, namely L1 conceptual transfer and concept internalisation.

L1 conceptual transfer describes a state of the conceptual system where L1-based concepts underlie both the L1 and the L2 linguistic systems. That is, L2 words and grammatical constructions are anchored on the already established L1-based conceptual system. Here, such transfer may be apparent in 1st and 2nd year learners, since they did not differ significantly from monolingual speakers of their L1. However, we need to be careful when interpreting this as L1 conceptual transfer, because this is not transfer of an existing grammatical gender system to the learning and use of an L2 system that differs from that of the L1, since the L1 in this case lacks grammatical gender. Therefore, the non-significant differences in behaviour between learners and monolingual English speakers is more accurately interpreted as incomplete internalisation of a new L2 grammatical system, rather than transfer of an existing L1 system.

Internalisation of new conceptual representations describes a process where a new conceptual representation enters the conceptual repertoire of L2 learners/users. This state of affairs seems to be the most apt to describe the phenomenon in operation in the current study. Native speakers of English (a language with no grammatical gender on common nouns) who are learning French (a language with an obligatory grammatical gender system on all nouns) began assigning male and female voices to objects consistent with their grammatical gender in French, and this tendency was significantly correlated with increasingly successful use of grammatical gender in the target language, with the strength of the correlation between VAT patterns and naming patterns progressively increasing from Time 1 through to Time 3 of testing. Thus, learners appear to be internalising the new grammatical structure at the conceptual level in an incremental way, the progress of which is parallel to the progress exhibited in learning the grammatical distinction at the linguistic level.

More broadly, our results corroborate previous findings (e.g. Sera et al., 1994, 2002; Flaherty, 2001; Boroditsky et al., 2003), and demonstrate the mediating role of language not only regarding a native language, but also in the context of a second language learnt in an instructed setting later in life. In this wider context, studies looking at cognitive restructuring in instructed

L2 learners are scarce. Recent attempts in another domain, namely motion categorisation, to probe the relationship between language and thought in L2 learners in a higher education learning context have yielded findings that corroborate the main finding of this study, that is, that frequency of exposure plays a crucial role in changing cognitive patterns. Specifically, Athanasopoulos, Damjanovic, Burnand and Bylund (2015) looked at the effect of length of L2 exposure on motion event cognition in classroom learners and found a progressive strengthening of the relationship between increasing L2 proficiency and shifting event cognition patterns towards the L2, very similar to the progressive strengthening of the relationship between VAT and naming patterns found in this study. A similar study by Bylund and Athanasopoulos (2015) found that Swedish speakers with English as a foreign language restructure their categorisation of motion events as a function of their proficiency and experience with the English language. The foreign language users' cognitive patterns correlated with exposure to English in everyday life, such that those who often used English-speaking audio-visual media approximated the cognitive behaviour of English native speakers.

Findings from those studies and from the current study strongly point to frequency of exposure and use as determining factors of successful cognitive restructuring in instructed L2 learning. Although it is too early to ferret out the pedagogical implications of these first attempts to examine cognitive restructuring in L2 learning (see Cook, 2015), some preliminary conclusions point to the use of cognitive categorisation tasks such as the VAT as classroom tools in a task-based, contextualised learning curriculum, as well as the use of multi-modal experiences and materials in the L2 learning classroom that may contribute towards successful acquisition of notoriously difficult grammatical categories such as gender. Further research has the potential to examine more comprehensively such pedagogical implications through dedicated intervention studies, towards which the current and similar studies may provide a useful theoretical starting point.

Note

(1) This was their 3rd year of study, which they need to spend in a university in France, hence there is no 3rd year group in this study.

References

Athanasopoulos, P. (2006) Effects of the grammatical representation of number on cognition in bilinguals. *Bilingualism: Language and Cognition* 9, 89–89.
Athanasopoulos, P., Dering, B., Wiggett, A., Kuipers, J.R. and Thierry, G. (2010) Perceptual shift in bilingualism: Brain potentials reveal plasticity in pre-attentive colour perception. *Cognition* 116, 437–443.

Athanasopoulos, P., Damjanovic, L, Burnand, J. and Bylund, E. (2015) Learning to think in a second language: Effects of proficiency and length of exposure in English learners of German. *Modern Language Journal*.

Boroditsky, L., Schmidt, L.A. and Phillips, W. (2003) Sex, syntax, and semantics. In D. Gentner and S. Goldin-Meadow (eds) *Language in Mind: Advances in the Study of Language and Thought* (pp. 61–80). Cambridge, MA: MIT Press.

Bylund, E., and Athanasopoulos, P. (2015) Televised Whorf: Cognitive restructuring in advanced foreign language learners as a function of audio-visual media exposure. *Modern Language Journal* 99 (1), 123–137. Supplement 2015.

Casasanto, D. (2008) Who's afraid of the Big Bad Whorf? Cross-linguistic differences in temporal language and thought. *Language Learning* 58, 63–79.

Cook, V., Bassetti, B., Kasai, C., Sasaki, M. and Takahashi, J.A. (2006) Do bilinguals have different concepts? The case of shape and material in Japanese L2 users of English. *International Journal of Bilingualism* 10, 137–152.

Cook, V. (2015) Discussing the language and thought of motion in second language speakers. *Modern Language Journal* 99 (1), 154–164. Supplement 2015.

Corbett, G.G. (1991) *Gender*. Cambridge: Cambridge University Press.

Dewaele, J.M. and Véronique, D. (2001) Gender assignment and gender agreement in advanced French interlanguage: A cross-sectional study. *Bilingualism: Language and Cognition* 4, 275–297.

Foundalis, H. (2002) Evolution of Gender in Indo-European Languages. Presented at the 24th annual meeting of the Cognitive Science Society, Mahwah, MJ.

Forbes, J.N., Poulin-Dubois, D., Rivero, M.R. and Sera, M. (2008) Grammatical gender affects bilinguals' conceptual gender: Implications for linguistic relativity and decision making. *The Open Applied Linguistics Journal* 1, 68–76.

Flaherty, M. (2001) How a language gender system creeps into perception. *Journal of Cross–Cultural Psychology* 32, 18–31.

Kurinski, E. and Sera, M.D. (2011) Does learning Spanish grammatical gender change English-speaking adults' categorization of inanimate objects? *Bilingualism: Language and Cognition* 14, 203–220.

Miles, L.K., Tan, L., Noble, G.D., Lumsden, J. and Macrae, C.N. (2011) Can a mind have two time lines? Exploring space–time mapping in Mandarin and English speakers. *Psychonomic Bulletin & Review* 18, 598–604.

Pavlenko, A. (ed.) (2011) *Thinking and Speaking in Two Languages*. Bristol: Multilingual Matters.

Pavlenko, A. (2014) *The Bilingual Mind and What it Tells us about Language and Thought*. Cambridge: Cambridge University Press.

Regier, T. and Kay, P. (2009) Language, thought, and color: Whorf was half right. *Trends in Cognitive Science* 13, 439–446.

Sera, M.D., Berge, C. and del Castillo Pintado, J. (1994) Grammatical and conceptual forces in the attribution of gender by English and Spanish speakers. *Cognitive Development* 9, 261–292.

Sera, M.D., Elieff, C., Forbes, J., Burch, M.C. and Dubois, D.P. (2002) When language affects cognition and when it does not: An analysis of grammatical gender and classification. *Journal of Experimental Psychology. General* 131, 377–397.

Szekely, A., Jacobsen, T., D'Amico, S., Devescovi, A., Andonova, E., Herron, D. et al. (2004) A new on-line resource for psycholinguistic studies. *Journal of Memory and Language* 51, 247–250.

Whorf, B.L. (1956) *Language, Thought, and Reality: Selected Writings of Benjamin Lee Whorf* (J.B. Carroll, ed.). Cambridge, MA: MIT Press.

Appendix

Experimental stimuli including all the items seen from the first to third session. Control items (clearly sexuated pictures) in italics.

French Gender	Stimulus	
Masculine	a magnet	(un aimant)
	a tree	(un arbre)
	an artichoke	(un artichaut)
	a desk	(un bureau)
	a bus	(un bus)
	a lock	(un cadenas)
	a mushroom	(un champignon)
	a lemon	(un citron)
	a knife	(un couteau)
	a pencil	(un crayon)
	a dolphin	(un dauphin)
	a snail	(un escargot)
	a fire	(un feu)
	a fridge	(un frigidaire)
	a glove	(un gant)
	a boy	*(un garçon)*
	a book	(un livre)
	a sailor	*(un marin)*
	a nose	(un nez)
	a cloud	(un nuage)
	an egg	(un œuf)
	a bone	(un os)
	a basket	(un panier)
	a piano	(un piano)
	a foot	(un pied)
	a fish	(un poisson)
	a tap	(un robinet)
	a sun	(un soleil)
	a telephone	(un téléphone)
	a train	(un train)

	a glass	(un verre)
Feminine	a spider	(une araignée)
	a bathtub	(une baignoire)
	a ball	(une balle)
	a branch	(une branche)
	a cassette	(une cassette)
	a chair	(une chaise)
	a key	(une clé)
	a bell	(une cloche)
	a ladybird	(une coccinelle)
	a lobster	(une écrevisse)
	a leaf	(une feuille)
	a girl	*(une fille)*
	an ant	(une fourmi)
	a strawberry	(une fraise)
	a frog	(une grenouille)
	a guitar	(une guitare)
	a clock	(une horloge)
	a nurse	*(une infirmière)*
	a lamp	(une lampe)
	a hand	(une main)
	a house	(une maison)
	a mountain	(une montagne)
	a fly	(une mouche)
	a pipe	(une pipe)
	a plant	(une plante)
	a pan	(une poêle)
	an apple	(une pomme)
	a bin	(une poubelle)
	a mouse	(une souris)
	a table	(une table)
	a tomato	(une tomate)
	a turtle	(une tortue)
	a car	(une voiture)

10 Crosslinguistic Influence in Third Language Acquisition

Ulrike Jessner, Manon Megens and Stefanie Graus

Introduction

Over the last 15 years research on third language acquisition or multilingualism has been progressively intensified. One of the main goals has been to describe multilingual phenomena in order to investigate differences and similarities between second and third language acquisition. So far studies have mainly focused on lexical transfer, the cognitive and linguistic effects of bilingualism on third language acquisition, child trilingualism and L3 teaching (see Jessner, 2006, 2008).

In this chapter, which will be informed by a dynamic systems and complexity theory (DCT) perspective, we will first deal with definitions used here. Second, differences between second language acquisition (SLA) and third language acquisition (TLA) will be presented with a special focus on the concept of crosslinguistic interaction, as introduced by Herdina and Jessner (2002) in their Dynamic Model of Multilingualism (DMM). Metalinguistic awareness in multilingual learning or rather multilingual awareness will be focused on as an emergent property of a multilingual system. In support of the crucial role that multilingual awareness plays in the complex processes in third language acquisition, we will present a number of examples of crosslinguistic interaction in multilingual learners stemming from recent studies at Innsbruck University. A conclusion and future research challenges will be presented at the end of the chapter.

Definitions

In the fields referred to in this chapter, a wide range of terms with a wide range of meanings have been used. Even though some of the terms describe the same phenomenon or express identical ideas, they differ due to the complexity of the multilingual's background or the scholar's theoretical framework. Like an increasing number of academics (e.g. Aronin & Hufeisen, 2009; Todeva & Cenoz, 2009) we argue that the process of learning a third language cannot be equated to learning a second one, and bilingualism thus should be treated as a form of multilingualism and not vice versa. In fact, it has been argued that complexity in multilingualism is greater than complexity in bilingualism (for a detailed discussion see Aronin & Jessner, 2015). In this vein, as proposed by De Angelis (2007: 11), *Third language acquisition* (TLA) is used here as a terminological shortcut for *third or additional language acquisition*.

Additionally, the hypernyms L1 for 'first language', L2 for 'second language', L3 for 'third language', etc. cannot easily be applied to a context where multiple languages are learnt, since dominance (in terms of proficiency or frequency of use) and/or the 'emotional weight' given to a certain language do/does not necessarily correspond to chronological order of acquisition. Additionally, in line with the new research perspective that the application of DCT-principles has contributed to our understanding of multilingual development we should also take into consideration that a multilingual system is in constant change, as are the components of the system. This issue becomes most relevant when we think about processes of interruption, that is, when learning one language is given up for a while due to changes in needs or motivation, and/or relearning of languages (see Jessner, 2015a, 2015b).

The Diversity of Multilingual Development

In contrast to second language learning or bilingualism, in third language learning or trilingualism the routes of learning or order of acquisition show greater diversity. In contrast to SLA where we have to deal with two kinds of how two languages are acquired, in TLA there are at least four orders of acquisition:

(1) the three languages can be learnt consecutively;
(2) the three languages can be learnt simultaneously;
(3) L1 and L2 are learnt simultaneously before learning the L3;
(4) L2 and L3 are learnt simultaneously after the acquisition of the L1 (see also Cenoz, 2000).

With an increase of number of languages the varieties of acquisition will increase exponentially (see Todeva & Cenoz, 2009). From the above it becomes clear that the description of individual multilingual development, that is, contact with more than two languages during the life-span, has to take changes in multilingual proficiency into account. The following figure (based on Herdina & Jessner, 2002: 124: fig. 29b) models the development of a multilingual system, that is, it shows how the speaker develops language proficiency in more than two languages during a certain period of time. While the primary language system of the speaker remains dominant

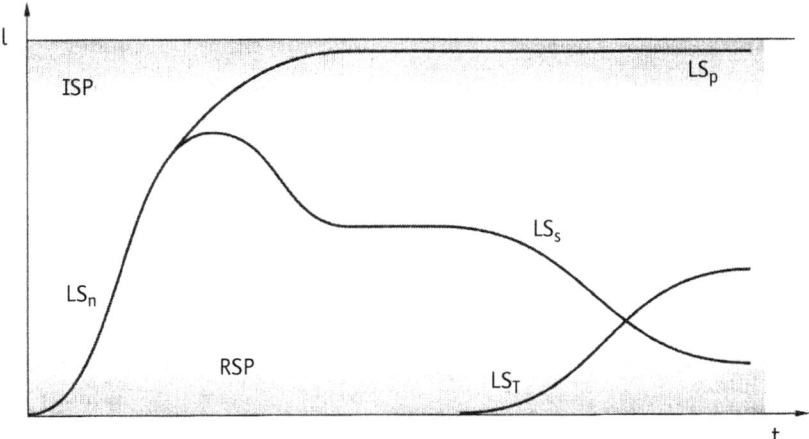

Figure 10.1 Learner multilingualism: Overall development (Herdina & Jessner, 2002: 124) LS_n = prior language system(s); LS_p = primary language system; LS_s = secondary language system; LS_T = tertiary language system; ISP = ideal native speaker proficiency; RSP = rudimentary speaker proficiency; t = time; l = language level

during this time, the secondary or incipient system undergoes development. The development of the third system is dependent on the acquisition of the first two systems, which in certain cases takes place at the same time as in simultaneous bilingualism. In fact, a closer look at the figure shows that transitional bilingualism forms an integrative part of the development of the third system. In this case, learner bilingualism, as it was called by Herdina and Jessner (2002: 125) to illustrate that bilingualism forms part of multilingualism, concerns the second and the third system and forms part of overall multilingual development.

As pointed out by Herdina and Jessner (2002: 88f), the graphs used in DMM 'simply relate language learning to time needed and predict the modifications in expected language growth due to the effect of certain factors assumed to affect multilinguals and ignore the fact that the level of achievement is heterogenous even in monolinguals, let alone multilinguals'.

In sum, we can state that the development of a multilingual repertoire or multilingual development acts in the following ways: it (a) changes over time, (b) is non-linear, (c) is reversible resulting in language attrition and/or loss and (d) is complex.

This discussion also makes it evident that learning another language like an L3 can counteract the maintenance of an L2 or L1, or in other words, language attrition or loss appear more often in multilingual than in bilingual contexts. In this case L3 will become more dominant than L2 due to limitations of resources for languages, as defined in Zipf's law of least effort (Zipf, 1968). Language attrition processes also point to the fact that language learning is made of non-linear and reversible processes: that is, development refers to both acquisition and attrition (Jessner, 2003a, 2015a, 2015b). Even if parts of the multilingual system can become fossilised or dormant, i.e. will in very general terms stop growing, they will still be able to exert an influence on the other parts of the system (Green, 1986).

Variation in multilingual development and use is strongly linked to the dependence of the system on social, psycholinguistic and individual factors (Herdina & Jessner, 2002), not to mention the mode of language learning in the form of either natural or instructional learning but also various combinations of both (see Cenoz & Genesee, 1998). Language choice depends on the perceived communicative needs of the multilingual user.

The Complexity of Crosslinguistic Influence in a Multilingual System

The key concept of this chapter is that of crosslinguistic influence (CLI), which can be defined as 'the influence of a person's knowledge of one language on that person's knowledge or use of another language' (Jarvis & Pavlenko, 2008: 1). This is an area that has received primary attention in the study of TLA and multilingualism (see e.g. Cenoz *et al.*, 2001a *inter alia*; De Angelis, 2007; De Angelis & Dewaele, 2011). As with most language acquisition and language use phenomena studied in multilingualism research, CLI has already established itself as a major area of bilingualism and SLA research (Jarvis & Pavlenko, 2008: xi). The study of CLI, as well as the term *crosslinguistic influence* itself, has its roots in the research into CLI in SLA carried out by Kellerman and Sharwood Smith (1986). They propose *crosslinguistic influence* as a theory-neutral term, 'allowing one to subsume under one heading such phenomena as "transfer", "interference", "avoidance", "borrowing", and L2-related aspects of language loss' (Kellerman & Sharwood Smith, 1986: 1). At the same time, they redefine the term *transfer* and narrow its notion to 'those processes that lead to the **incorporation** of elements from one language to another' (Kellerman & Sharwood Smith, 1986; emphasis in original).

Herdina and Jessner (2002) argue that, from a dynamic systems perspective of multilingualism, the phenomenon of transfer needs reconsideration. While in the Dynamic Model of Multilingualism (DMM) they recognise transfer phenomena as significant features in multilingual systems, they assume that the traditional distinction between code switching in research on bilingualism and transfer in SLA research is historically understandable but methodologically unfounded, impeding research on transfer in multiple language systems (Herdina & Jessner,

2002: 19). In view of that, Herdina and Jessner (2002: 28f.) suggest a distinction between language processing features and systems-relevant phenomena and argue that transfer should be seen as a dynamic process. They are therefore obliged to distinguish between transfer, interference, crosslinguistic influence and crosslinguistic interaction:

- transfer, either positive or negative, i.e. leading to either development or deviation in the learner system, is restricted to the monotonous phenomenon of the transfer of (the same) structures of L1 to L2;
- interference is what SLA describes as negative transfer, but in DMM it is argued that the term should be used to describe language processing, rather than language structure;
- crosslinguistic interaction suggests 'an extension of the concept of crosslinguistic influence (CLI) as the commonly used concept in language learning studies'. (Herdina & Jessner, 2002: 61)

In DMM the concept of crosslinguistic interaction (CLIN), resulting from the interplay of two or more language systems, can be taken to include not only transfer and interference but also code switching and borrowing phenomena, and 'is thus reserved as an umbrella term for all the existing transfer phenomena' (Jessner, 2003b: 49). Accordingly, Herdina and Jessner (2002: 66) relate that the contact between three language systems in a multilingual speaker can develop more forms, that is, apart from the bidirectional relationship between L1 and L2; L3 can influence L1 and vice versa and L2 and L3 can influence each other too. Thus, the term *crosslinguistic interaction*, in contrast to *crosslinguistic influence*, implies a multidirectional interplay between all the language systems of a multilingual person, rather than suggesting that there is a dominant, more active language system which influences a weaker one in a unidirectional way (see Jessner & Megens, 2014). Additionally, CLIN is intended to cover another set of phenomena as non-predictable dynamic effects which determine the development of the systems themselves and are particularly observable in multilingualism (Jessner & Megens, 2014: 29). Such influences can not only be interpreted as synergetic and interferential (Jessner & Megens, 2014), but also as affecting a multilingual's crosslinguistic awareness, as will be discussed later.

In addition to the idea of bidirectional transfer and opposed to traditional CLI as a one-to-one type relation between a source language (SL) and target language (TL), De Angelis (2007: 20f.) proposed *combined CLI*: 'the simultaneous influence of more than one language upon a target language, i.e. a many-to-one-type' – expanding the idea of transfer to multidirectional transfer. Still, in most cases, it will be rather difficult to attribute CLI to only one specific SL amongst several that are interacting. The more languages that are involved, the more relationships between the language systems have to be considered, since the number of possible interactions in multilinguals increases with every additional language.

Influential Factors

Of major interest in CLI research is the identification and study of factors likely to activate/stimulate or to decelerate and/or inhibit crosslinguistic interactions. These factors can be related to the language learner (e.g. her or his proficiency in the acquired languages; see Lindqvist, 2010; Williams & Hammarberg, 1998), to the languages (e.g. language distance; see Cenoz, 2001; Ringbom, 1987) or to the context (e.g. formality of the situation; see Dewaele, 2001). Researchers focus on different aspects and suggest different categorisations of such factors. De Angelis (2007: 19–40), for instance, places special emphasis on factors which trigger CLI from a non-native language, comprising language distance/proximity, target and source language proficiency, recency of use, length of residence and exposure to a non-native language environment, order of acquisition and formality of context. Cenoz (2003a: 104), by contrast, suggests a categorisation of the factors and distinguishes between two main domains: (1) 'individual and contextual factors such as age, anxiety, metalinguistic awareness, characteristics of the task, characteristics of the interlocutors, etc.' and (2) 'characteristics of the languages involved such as typology or proficiency'.

Researchers have found occurrences of language transfer in various areas. The scope of CLI research has been broadened, and the range of topics now spans phonology (e.g. Leather & James, 1996; Wunder, 2011), morphosyntax (e.g. Dewaele & Veronique, 2001; Helms-Park, 2001; Pavlenko & Jarvis, 2002; Sjöholm 1995) and discourse (e.g. Kellerman, 2001). De Angelis (2007: 41) indicates the domains of syntax (e.g. Klein, 1995), morphology (e.g. Jarvis & Odlin, 2000), phonetics and phonology (e.g. Hammarberg & Hammarberg, 1993; Williams & Hammarberg, 1998) and lexis (e.g. Ringbom, 1987 *inter alia*) as areas where non-native language transfer takes place. Additionally, Jarvis and Pavlenko (2008: 14) mention, that '[r]ecent studies have pushed the boundaries of the field outward, demonstrating that CLI is not limited to production and acquisition and can be identified in a variety of psycholinguistic processes'. They emphasise the fields of comprehension (e.g. Su, 2001), tip-of-the-tongue states (e.g. Ecke, 2001), nonverbal communication (e.g. Kellerman, 2001) and conceptual transfer, which is particularly interesting in the field of emotions (Pavlenko, 2002). Another area of transfer occurrence has been examined by Gabrys-Barker (2011: 97) who highlights the importance of 'transfer of learning and transfer of training' in TLA, which involves '[e]xplicit learner training in learning based [...] on the *learners' former L2* experiences' (Gabrys-Barker, 2011: 97) (see also Allgaeuer-Hackl & Jessner, 2014).

L2 Status

Among the many directions CLI can take, several researchers highlight the influence of the L2 on performance in an additional foreign language (e.g. Bono, 2011; Cenoz, 2001 *inter alia*; De Angelis, 2005a *inter alia*; De Angelis & Selinker, 2001; Dewaele, 1998; Jessner, 1999; Müller-Lancé, 2003; Selinker & Baumgartner-Cohen, 1995; Williams & Hammarberg, 1998). Hammarberg (2001: 23) explains that 'there appears to be a general tendency to activate an earlier secondary language in L3 performance rather than L1', whereas Meisel (1983) termed this 'L2 reliance in L3 production' as *foreign language effect* which can be equated to Williams and Hammarberg's (1998) *L2 status*. Similar terms such as *L2 effect* or *L2 factor* (see e.g. Clyne, 1997; De Angelis, 2005 *inter alia*; De Angelis & Selinker, 2001) have also been suggested.

In research conducted with learners whose first language is a non-Indo-European language, several scholars have found evidence that, if the L2 and the L3 are typologically similar, language learners tend to rely more on their L2 in their L3 production (e.g. Ahukanna *et al.*, 1981; Cenoz, 2001; Chandrasekhar, 1978; Wei, 2003; see Jessner, 2006). This dependence on an earlier L2 rather than on the L1 can be observed even when all the multilingual learner's languages are Indo-European languages. Williams and Hammarberg (1998: 323), for instance, identify L2 status as a decisive factor in language transfer. Their comprehensive study provides the framework for the concept of the *instrumental* and *supplier role* of the learner's background languages, a theory which has found strong support in later research (e.g. Bardel & Lindqvist, 2006). The subject of Williams and Hammarberg's (1998: 305) study (Sarah Williams, the first author of the paper) was an English native speaker who was fluent in German, advanced in French, had elementary knowledge of Italian and was acquiring Swedish as L3 at the time of the study. A considerable data sample was gathered through the recording of conversations and stories approximately every second week (Williams & Hammarberg, 1998). Data analysis showed language switches with different purposes, among which the authors identified four different types, neither morphologically nor phonologically adapted to the L3 Swedish. Williams and Hammarberg (1998: 295) explain that the first three 'had pragmatic purpose, namely (1) EDIT (marking self-repair, beginning of turntake etc.), (2) META (used for asides, to comment on L3 performance or ask for help) and (3) INSERT (use of non-L3 items to overcome lexical problems in L3)' whereas the last category, the so-called WIPP switch was explained to be 'Without Identified Pragmatic Purpose'. The last category is partially equivalent to the 'non-intentional language switches' identified by Poulisse and Bongaerts (1994) (Hammarberg, 2001: 27). The analysis of the language switches led to the conclusion that previously acquired languages were ascribed different roles in the subject's Swedish production. Basing their claim on the examination of 844 occurrences of switches, they claim that, since approximately 92% of the WIPP switches were from German, one of the subject's L2s, this language was defined as the *Default Supplier* (Williams & Hammarberg, 1998: 318). They explain that, since German was of major importance for lexical constructions in the third language (Williams & Hammarberg, 1994; referred to in Williams & Hammarberg, 1998: 295) and was also found to be influential in the case of INSERT switches in L3 and even L1, it 'is activated in parallel to the L3 interlanguage' (Williams & Hammarberg, 1998: 296). L1 English, contrariwise, occupied a different role: it was primarily used 'as a tool to facilitate communication in the form of metalinguistic comments, asides, requests for help, etc' (Williams & Hammarberg, 1998: 304). Williams and Hammarberg (1998: 297) term *metalinguistic communication* as instances 'where the thematic continuity is broken in the sense that the communication situation itself is commented on'. Thus, given that switches identified as belonging to the META category nearly only occurred in the participant's first language, the subject's L1 English was ascribed an *Instrumental Role* (Williams & Hammarberg, 1998: 295). With an increase of L3 proficiency, the L3 slowly becomes more independent and takes on the default supplier as well as the instrumental role (Williams & Hammarberg, 1998), which is why Williams and Hammarberg (1998: 325) state that their 'model is a developmental one'.

In her study with learners of Spanish whose first language was predominantly French, and whose L2 was English for one half and German for the other half of the group, Bono (2011: 34ff.) additionally supports the importance of the L2 status in L3 performance. The participants' conversations in the Spanish target language were analysed according to language switches and metalinguistic comments. Relying on William's and Hammarberg's (1998) theory of the default supplier role, Bono (2011) points out that, even though the participants' L1 French would achieve higher scores in proficiency, frequency of use and typology, the learners still predominantly relied on their L2 English as a supplier language. Bono (2011: 44f.) concludes that the L2 factor is of major importance and, thus, the effect of the other 'variables [...] seem to be neutralised'. She goes even further by stating that this hypothesis of a foreign language effect is in fact strengthened by the comparatively greater typological distance between L2 and L3. Additionally, she notes that in cases where the learners had learnt both English and German as a second language they predominantly relied on their English knowledge. She explains this by stating that 'English enjoys a special status [...], and this may reinforce the foreign language effect'.

Similarly, Cenoz (2001: 17f.) argues that the L2 status is an essential factor for CLI because learners of English as L3 whose native language was Basque appeared to show more CLI from Spanish than those whose L1 was Spanish. In this case, the L2 status and language distance contribute to the preference for Spanish as source language (SL). In the same vein, regarding the role the L2 factor plays, Sanchez (2011: 98) even goes so far as to state that, in the context of her study on syntactic transfer, 'in TLA, non-native languages may be activated more straightforwardly than the mother tongue, irrespective of typology'.

Researchers have suggested different explanations for this reliance on an earlier second language. Selinker and Baumgartner-Cohen (1995: 115) argue that 'there is an "interlanguage logic" in multiple language acquisition, where the learner is in a cognitive mode we can call "talk foreign"'. In the same vein, De Angelis and Selinker (2001: 56), who have found lexical (whole word) and morphological (restricted to a morpheme) transfer from the subject's non-native languages, argue for a 'cognitive mode called "talk foreign" or "foreign language mode"' which promotes non-native language influence. Williams and Hammarberg (1998: 323) explain that, particularly at the initial stages of L3 acquisition, the general higher likelihood of L2 transfer may be caused, firstly, by the 'reactivation of the same acquisition mechanism as was in previous L2 acquisition, which in turn reactivates other L2s', and, secondly, by the learner's attitude, or more precisely, a 'desire to suppress L1 in the belief that this is inherently "non-foreign"'. The latter suggestion is based on various introspective comments stating that the participant 'did not want to sound English' (Hammarberg & Hammarberg, 1993; referred to in Williams & Hammarberg, 1998: 323).

Taking a similar line, De Angelis (2005b: 11) suggests two possible reasons which favour transfer from non-native languages. She explains that system shifts might occur, first, due to a factor she calls *perception of correctness*, i.e. 'multilingual's resistance to incorporating L1 linguistic knowledge into interlanguage production when other information is available' because words from the mother tongue are immediately perceived as wrong. She further suggests that this factor might be related to the learner's level of proficiency in L3. The fact that learners are not always able to tell 'whether a word from a non-native language is correct or incorrect in another non-native language' leads to 'an increased acceptance level for non-native words into target language production' (De Angelis, 2005b: 11). The second reason suggested is *association of foreignness*, which she explains is caused by the fact that 'learners assign to non-native languages the status of "foreign languages", which results in a cognitive association between foreign languages' (De Angelis, 2005b: 12).

Several scholars attempt to explain the influence of the L2 factor on the basis of language production models. De Angelis and Selinker (2001: 45) refer to Green's (1986) model which postulates that languages have different levels of activation. Dewaele (1998) conducted a study on CLI with Dutch L1 learners comparing the lexical inventions in French of one group, whose L2 was French and L3 English, with a second group, whose L2 was English and L3 French. The category *lexical inventions* is similar to Ringbom's (2007) category of hybrids, blends and relexifications, 'lexemes [...] which are morpho-phonologically adapted to the target language (TL) but which are never used by native speakers' (Dewaele, 1998: 471). The French production of both groups showed a number of instances of CLI. However, the lexical inventions of the L2 French speakers were influenced more by their L1 Dutch, whereas the lexical creations of the L3 French speakers showed more L2 English influence. Referring to Green (1986) and Poulisse and Bongaerts (1994), Dewaele (1998: 471) concludes that this result 'suggests principles blocking L1 transfer in L3 learners in terms of spreading activation'.

Burton (2013), too, refers to language production models to explain language transfer from non-native languages. He follows De Bot (2004: 27) who suggests that, even though the learner's mother tongue is assumed to have a higher level of activation, owing to the fact that the L1 has a more structured network, it may also be deactivated more easily. Thus, Burton (2013: 50) argues that 'transfer from a non-target non-native language becomes more likely, simply because the non-native language is likely to be less easy to inhibit'. Keeping in mind De Bot's (2004) arguments, Burton (2013) furthermore proposes that items do not only have tags according to the languages they belong to, but also depending on whether they are items from a native or non-native language. Accordingly, he concludes that '[t]he existence of a "foreign" tag would help to explain the occurrence of unintentional CLI involving cognates and homophones, and in addition that involving lexical items with no cross-linguistic similarity' (Burton, 2013: 57). Yet, in the meantime, De Bot has also moved away from static modelling to dynamic modelling (De Bot *et al.*, 2007).

In sum, most research studies on the positive effect of the L2 relate the advantages presented to the influence of bilingualism on cognitive development: creativity, conceptualisation, spatial perception, lateral thinking, and specifically to metalinguistic awareness and communicative skills (see e.g. Cenoz, 2003; Cenoz & Genesee, 1998; Jessner, 1999). Thus, in studies on TLA and multilingualism both *L2 status* and *metalinguistic awareness* are of unique nature in a TLA-context and therefore of major importance for the discussion of CLIN in TLA. Studies on these two factors allow us not only to regard CLIN as a linguistic phenomenon, but broaden the concept and connect it with cognitive abilities, regarding CLIN from a cognitive point of view.

The Role of Metalinguistic Awareness in Multilingual Learning and Use

Metalinguistic awareness, or, as Baker (2011: 152) defines it, 'thinking about and reflecting upon the nature and functions of language', is an important factor in the language development of multilinguals (e.g. Bialystok, 2001; Herdina & Jessner, 2002; James, 1996). It can also be described as 'the ability to focus on linguistic form and to switch focus between form and meaning' (Jessner, 2008: 277). The concept of language awareness has been studied by numerous researchers in different academic disciplines. In the last decades, a substantial amount of research has been conducted with the aim of exploring the field of bilingualism related to bilinguals' cognitive skills. Particularly after the seminal work by Peal and Lambert (1962), who found out that bilingual children not only outperformed their monolingual counterparts in linguistic tasks but also showed cognitive advantages – thus proving the positive effect of bilingualism on children's cognitive skills, more attention has been paid to the nature of metalinguistic awareness (Jessner, 2008). In their early work on DCT, Herdina and Jessner (1997) refer to this phenomenon as the 'paradox of transfer'.

Also, multilinguals are believed to develop additional cognitive abilities that are not found in monolinguals, or even in bilinguals. In their Dynamic Model of Multilingualism (DMM) Herdina and Jessner (2002) refer to these multilingual abilities as the M(ultilingualism)-factor. The M-factor can be defined as an emergent property of the multilingual system, and can be specified as a function of the interaction between more than one language system (Herdina & Jessner, 2002: 129). Since 'it is difficult to decide whether it constitutes a precondition or a result of multilingualism', Jessner (2008a: 275) proposes that the M(ultilingualism)-factor might also be referred to as the M-effect. The key factor of the M-effect is metalinguistic awareness and the practical application of this awareness to tasks or use of language is referred to as metalinguistic ability.

Along with explicit metalinguistic knowledge, metalinguistic abilities are also developed in foreign language learning. At the same time this acquired awareness, i.e. prior language knowledge, has been observed to facilitate additional language acquisition to a considerable extent (e.g. Cenoz, 2003a; Herdina & Jessner, 2002; Jessner, 1999). This includes crosslinguistic associations the multilingual learner has at her or his disposal from which s/he can derive benefits. Nevertheless, 'for L2 influence to become a learning accelerator, CLIN needs to be coupled with metalinguistic awareness' (Bono, 2011: 25f.). Exactly these two factors were analysed in Jessner's (2006: 87) study which had the goal 'to explore the relationship between cross-linguistic interaction and linguistic awareness in the use of multilingual compensatory strategies'. The participants of her study were South Tyrolean ambilingual balanced bilinguals in Italian and German (Jessner, 2006: 86) as well as students, who were studying English at university. They were asked to fulfil three writing tasks in their L3: they had to write an essay, a summary and a letter while simultaneously saying out loud (in any language) what they were thinking while writing, an introspective method called think-aloud protocol (henceforth TAP) (Jessner, 2006: 85). It was hypothesised that the learners would choose compensatory strategies in order to overcome their lexical inadequacies or deficits which may become apparent in the TAPs, the main subject of analysis containing 'the metalanguage of the multilingual learners [...] as the most explicit expression of metalinguistic awareness in multilingual speech used in the TAPs' (Jessner, 2006: 88–90). However, the researcher also reports Singleton's concern (1999: 244f.; referred to in Jessner, 2006: 90) as to the traceability of these thinking processes, stating that 'there were cases where the cross-linguistic processing left no trace in the actual product and [...] many of the solutions which indicated a cross-linguistic dimension were not accompanied by an introspective comment mentioning cross-lexical consultation' (see also below). The identified functions of the strategies were either to compensate for lexical insecurity or for a total lack of target language knowledge, or they were employed in the search for alternatives. The analysis of the TAPs provided evidence that the learners indeed resorted to languages other than the target language and, thus, depending on the source language, different strategies could be identified: '(1) German-based strategies, (2) Italian-based strategies and (3) combined strategies' (Jessner, 2006). With regard to MLA, Jessner (2006: 101) observes that those participants who made strong use of combined strategies (i.e. strategies including both Italian and German) in their cross-lexical consultation were regularly in contact with the languages, studied English and Italian, and were therefore argued to have a higher proficiency level in the languages, factors which 'might be seen as an indication for a high level of metalinguistic awareness'.

As to the roles of the supporter languages in lexical search, Jessner (2006) identified two different functions of the learner's background languages. The analysis of the ambilingual students' thoughts while completing tasks in L3 English led her to the conclusion that German and Italian fulfilled different roles. She identified instances of German and Italian switches either before or after the English target item and argues that the language which is used before the L3 items serves in the role of supporter in the sense of initiating lexical search, whereas the language which is activated after the L3 item in most cases has the role of a confirming supporter. Whereas German 'served as a springboard' and, similar to Williams and Hammarberg's (1998) study, 'also had an instrumental role', Italian was the language which confirmed language choice (Jessner, 2006: 101).

Jessner (2006) ascribes an important role to the learners' use of cognates in their lexical search. Based on the analysis of the TAPs, she suggests that 'intentional switches during lexical search' indicate tacit crosslinguistic awareness, which 'was expressed in particular through the use of cognates in the supporter languages' (Jessner, 2006: 114). On the other hand, 'switches which were either introduced by metalinguistic expressions or commented on by the informants' indicated explicit awareness (Jessner, 2006). Employing Bialystok's (e.g. 1991, 2001) concept of analysis and control, and drawing from Kellerman and Bialystok (1997), Jessner (2006: 114) suggests that the use of metalanguage might be seen as one form of interaction between the processes of analysis and control. Moreover, assuming that 'manipulation of language reflects implicit knowledge and theorizing reflects explicit knowledge, one can furthermore argue that metalinguistic awareness expressed by ML [metalanguage] can be found at the interface between implicit and explicit learning' (Jessner, 2006: 115; see also Jessner, 2005).

With regard to the use of languages other than the intended one, Jessner (2006: 90) points out that, in comparison to the instances of transfer in other studies, in her study '[a]ll the instances of other language use in the English text production were identified as non-adapted switches'.

Cross-lexical consultation, or 'how bi- and multilinguals search for words in their other languages when they meet linguistic problems in the target language' (Jessner, 2008: 278) has been a subject of interest for other researchers, too. Herwig (2001: 128), notes that when multilinguals are unable to access a word, they automatically but also deliberately consult their other languages.

In the same line of thought, in the context of her small-scale study on lexical attrition in the English L2 oral production of multilingual language learners, Megens (2011) revealed crosslinguistic consultation to be at work: participants tended to draw from German (L1) and/or French (L3) when they did not find the right word or expression in English (L2):

- German/German dialect CLINs:
  ... small rain, just a few: <L1.ger> Tropfen [drops] <L1.ger>... (excerpt eldü_01)
  ...the man has –ahm- long hair, <L1.terdia> halt (xx) also, Bart ischt des [you know (xx) so, beard is this] <L1.gerdia>... (excerpt kado_01)
- French CLINs:
  ... and her they (.) <L3.fr> bon [well] <L3.fr> I don't see their faces... (excerpt mila_02)
  ...short black hair (.) an a <?> <L3.fr> barbe [beard] <L3.fr>... (excerpt pama_02)
  (Megens, 2011: 116)

The strong increase of French CLINs (crosslinguistic interactions) between the two testing times before and after the attrition period of four months showed that the French language system had become more prominent (and easier to access), and accordingly had become a more important supporter language. The reasons for the changes seem to be found in the French L3 being another foreign language of the participants and so following the notion of *association of foreignness*, as proposed by De Angelis (2005b: 12). Furthermore, since the participants had spent the four months of non-use in a French (L3) linguistic environment, their French L3 proficiency had increased strongly, allowing the participants' French L3 to take on the instrumental role at the second time of testing in addition to the default supplier role of a learner's background languages.

In their research on learners' written production De Angelis and Jessner (2012) obtain evidence that in lexical search previously acquired languages can serve as *supporter* or *bridge languages*. The researchers carried out a study in South Tyrol analysing the Italian (L1), German (L2) and English (L3) writing performance of multilingual learners in a school context with the aim of exploring the '***interaction*** between all the languages known by participants and how such interactions may influence writing development over time' (De Angelis & Jessner, 2012: 47; emphasis in original). They analysed the relationship between fluency and proficiency level in the non-native languages and interpreted the results from a Dynamic Systems Theory perspective, finding that 'multilingual awareness and language learning awareness guide transfer or crosslinguistic interaction' (De Angelis & Jessner, 2012: 64). They provide some examples as to the support of German and Italian in English production such as 'I like eating pizza, spaghetti, eis-creams (It. Gelato; Germ. Eis) and cakes' (De Angelis & Jessner, 2012).

This is clearly in accord with Bono's (2011) arguments. In her study, which aimed to answer the question of whether 'multilingual learners [are] aware of CLIN phenomena', and whether they are 'able to exploit crosslinguistic associations in the learning process' (Bono, 2011: 25), she found that, while the first language was mainly used for metalinguistic comments, the second language was strongly used to draw comparisons between the non-native languages. Not only language switches led to this hypothesis, but even more so reference to a language or languages, for instance, when a learner asked whether the meaning of the Spanish term *librería* was more similar to the French word for *bookshop*, or like the English word for *library* (Bono, 2011: 46f.).

Metalinguistic Awareness in CLIN

When linguists talk about awareness, they do not only refer to awareness in/of a single language, but also to the relationship between the languages in a learner's mind. James (1996: 138f.), for instance, describes different types of knowledge with regard to language. One can know different languages, for instance, German, Dutch and English, but one can also know about the relation between these languages. According to him, this knowledge can be found 'at the procedural level of performance (being manifest in MT [mother tongue] interference on FL [foreign language] use), or at the cognitive level of intuition, in which case we talk of Cross-linguistic Intuition (XLI). Or knowledge can be held at the explicit (declarative) level of metacognition, which we shall call Cross-linguistic Awareness (XLA)' (James, 1996: 139).

Thus James (1996) introduced the cognitive turn in the study of language contact, that is, 'the language transfer issue of classical Contrastive Analysis becomes a new issue of metalinguistic transfer – and its relationship to cross-linguistic awareness' (James, 1996: 143). The search for crosslinguistic equivalents is marked by the search for similarities, which forms a considerable part of the metalinguistic thinking going on during L3 production and thus refers to the relationship between CLIN and metalinguistic awareness, thereby pointing to the dynamic interplay which sheds light on key variables that form part of the M-factor (see Jessner, 2008: 279). According to Jessner (2008: 279; referring to her 2006 study) XLA 'in multilingual production is described as (a) tacit awareness shown by the use of cognates in the supporter languages (mainly in the use of combined strategies) and (b) explicit awareness in the case of switches that are introduced by meta-language' (see also Jessner, 2005).

In her study on crosslinguistic lexical influence from English (L2) on Italian (L3) in spontaneous written production, regarding the multilinguals' awareness Graus (2014: 142) 'assumed that with a higher number of switches accompanied by metalanguage indicating XLA, there would be more occurrences of CLI where a positive influence may be observed'. She found (in the TAPs) that the majority of positive crosslinguistic influence occurred along with metalanguage:

- *(...) und ich schreibe* molto delizioso *weil* delizioso *denke ich dass das schon das richtige Wort ist* deli zioso *weil in Englisch ist es auch* delicious ähm [=?un dessert] era molto delicioso *(...)* [and I'll write *molto delizioso* because I think *delizioso* is the right word *delizioso* because in English it is also *delicious* ähm [=?un dessert] era molto delicioso].
- *(...) jetzt muss ich überlegen was Einladung geheißen hat ähm (.) fällt mir jetzt nicht genau ein aber [=?also]* invent *wär's englische Wort dann wird's vielleicht in Italienisch ähm so was wie* inventazione *sein oder so (...)* [now I have to think what the word for invitation was ähm (.) I can't think of it just now [=?so] *invent* would be the English word then in Italian it will probably be *inventazione* or something like that]. (Graus 2014, 121)

Still, like Jessner (2005), Graus (2014: 142) notes that there were not many references, and these were only detected if accompanied by metalanguage because most instances of XLA stay undetected due to lack of metalinguistic comments in the TAPs. Nevertheless, absence of proof does not mean proof of absence.

So far we can conclude that a definition of multilingual awareness as key part of multilingual proficiency would have to include at least two dimensions of awareness in the form of crosslinguistic awareness and metalinguistic awareness. The definitions

- 'seeing MT and FL "objectively", first in terms of their immanent systemicity, and then in terms of each other, is to develop one's linguistic metacognitions of each' (James, 1996: 142)
- 'awareness of the links between their language systems expressed tacitly and explicitly during language production and use' (Jessner, 2006: 116)

should therefore be regarded as complementary.

With reference to this last notion, MLA and XLA appear to be difficult to disentangle. It has become clear that the two components interact and that the levels of awareness exert influence on the organisation of the multilingual mental lexicon because the levels of awareness show influence on the activation of the individual languages in multilingual production (Jessner, 2006: 116). Whereas crosslinguistic awareness can be defined as the awareness (tacit and explicit) of the interaction between the languages in a multilingual's mind, metalinguistic awareness adds to crosslinguistic awareness in so far that it makes objectification possible (see Jessner & Megens, 2014).

Outlook

Current research on crosslinguistic influence in TLA/multilingualism has shown that a focus on more than two languages is necessary to provide stimulating insights into the acquisition processes in multilingual learning. The multilingual turn, which has certainly been strongly influenced by work on TLA, has brought considerable insight into the acquisition processes in the multilingual learner.

In this chapter we discussed the concept of crosslinguistic influence (CLI) in third or additional language acquisition (TLA). Informed by dynamic systems and complexity theory (DCT), we argued for the term crosslinguistic interaction (CLIN), as proposed in Herdina and Jessner's (2002) Dynamic Model of Multilingualism (DMM) and broadened to the concept of CLI, since CLIN covers all the existing transfer phenomena, resulting from the dynamic, multidirectional interplay of a multilingual learner's language systems. In addition, CLIN comprises the cognitive consequences of multilingual development, i.e. it considers individual, unexpected and dynamic aspects in crosslinguistic activities, affecting a learner's multilingual awareness too.

A discussion of the L2 status (used here as the effect of any given foreign language within the multilingual learner's repertoire) as a psycholinguistic influential factor showed previously acquired (foreign) languages to be of major importance to TLA and cognitive development; specifically to metalinguistic awareness and communicative skills. Hence both *L2 status* and *metalinguistic awareness* are of a unique nature in the context of TLA and therefore highly important when discussing CLIN in TLA. Still, for previously acquired non-native languages to facilitate TLA, CLIN actually needs to be coupled with metalinguistic awareness. Exactly these two factors were analysed in Jessner's (2006) study, in which it was hypothesised that the learners would choose compensatory strategies in order to overcome their lexical inadequacies or deficits which may become apparent in the think-aloud-protocols (TAP). Based on the analysis of the TAPs, Jessner suggested that 'intentional switches during lexical search' indicate tacit crosslinguistic awareness, which 'was expressed in particular through the use of cognates in the supporter languages' (Jessner, 2006: 114). Then again, 'switches which were either introduced by metalinguistic expressions or commented on by the informants' indicated explicit awareness (Jessner, 2006). Also, Megens (2011) and Graus (2014) found crosslinguistic consultation, i.e. the use of supporter languages, to be at work and that the majority of crosslinguistic interactions occurred along with metalanguage. Thus, we concluded this chapter with a definition of multilingual awareness which has to include both crosslinguistic awareness (XLA) and metalinguistic awareness (MLA), since this way, multilingual awareness guides CLIN in TLA and allows us not only to regard CLIN as a linguistic phenomenon, but broadens the concept and connects it with cognitive abilities (see also De Angelis *et al.*, 2015).

Nonetheless, there are many research areas that still need more attention in future studies on language contact on an individual level. Work on inferencing and guessing, for instance, needs to be combined with research on cognates. The trainability of crosslinguistic awareness in institutionalised multilingual contexts needs further consideration (see Allgäuer-Hackl *et al.*, under review) as well as the relation between XLA and multilingual attrition (see Megens, forthcoming). Additionally, it also becomes clear that the current work on crosslinguistic influence/interaction needs to draw on other disciplines such as cognitive psychology and/or neurolinguistics to gain better insight into multilingual processing.

Acknowledgements

This research has partly been supported by The Austrian Science Fund (FWF) P 23146.

References

Ahukanna, J.G.W., Lund, N.J. and Gentil, R.J (1981) Inter- and intra-lingual interference effects in learning a third language. *Modern Language Journal* 65 (3), 281–287.

Allgaeuer-Hackl, E. and Jessner, U. (2014) Und was sagt die Mehrsprachigkeitsforschung dazu? Neue Perspektiven in der Mehrsprachigkeitsforschung und deren Relevanz für Unterricht und LehrerInnenbildung. In A. Wegner and E. Vetter (eds) *Mehrsprachigkeit und Professionalisierung in pädagogischen Berufen. Interdisziplinäre Zugänge zu aktuellen Herausforderungen im Bildungsbereich* (pp. 125–45). Opladen/ Berlin/Toronto: Budrich.

Allgaeuer-Hackl, E., Hofer, B. and Jessner, U. (2015; under review) Emerging plurilingual awareness in educational contexts: From theory to practice. *Canadian Modern Language Review*.

Aronin, L. and Hufeisen, B. (2009) Methods of research in multilingualism studies: Reaching a comprehensive perspective. In L. Aronin and B. Hufeisen (eds) *The Exploration of Multilingualism* (pp. 103–121). Amsterdam: Benjamins.

Aronin, L. and Jessner, U. (2015) Understanding current multilingualism: What can the butterfly tell us? In U. Jessner and C. Kramsch (eds) *The Multilingual Challenge: Cross-disciplinary Perspectives*. Berlin, New York: Mouton de Gruyter.

Baker, C. (2011) *Foundations of Bilingual Education and Bilingualism* (5th edition). Bristol: Multilingual Matters.

Bardel, C. and Lindqvist, C. (2006) The role of proficiency and psychotypology in lexical cross-linguistic influence: A study of a multilingual learner of Italian L3. In M. Chini, P. Desideri, M. Favila and G. Pallotti (eds) *Atti del VI Congresso di Studi dell'Associazione Italiana di Linguistica Applicata* (pp. 123–145). Perugia: Guerra Editore.

Bialystok, E. (1991) Metalinguistic dimensions of bilingual language proficiency. In E. Bialystok (ed.) *Language Processing in Bilingual Children* (pp. 113–140). Cambridge: Cambridge University Press.

Bialystok, E. (2001) Metalinguistic aspects of bilingual processing. *Annual Review of Applied Linguistics* 21, 169–181.

Bialystok, E. (2005) Consequences of bilingualism for cognitive development. In J.F. Kroll and A.M.B. De Groot (eds) *Handbook of Bilingualism: Psycholinguistic Approaches* (pp. 417–432). Oxford: Oxford UP.

Bono, M. (2011) Crosslinguistic interaction and metalinguistic awareness in third language acquisition. In G. De Angelis and J.M. Dewaele (eds) *New Trends in Crosslinguistic Influence and Multilingualism Research* (pp. 25–52). Bristol: Multilingual Matters.

Burton, G. (2013) Cross-linguistic influence in non-native languages: Explaining lexical transfer using language production models. *International Journal of Multilingualism* 10 (1), 46–59.

Cenoz, J. (2000) Research on multilingual acquisition. In J. Cenoz and U. Jessner (eds) *English in Europe. The Acquisition of a Third Language* (pp. 39–53). Clevedon: Multilingual Matters.

Cenoz, J. (2001) The effect of linguistic distance, L2 status and age on cross-linguistic influence in third language acquisition. In J. Cenoz, B. Hufeisen and U. Jessner (eds) *Cross-Linguistic Influence in Third Language Acquisition: Psycholinguistic Perspectives* (pp. 8–20). Clevedon: Multilingual Matters.

Cenoz, J. (2003a) The Role of typology in the organization of the multilingual lexicon. In J. Cenoz, B. Hufeisen and U. Jessner (eds) *The Multilingual Lexicon* (pp. 103–116). Dordrecht: Kluwer Academic Publishers.

Cenoz, J. (2003b) Cross-linguistic influence in third language acquisition: Implications of the organization of the multilingual lexicon. *Bulletin VALS/ ASLA* 78, 1–11.

Cenoz, J. (2005) Learning a third language: Cross-linguistic influence and its relationship to typology and age. In B. Hufeisen and R.J. Fouser (eds) *Introductory Readings in L3* (pp. 1–9). Tübingen: Stauffenburg.
Cenoz, J. and F. Genesee (1998) Psycholinguistic perspective on multilingualism and multilingual education. In J. Cenoz and F. Genesee (eds) *Beyond Bilingualism: Multilingualism and Multilingual Education* (pp. 16–32). Clevedon: Multilingual Matters
Cenoz, J., Hufeisen, B. and Jessner, U. (eds) (2001a) *Cross-linguistic Influence in Third Language Acquisition: Psycholinguistic Perspectives*. Clevedon: Multilingual Matters.
Cenoz, J., Hufeisen, B. and Jessner, U. (eds) (2001b) *Looking Beyond Second Language Acquisition: Studies in Third Language Acquisition and Trilingualism*. Tübingen: Stauffenburg.
Cenoz, J., Hufeisen, B. and Jessner, U. (eds) (2003) *The Multilingual Lexicon*. Dordrecht: Kluwer.
Chandrasekhar, A. (1978) Base language. *International Review of Applied Linguistics in Language Teaching* 16 (1), 62–65.
Clyne, M. (1997) Some of the things trilinguals do. *International Journal of Bilingualism* 1 (2), 95–116.
De Angelis, G. (2005a) Interlanguage transfer of function words. *Language Learning* 55 (3), 379–414.
De Angelis, G. (2005b) Multilingualism and non-native lexical transfer: An identification problem. *International Journal of Multilingualism* 2 (1), 1–25.
De Angelis, G. (2007) *Third or Additional Language Acquisition*. Clevedon: Multilingual Matters.
De Angelis, G. and Dewaele, J.M. (2009) The development of psycholinguistic research on crosslinguistic influence. In L. Aronin and B. Hufeisen (eds) *The Exploration of Multilingualism* (pp. 63–77). Amsterdam: Benjamins.
De Angelis, G. and Dewaele, J.M. (eds) (2011) *New Trends in Crosslinguistic Influence and Multilingualism Research*. Bristol: Multilingual Matters.
De Angelis, G. and Jessner, U. (2012) Writing across languages in a bilingual context: A Dynamic Systems Theory approach. In R. Manchón (ed.) *L2 Writing Development: Multiple Perspectives* (pp. 47–68). Boston: De Gruyter Mouton.
De Angelis, G. and L. Selinker (2001) Interlanguage transfer and competing linguistic systems in the multilingual mind. In J. Cenoz, B. Hufeisen and U. Jessner (eds) *Cross-Linguistic Influence in Third Language Acquisition: Psycholinguistic Perspectives* (pp. 42–58). Clevedon: Multilingual Matters.
De Angelis, G., Jessner, U. and Krésic, M. (eds) (2015) *Crosslinguistic Influence and Crosslinguistic Interaction in Multilingual Language Learning*. London: Bloomsbury.
De Bot, K. (2004) The multilingual lexicon: Modelling selection and control. *International Journal of Multilingualism* 1 (1), 17–32.
De Bot, K., Lowie, W. and Verspoor, M. (2007) A Dynamic Systems Theory approach to second language acquisition. *Bilingualism: Language and Cognition* 10 (1), 7–21.
Dewaele, J.M. (1998) Lexical inventions: French Interlanguage as L2 versus L3. *Applied Linguistics* 19 (4), 471–490.
Dewaele, J.M. (2001) Activation or inhibition? The interaction of L1, L2 and L3 on the Language Mode Continuum. In J. Cenoz, B. Hufeisen and U. Jessner (eds) *Cross-Linguistic Influence in Third Language Acquisition: Psycholinguistic Perspectives* (pp. 69–89). Clevedon: Multilingual Matters.
Dewaele, J.M. and Véronique, D. (2001) Gender assignment and gender agreement in advanced French interlanguage: A cross-sectional study. *Bilingualism: Language and Cognition* 4 (3), 275–297.
Ecke, P. (2001) Lexical retrieval in a third language: Evidence from errors and tip-of-the-tongue states. In J. Cenoz, B. Hufeisen and U. Jessner (eds) *Cross-Linguistic Influence*

in Third Language Acquisition: Psycholinguistic Perspectives (pp. 90–114). Clevedon: Multilingual Matters.

Gabrys-Barker, D. (2011) Appraisal systems in L2 vs. L3 learning experiences. *International Journal of Multilingualism* 8 (2), 81–97.

Graus, S. (2014) Crosslinguistic lexical influence from English (L2) on Italian (L3) in spontaneous written production. Master's thesis, University of Innsbruck, Austria.

Green, D.W. (1986) Control, activation, and resource: A framework and a model for the control of speech in bilinguals. *Brain and Language* 27, 210–223.

Hammarberg, B. (2001) Roles of L1 and L2 in L3 production and acquisition. In J. Cenoz, B. Hufeisen and U. Jessner (eds) *Cross-Linguistic Influence in Third Language Acquisition: Psycholinguistic Perspectives* (pp. 21–41). Clevedon: Multilingual Matters.

Hammarberg, B. and Hammarberg, B. (1993) Articulatory re-setting in the acquisition of new languages. *Reports from the Department of Phonetics, University of Umeå, PHONUM* 2, 61–67.

Helms-Park, R. (2001) Evidence of lexical transfer in learner syntax: The acquisition of English causatives by speakers of Hindi-Urdu and Vietnamese. *Studies in Second Language Acquisition* 23 (1), 71–102.

Herdina, P. and Jessner U. (2002) *A Dynamic Model of Multilingualism: Perspectives of Change in Psycholinguistics*. Clevedon: Multilingual Matters.

Herdina, P. and Jessner, U. (2013) The implications of language attrition for dynamic system theory: Next steps and consequences. *International Journal of Bilingualism* 17 (6), 752–756.

Herwig, A. (2001) Plurilingual lexical organisation: Evidence from lexical processing in L1-L2-L3-L4 translation. In J. Cenoz, B. Hufeisen and U. Jessner (eds) *Cross-linguistic Influence in Third Language Acquisition: Psycholinguistic Perspectives* (pp. 115–137). Clevedon: Multilingual Matters.

James, C. (1996) A cross-linguistic approach to language awareness. *Language Awareness* 4, 138–148.

James, C. (1999) Language awareness: Implications for the language curriculum. *Language, Culture and Curriculum* 12 (1), 94–115.

Jarvis, S. and T. Odlin (2000) Morphological type, spatial reference, and language transfer. *Studies in Second Language Acquisition* 22 (4), 535–56.

Jarvis, S. and A. Pavlenko (2008) *Crosslinguistic Influence in Language and Cognition*. New York: Routledge.

Jessner, U. (1999) Metalinguistic awareness in multilinguals: Cognitive aspects of third language learning. *Language Awareness* 8 (3–4), 201–209.

Jessner, U. (2003a) A dynamic approach to language attrition in multilingual systems. In V. Cook (ed.) *Effects of the Second Language on the First* (pp. 234–247). Clevedon: Multilingual Matters.

Jessner, U. (2003b) The nature of cross-linguistic interaction in the multilingual system. In J. Cenoz, B. Hufeisen and U. Jessner (eds) *The Multilingual Lexicon* (pp. 45–55). Dordrecht: Kluwer Academic Publishers.

Jessner, U. (2005) Multilingual metalanguage, or the way multilinguals talk about their languages. *Language Awareness* 14 (1), 56–68.

Jessner, U. (2006) *Linguistic Awareness in Multilinguals: English as a Third Language*. Edinburgh: Edinburgh UP.

Jessner, U. (2008) A DST model of multilingualism and the role of metalinguistic awareness. *The Modern Language Journal* 92 (2), 270–283.

Jessner, U. (2015a) Multicompetence approaches to language proficiency development in multilingual education. In O. García and A. Lin (eds) *Encyclopedia of Language and Education*, Vol 5: Bilingual Programs. New York: Springer.

Jessner, U. (2015b) Multilingualism. In J. Wright (ed.) *International Encyclopedia of the Social and Behavioral Sciences*. Oxford: Elsevier.
Jessner, U. and Megens, M. (2014) On crosslinguistic awareness (XLA). Paper presented at the International Conference on Third Language Acquisition and Multilingualism, Uppsala University, Uppsala, Sweden, 12–14 June, 2014.
Kellerman, E. (2001) New uses for old language: Cross-linguistic and cross-gestural influence in the narratives of non-native speakers. In J. Cenoz, B. Hufeisen and U. Jessner (eds) *Cross-Linguistic Influence in Third Language Acquisition: Psycholinguistic Perspectives* (pp. 170–191). Clevedon: Multilingual Matters.
Kellerman, E. and Bialystok, E. (1997) On psychological plausibility in the study of communication strategies. In G. Kasper and E. Kellerman (eds) *Communication Strategies. Psycholinguistic and Sociolinguistic Perspectives* (pp. 31–48). London: Longman.
Kellerman, E. and Sharwood Smith, M. (eds) (1986) *Crosslinguistic Influence in Second Language Acquisition*. New York: Pergamon Press.
Klein, E.C. (1995) Second versus third language acquisition: Is there a difference? *Language Learning* 45 (3), 419–466.
Leather, J. and James, A. (1996) Second language speech. In W. Ritchie and T. Bhatia (eds) *Handbook of Second Language Acquisition* (pp. 269–316). New York: Academic Press.
Lindqvist, C. (2010) Inter- and intralingual lexical influences in advanced learners' French L3 oral production. *International Review of Applied Linguistics in Language Teaching* 48 (2–3), 131–157.
Megens, M. (2011) Language attrition after four months of non-use? Emergence of lexical attrition in the English L2 oral production of multilingual learners. Master's thesis, University of Innsbruck, Austria.
Megens, M. (forthcoming) Crosslinguistic Awareness in Processes of Multilingual Attrition. Doctoral Dissertation. University of Innsbruck, Austria.
Müller-Lancé, J. (2003) A strategy model of multilingual learning. In J. Cenoz, B. Hufeisen and U. Jessner (eds) *The Multilingual Lexicon* (pp. 117–132). Dordrecht: Kluwer Academic Publishers.
Odlin, T. (1989) *Language Transfer: Cross-linguistic Influence in Language Learning*. Cambridge: Cambridge UP.
Pavlenko, A. (2002) Bilingualism and emotions. *Multilingual* 21, 45–78.
Pavlenko, A. and Jarvis, S. (2002) Bidirectional transfer. *Applied Linguistics* 23 (2), 190–214.
Peal, E. and Lambert, W.E. (1962) The relation of bilingualism to intelligence. *Psychological Monographs* 76, 1–23.
Poulisse, N. and Bongaerts, T. (1994) First language use in second language production. *Applied Linguistics* 15 (1), 36–57.
Ringbom, H. (1987) *The Role of the Mothertongue in Foreign Language Learning*. Clevedon: Multilingual Matters.
Ringbom, H. (2001) Lexical Transfer in L3-Production. In J. Cenoz, B. Hufeisen and U. Jessner (eds) *Cross-Linguistic Influence in Third Language Acquisition: Psycholinguistic Perspectives* (pp. 59–68). Clevedon: Multilingual Matters.
Ringbom, H. (2007) *Cross-linguistic Similarity in Foreign Language Learning*. Clevedon: Multilingual Matters.
Sanchez, L. (2011) 'Luisa and Pedrito's Dog will the Breakfast Eat': Interlanguage transfer and the role of the second language factor. In G. De Angelis and J.M. Dewaele (eds) *New Trends in Crosslinguistic Influence and Multilingualism Research* (pp. 86–104) Bristol: Multilingual Matters.
Selinker, L. and Baumgartner-Cohen, B. (1995) Multiple language acquisition: 'Damn it, why can't I keep these two languages apart?' *Language, Culture and Curriculum* 8 (2), 115–121.

Singleton, D. (1999) *Exploring the Second Language Mental Lexicon*. Cambridge: Cambridge University Press.

Sjöholm, K. (1976) A comparison of the test results in grammar and vocabulary between Finnish- and Swedish-speaking applicants for English. In H. Ringbom and R. Palmberg (eds) *Errors Made by Finns and Swedish-speaking Finns in the Learning of English* (pp. 54–137). Åbo: Åbo Academy, Publications of the Department of English.

Su, I. (2001) Transfer of sentence processing strategies: A comparison of L2 learners of Chinese and English. *Applied Psycholinguistics* 22, 83–112.

Todeva, E. and Cenoz, J. (eds) (2009) *The Multiple Realities of Multilingualism: Personal Narratives and Researchers' Perspectives*. Berlin, New York: Mouton de Gruyter.

Wei, L. (2003) Activation of lemmas in the multilingual mental lexicon and transfer in third language learning. In J. Cenoz, B. Hufeisen and U. Jessner (eds) *The Multilingual Lexicon* (pp. 57–70). Dordrecht: Kluwer Academic Publishers.

Williams, S. and Hammarberg, B. (1998) Language switches in L3 production: Implications for a polyglot speaking model. *Applied Linguistics* 19 (3), 295–333.

Wunder, E.M. (2011) Crosslinguistic influence in multilingual language acquisition: Phonology in third or additional language acquisition. In G. De Angelis and J.M. Dewaele (eds) *New Trends in Crosslinguistic Influence and Multilingualism Research* (pp. 105–125). Bristol: Multilingual Matters.

Zipf, G. (1968) *The Psycho-biology of Language. An Introduction to Dynamic Philology*. Cambridge: Cambridge University Press.

11 Contemporary Perspectives on Crosslinguistic Influence

Janusz Arabski and Adam Wojtaszek

Finding a common denominator for such an extensive array of topics discussed in the present volume is not an easy enterprise. The difficulty can be partly attributed to the comprehensiveness of crosslinguistic influence as a theme in contemporary SLA research. The fact that certain issues raised in particular chapters extend the vast perspectives offered by Odlin (1989) or Jarvis and Pavlenko (2008) is quite symptomatic in this context. On the other hand, it also demonstrates the prolific nature and developmental potential of this area of investigation. In this situation a different alternative seems to be more compelling than looking for common themes. Bearing in mind potential readers of the volume, the decision was made to highlight some of the issues raised by particular chapter authors, developing certain ideas and offering some food for thought which might inspire future research. The authors of the present chapter resolved to structure the discussion around two major pivots: the first one related to important contributions to the theoretical background of crosslinguistic influence as a field of study, and the second one highlighting the value of the cognitive linguistic approach in research design and results interpretation.

The word *transfer* reappears multiple times in the book, especially in the first three chapters, all of which undertake the task of terminology-related reflection revolving around the most frequently employed notions. Odlin (Chapter 1) extends the perspective beyond the commonly assumed background involving the work of Weinreich (1953), Lado (1957) and behaviourist psychology, Cook (Chapter 2) presents the notion against a wider perspective of multi-competence, while Ringbom (Chapter 3) discusses its diverse senses and properties in relation to comprehension, production, items, system and genetic distance between languages.

The importance of Odlin's elaboration lies in the enlightening character of his discussion, arguably even for specialists in the field, many of whom might not have had an opportunity or compulsion to explore the origins of this ubiquitous term. Chapter 1 gives us a unique chance to embrace the more distant ancestors of *transfer* and reshape our appreciation and understanding of the notion. In Chapter 2, Cook argues for an extended understanding of transfer or crosslinguistic influence, pointing to the fact that two languages interact in the mind of the learner, and that the influences are evident in both directions. Cook also argues that in most papers no distinction has been made between transfer as a phenomenon occurring in speech, in actual language use, and as something which in some way influences the whole acquisition or language development. Additionally, the necessity of including other phenomena within the multi-competence perspective stems from the fact that the discussion of transfer usually entailed the direction of the influence (almost exclusively from L1 to L2) and positive versus negative effect. Ringbom, on the other hand, highlights the fact that there hasn't been sufficient attention given to comprehension, as most SLA studies focus on production. Comprehension is, according to Ringbom, the pre-requisite of learning. An important difference between comprehension and production is that production places a much heavier burden on accuracy and precision than comprehension. One of the central claims presented in Chapter 3 is that L2 comprehension involves many more opportunities and instances of transfer than L2 production, especially when crosslinguistic formal similarities between related languages invite exploitation of familiar patterns. Ringbom's unique contribution to this field of research lies in the fact that he was the first specialist in Europe to investigate crosslinguistic influences between Indo-European (Swedish, English) and Fenno-Ugric language (Finnish) in language acquisition context (Ringbom, 1976, 1987). His investigations led him to the conclusion that since comprehension in an unrelated L2 is more difficult, mainly because the crosslinguistic similarities may only be assumed and not perceived, there will also be less opportunities for transfer between genetically unrelated languages.

Another intriguing theme is verbalised in the title of Odlin's chapter, which might come as shocking to many scholars investigating the mysteries of second language acquisition. Putting to question the status of one of the cornerstones of SLA theory, the Contrastive Analysis Hypothesis (CAH), must be considered an act of remarkable bravery. At the same time, such a title undoubtedly performs a strong attention-getting function, awakening the curiosity of many experts in the field. The author claims that linking CAH with behaviourism (according to him unfounded) stems from the fact that both Lado and Weinreich (as well as other linguists) used the word *habit* in their texts. This word, however, does not necessarily have to be linked to behaviourism. Some researchers did not in fact see a considerable difference between habit and rule-governed behaviour. Besides, CAH has only come into widespread use after the publication of Wardhaugh's (1970) article, so its links with Lado are not well founded. In fact, however, it is extremely difficult to show when the idea, in terms of the importance of crosslinguistic influence in SLA, was actually born. This, in turn, forces us to reconsider the estimation of the starting point of SLA studies and research. In spite of the genetic and theoretical problems related to CAH (both in the context of Contrastive Analysis as such, as well as its status as a hypothesis), it will probably remain a very influential concept for the years to come. If approached with a proper care and reservation, it is capable (as an approach more than a hypothesis) to yield a number of interesting and valuable predictions about the nature of multilingual acquisition.

The central theme of Chapter 2 is Cook's original term multi-competence, whose origin can be traced back to the absence of a term which would encompass the totality of learner's L1 and interlanguage, originally defined as 'the compound state of a mind with two grammars' (Cook, 1991). Subsequently, it has been expanded to also include the scope of a community, and to allow for any number of languages which are known beyond the first (Cook, 2015). Language is also viewed in a broader perspective, not only as grammar, but as a multi-faceted cognitive system. Cook's new approach is additionally in line with the recent trends viewing second and subsequent language acquisition from the L2 user's point of view rather than assuming the native speaker's point of reference. The author speaks in one voice with Jessner, Megens and Graus (Chapter 10), who stress the dynamic character of inter-relationships between languages in the mind, which are in constant flux and diverse states of activation. Beside traditional transfer, multi-competence encompasses also such phenomena as code switching and attrition. This again reverberates in Jessner *et al.*'s concept of crosslinguistic interaction, elucidated in Chapter 10. The instances of code switching are seen by Cook as especially excellent illustrations of a complex multilingual system in action.

Implementation of the cognitive view of language is not a matter of following fashionable trends anymore. The implicit assumption that the use and acquisition of language is intrinsically and inseparably immersed in the complex network of cognitive processes seems to permeate the bulk of contemporary literature on the subject. It is also clearly visible in the contributions to the present volume, some of which make explicit references to the cognitively biased elaborations of the issues discussed in them. The notion of construal, for example, which is one of the fundamental concepts in Cognitive Linguistics (Croft & Cruse, 2004; Geeraerts & Cuyckens, 2007; Langacker, 2008; Lee, 2001; Robinson & Ellis, 2008), is applied and elaborated explicitly in Chapters 4, 6, 7 and 8, and evoked in a more indirect way also in Chapters 2, 5 and 9.

Alonso, Cadierno and Jarvis (Chapter 6) highlight the distinction between individual-level and language-level character of construal, which is vital in demonstrating the role of crosslinguistic influence. While a more individual perspective on the perception and construction of spatial relationships, and ultimately on their linguistic encoding, inherited from Langacker (1987) or Tyler (2014), seems to be closer to the original formulations, it is the collective, language-level understanding of construal, based on Littlemore (2009), which lends itself to the explanatory accounts offered by the authors. The suggestion made by Lee (2001: 27) that the patterns of individual construals may lead to language-specific conventions is very much in line with the more recent formulations within the Dynamic Model of Meaning (Kecskes, 2008), describing how frequently repeated uses of a particular item in specific contextual frames become imprinted on its 'coresense' – the denotational, diachronically shaped, relatively constant sense shared by all members of a given speech community (2008: 393–394).

Seen in such a perspective, the use of a particular prepositional construction by speakers of a given language may be treated as evidence of a specific mental conceptualisation of space relationships which has been conventionalised to such a degree that it shapes individual construals in a pervasive way. In other words, such conventions promote particular choices made by individual speakers in given situations, which in effect functions as a self-propelling mechanism responsible for conventionalising semantic landscapes of a language. The differences between those landscapes may be attributed to different criteria for spatial encoding applied in different languages; as a consequence, the formal exponents of those encodings tend to overlap only, instead of being one-to-one equivalents (the authors of Chapter 6 quote interesting examples from Finnish and English after Bowerman, 1996). In this way, the linguistic performance of L2 learners, compared to native speakers, could be used as evidence of crosslinguistic influence.

Following Jarvis' (2000) criteria, the authors of Chapter 6 were successful in demonstrating clear cases of L1 influence on subjects' L2 English, whose magnitude appeared to be directly proportional to the genetic distance between L1 and L2, at least taken at face value. However, one has to be careful, in this context, not to misinterpret the results as showing that the influence of L1 Spanish on the construal of spatial relationships in L2 English is necessarily greater than the influence of L1 Danish. What the study does demonstrate is the distinct preponderance of crosslinguistic visible effects that can be found in the spatial reference of L1 Spanish learners, which does not equate with the level of such influence, as many of its potential effects in the case of genetically close languages, such as Danish and English, might simply not be detectable. This echoes the classic distinction between positive and negative transfer (Larsen-Freeman & Long, 1991; Stockwell *et al.*, 1965), as positive influences, albeit invisible, may nevertheless be present (Weinreich, 1953). Alonso, Cadierno and Jarvis warn the readers that '[t]he source of crosslinguistic influence in this domain is more difficult to isolate, partly because the possible sources are manifold (e.g. structural, semantic, conceptual), and partly because of the lack of well-developed methods for disambiguating the sources' (p. 99).

Following this warning is essential for appropriate interpretation of the results reported in Chapter 6.

It follows from the juxtaposition of Chapter 6 and Chapter 7 that the magnitude of discernible crosslinguistic effects is an interesting function of the genetic (and typological) distance between L1 and L2. In their study of the acquisition of motion event construal (Talmy, 1985, 2000) by L1 Mandarin Chinese learners of L2 English, Treffers-Daller and Xu (Chapter 7) have found some evidence of covert transfer (Mougeon *et al.*, 2005) of L1 frequencies of motion verbs use, but they admit that the 'push-effect' was less significant than expected. It seems that the learners do not depend so much on their L1 experience in this case; instead, in the process of L2 acquisition they employ mainly the L2 data for the purpose of shaping the motion event construals. This goes hand-in-hand with Ringbom's remarks (Chapter 3) that transfer between unrelated languages is less likely mainly because the crosslinguistic similarities may only be assumed and not perceived. As a result, less visible traces of L1-induced linguistic behaviour will be observed in the performance of learners of an unrelated L2.

This is indirectly confirmed also by Han and Ekiert's findings (Chapter 8), who studied the acquisition of linguistic exponents of definiteness, i.e. the article system, by L2 English learners with L1 Slavic background. In the context of definiteness as a grammatical category, English on the one hand and Polish, Russian and Ukrainian on the other hand may be treated as completely unrelated in the typological dimension. For that reason, in line with Ringbom's assumptions, the likelihood of finding any traces of L1 transfer should be minute. The observations reported by Han and Ekiert confirm that expectation, as significant variability was found between individual learners who were asked to reflect on their choices in the qualitative recall task. The learners' construals of definiteness in form of the articles they used turned out to be related exclusively to their temporal, situated perspective as speakers in a given situation. Thus, the first of Jarvis' (2000) criteria for demonstrating L1 influence (i.e. intra-L1-group homogeneity in learners' target-language behaviour) has not been met. In the context of those observations it seems plausible to suggest that the magnitude of visible crosslinguistic effects in the form of non-target-like L1 patterns will take the shape represented in Figure 11.1. Where the genetic and typological distance between L1 and L2 is small, the influences will be insignificant due to the fact that the patterns of L1 and L2 are to a large extent similar. In cases of considerable typological and genetic unrelatedness, however, a small degree of discernible L1 patterning will be attributed to the difficulty of discovering any transferable crosslinguistic configurations. Only in situations involving moderate typological or genetic distance is there a place for more significant exploitation of L1 patterns which lead to erroneous L2 forms.

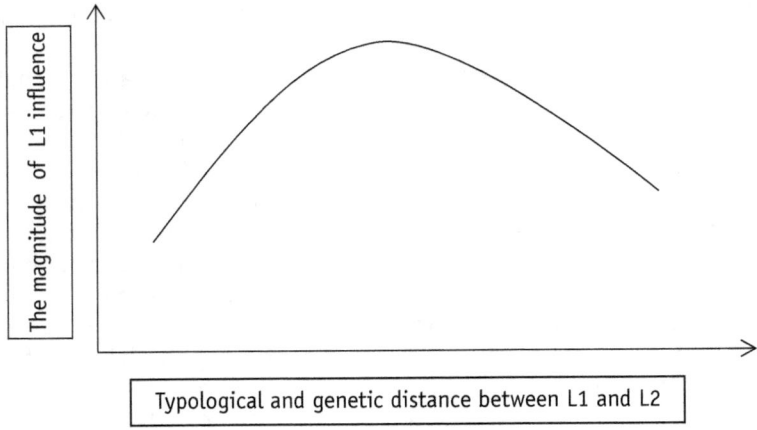

Figure 11.1 The magnitude of visible L1-effects as a function of typological/genetic distance

The visible non-target-like forms in L2 are obviously only one of many faces of crosslinguistic influence. In his elaboration on the notion of transfer, Ringbom (Chapter 3) points to an important distinction between the availability of crosslinguistic influences in comprehension and in production. Since L2 input is available to learners only through the channel of comprehension, Ringbom's remark that comprehension in an unrelated L2 is more difficult mainly due to lack of perceivable crosslinguistic similarity may also be used to account for the remaining piece of findings reported by Treffers-Daller and Zijyan (Chapter 7), i.e. the less significant than expected effect of statistical learning (Romberg & Saffran, 2010) in advanced Chinese L1 learners of L2 English. Apart from the shortage of facilitating input which could be obtained during a longer period of residence in an English-speaking country, the authors point to a large typological distance between English and Chinese as a contributing factor (p. 140–141). The usefulness of L2 input as a driving force for statistical learning is smaller when L1 and L2 are genetically and typologically distant. It is more difficult to attend to and analyse frequency patterns in an unrelated L2. The authors of Chapter 7 nevertheless believe that it is possible. The frequency distribution of motion verbs in L2 input may be 'only one piece of the puzzle' (p. 141), but it definitely constitutes an important cue.

In the context of the cognitive perspective inclusion, going beyond mere language system accounts, an important contribution comes in the form of the already mentioned investigation by Han and Ekiert (Chapter 8). Apart from raising a number of vital methodological concerns, such as operationalising the variable of 'difficulty', it comes as an inspiring illustration of the emergence of a cognitive category initially not explicitly present in learners' minds. The combination of quantitative and qualitative approaches allowed the authors not only to expound an ingenious scale of difficulty mirroring the cognitive complexities of definiteness encoding, but also to shed light on the emergence of learners' construals leading to the development of the article system in their L2.

A very important contribution, integrating the perspectives of language learning/acquisition with linguistic relativity, is Chapter 4 by Lucy. Linking the two themes is very much in line with the application of cognitive linguistic perspective, that is, seeing human perception of the world mediated by language on the one hand and language learning on the other as mutually dependent and inseparable processes. Evidence for effects of linguistic relativity is abundant: Lucy presents multiple references in his chapter. It is important in this context that linguistic relativity should be understood as the claim that the linguistic encoding and categorisation of the surrounding reality affects our cognition in general, not just the second or subsequent language use. Lucy's examples of L1 English-speaking children tested for the correct use of the article system resemble in some ways Polish L1 users of L2 English who have not yet developed the target-like construals embodied in article use, described in Chapter 8 by Han and Ekiert. However, the difference between the two groups lies in the ultimate attainment, as the L1 English-speaking children will invariably reshape their cognitive constitution under the influence of their mother tongue, whereas for the Polish adult learners the task is predicted to be much more difficult, which clearly follows from the study by Han (2010) evoked by Lucy in his chapter.

The aspects of linguistic relativity elaborated by Lucy add yet another dimension to Cook's multi-competence perspective. Interestingly, the observations and suggestions articulated by Cook at the end of Chapter 2 provide an excellent illustration. Echoing one of the groundbreaking works in cognitive linguistics, Rosch's (1973; 1975) investigation of colour terminology in language, and commenting on the pioneering expansion of the theme to the realm of SLA, Athanasopoulos' (2009) investigation of the colour terminology acquisition by Greek L1 learners of L2 English, the author outlines four possible cognitive scenarios for the modification of the learners' cognitive perception and encoding of colours, as a consequence of crosslinguistic influence (pp. 33–34). What comes as an unexpected revelation of the aforementioned study is the emergence of a completely new mental concept in the minds of Greek learners of L2 English, which is not predictable from the relationships and comparisons between the two languages. Thus, Cook points to a very important direction in future investigation of crosslinguistic influence: the theoretical possibility that bilingualism (and also multilingualism) involves the emergence of cognitive constructs which cannot be related in any straightforward way to simple interactions between L1 and L2 conceived as autonomous systems.

Postulating crosslinguistic influence and transfer seen as mutual re-shaping of isolated mental spaces is, in Cook's opinion, only a partial explanation of second language acquisition, if unique states of L2 users can be found which are not derivable from their L1 and L2.

One of the manifestations of such a unique state is the simultaneous activation of L1 and L2 lexicons, often called upon as an explanation of cognate facilitation (Helms-Park & Dronjic, Chapter 5). Viewed in the light of the discussion above, it should probably be slightly modified as a postulate of emergence of a unique collective lexicon in the process of second language acquisition, better than sticking to the traditional separationist treatment of L1 and L2. The facilitating power of cognates is observable, as Helms-Park and Dronjic claim, after a certain threshold level has been achieved by the learners, when they start realising that there exist items in their developing lexicon which share not only semantic properties (like traditional translational equivalents), but are additionally formally closely related. Such an additive (as opposed to competitive) view of lexical development seems to constitute a powerful explanatory basis for a large number of phenomena found in the research on code-mixing and multiple language use.

The discussion so far, for reasons of convenience rather than conviction, has largely assumed a bilingual bias, i.e. it has restricted the number of interacting languages to two. However, as Jessner, Megens and Graus clarify in Chapter 10, bilingualism is but a special kind of multilingualism. Because of this, the authors claim, third and subsequent language acquisition should constitute the central territory for crosslinguistic influence. The perspective of L3 acquisition (where L3 stands for the third, but also for any other subsequent language), necessarily incorporating the factors of metalinguistic and crosslinguistic awareness and learning experience, is even more clearly biased towards the complementary holistic cognitive view of crosslinguistic influence. To highlight the dynamic and heterogeneous character of the cognitive systems shaped by multiple language acquisition, the authors propose their own new term: crosslinguistic interaction (CLIN). Drawing upon the definition of crosslinguistic influence (CLI) from Jarvis and Pavlenko (2008) and following Kellerman and Sharwood Smith (1986), they explain that the new term allows the covering of such diverse phenomena as transfer (also lateral – c.f. Ringbom, Chapter 3), interference, avoidance, borrowing, code switching and attrition, subsuming processes working in all directions and between any component systems in a multilingual mind.

An excellent illustration of thus defined crosslinguistic interaction is presented in Chapter 9, where Athanasopoulos and Boutonnet demonstrate a peculiar modification in the cognitive system of learners which is the result of interaction between a language encoding grammatical gender and a language with natural gender marking. Making an explicit reference to

Linguistic Relativity Hypothesis (Whorf, 1956), the authors show how peculiar cognitive effects may result from second language acquisition and modify the semantic landscapes shaped by the first language. It turns out that English L1 learners of L2 French, in comparison with monolingual speakers of English, develop a modified perception of inanimate objects which are grammatically marked for gender in L2. Most generally, the study corroborates many previous findings that learning a second language results in some degrees of cognitive restructuring, in both directions (L1 influencing L2 and the other way round). Thus, learning another language does not quite endow us with a new personality, but it actually enriches and modifies our cognitive composition, also those aspects which are manifested through our L1.

The overall picture of crosslinguistic influence studies emerging from the contributions to the present volume is quite optimistic. Thanks to the re-orientation of focus and inclusion of a broader view of language-related processes as components of the overall human cognitive structure, stimulating research opportunities and directions emerge. They include such recommendations as a shift towards studies on comprehension and cognitive construction of surrounding reality mediated by language, taking advantage of modern technology in psycholinguistic and neurolinguistic research and turning to investigation of instances involving the use of multiple languages in acts of multilingual communication, which become increasingly common in the contemporary world.

References

Athanasopoulos, P. (2009) Cognitive representation of colour in bilinguals: The case of Greek blues. *Bilingualism: Language and Cognition* 12, 83–95.

Bowerman, M. (1996) The origins of children's spatial semantic categories: Cognitive vs. linguistic determinants. In J.J. Gumperz and S.C. Levinson (eds) *Rethinking Linguistic Relativity* (pp. 145–176). Cambridge: Cambridge University Press.

Cook, V.J. (1991) The poverty-of-the-stimulus argument and multi-competence. *Second Language Research* 7 (2), 103–117.

Cook, V.J. (2015) Premises of multi-competence. In V.J. Cook, and L. Wei (eds) *The Cambridge Handbook of Linguistic Multi-competence*. Cambridge: Cambridge University Press.

Croft, W. and Cruse, D.A. (2004) *Cognitive Linguistics*. Cambridge: Cambridge University Press.

Geeraerts, D. and Cuyckens, H. (eds) (2007) *The Oxford Handbook of Cognitive Linguistics*. New York: Oxford University Press.

Han, Z. (2010) Grammatical morpheme inadequacy as a function of linguistic relativity: A longitudinal study. In Z. Han and T. Cadierno (eds) *Linguistic Relativity in SLA: Thinking for Speaking* (pp. 154–182). Bristol: Multilingual Matters.

Jarvis, S. (2000) Methodological rigor in the study of transfer: Identifying L1 influence in the Interlanguage lexicon. *Language Learning* 50, 245–309.

Jarvis, S. and Pavlenko, A. (2008) *Crosslinguistic Influence in Language and Cognition*. New York and London: Routledge.

Kecskes, I. (2008) Duelling contexts: A dynamic model of meaning. *Journal of Pragmatics* 40, 385–406.
Kellerman, E. and Sharwood-Smith, M. (1986) *Crosslinguistic Influence in Second Language Acquisition*. New York: Pergamon Press.
Lado, R. (1957) *Linguistics across Cultures. Applied Linguistics for Language Teachers*. Ann Arbor: University of Michigan Press.
Langacker, R.W. (1987) *Foundations of Cognitive Grammar, Vol. 1: Theoretical Prerequisites*. Stanford, CA: Stanford University Press.
Langacker, R.W. (2008) *Cognitive Grammar: A Basic Introduction*. New York: Oxford University Press.
Larsen-Freeman, D. and Long, M. (1991) *An Introduction to Second Language Acquisition Research*. London: Longman.
Lee, D. (2001) *Cognitive Linguistics: An Introduction*. Oxford: Oxford University Press.
Littlemore, J. (2009) *Applying Cognitive Linguistics to Second Language Learning and Teaching*. Basingstoke/New York: Palgrave Macmillan.
Mougeon, R., Nadasdi, T. and Rehner, K. (2005) Contact-induced linguistic innovations on the continuum of language use: The case of French in Ontario. *Bilingualism: Language and Cognition* 8 (2), 99–115.
Odlin, T. (1989) *Language Transfer: Cross-linguistic Influence in Language Learning*. Cambridge: Cambridge University Press.
Ringbom, H. (1976) What differences are there between Finns and Swedish-speaking Finns learning English? In H. Ringbom and R. Palmberg (eds) *Errors Made by Finns and Swedish-speaking Finns in the Learning of English* (pp. 1–14). Abo: Department of English, Abo Akademi.
Ringbom, H. (1987) *The Role of the First Language in Foreign Language Learning*. Clevedon: Multilingual Matters.
Robinson, P. and Ellis, N.C. (eds) (2008) *Handbook of Cognitive Linguistics and Second Language Acquisition*. New York: Routledge.
Romberg, A.R. and Saffran, J.R. (2010) Statistical learning and language acquisition. *Wiley Interdisciplinary Reviews: Cognitive Science* 1 (6), 906–914.
Rosch, E.H. (1973) On the internal structure of perceptual and semantic categories. In T.E. Moore (ed.) *Cognitive Development and the Acquisition of Language* (pp. 111–144). New York: Academic Press.
Rosch, E.H. (1975) The nature of mental codes for color categories. *Journal of Experimental Psychology – Human Perception and Performance* 1, 303–322.
Stockwell, R.P., Bowen, J.D. and Martin, J.W. (1965) *The Grammatical Structures of English and Spanish*. Chicago: University of Chicago Press.
Talmy, L. (1985) Lexicalization patterns: Semantic structure in lexical forms. *Language Typology and Syntactic Description* 3, 57–149.
Talmy, L. (2000) *Toward a Cognitive Semantics. Vol. II: Typology and Process in Concept Structuring*. Cambridge, MA: The MIT Press.
Tyler, A. (2014) Cognitive linguistics and language learning. In P. C. Hogan (ed.) *Cambridge University Encyclopedia of Language Sciences*. Cambridge: Cambridge University Press.
Wardhaugh, R. (1970) The contrastive analysis hypothesis. *TESOL Quarterly* 4, 123–130.
Weinreich, U. (1953) *Languages in Contact*. The Hague: Mouton.
Whorf, B.L. (1956) *Language, Thought and Reality: Selected Writings of Benjamin Lee Whorf.* (J.B. Carroll, ed.) Cambridge, MA: The MIT Press.

Index

Adjémian, C. 128, 143
Ahlqvist, A. 5, 21
Ahukanna, J.G.W., Lund, N.J. & Gentil, R.J. 199, 210
Albert, M.L. & Obler, L.K. 49, 50
Allan, K. 151, 168
Allgäeuer-Hackl, E. & Jessner, U. 198, 210
Allgaeuer-Hackl, E., Hofer, B. & Jessner, U. 210
Alonso, R. xiii, xv, 217, 218
Amengual, M. 86, 89
Andersen, R. 29, 35
Anderson, B. 32, 35
Antonijević, S., & Berthaud, S. 141, 143
Arabski, J. xiii, xv, 22, 36
Ard, J.& Homburg, T. 71, 89
Aronin, L. & Hufeisen, B. 193, 210, 211
Aronin, L. & Singleton, D. 29, 35
Aronin, L. & Jessner, U. 194, 210
Aske, J. 128, 143
Athanasopoulos, P. 33, 34, 35, 66, 68, 189, 190, 221, 223
Athanasopoulos, P., Damjanovic, L. Burnand, J. & Bylund, E. 189, 190
Athanasopoulos, P., Dering, B., Wiggett, A., Kuipers, J.R. & Thierry, G. 189

Baayen, R.H., Piepenbrock, R., & Van Rijn, H. 130, 143
Baker, C. 202, 210
Bardel, C.& Lindqvist, C. 199, 210
Beauvillain, C. & Grainger, J. 28, 35
Beavers, J., Levin, B., & Wei Tham, S. 124, 125, 143
Becker, A., Carroll, M. & Kelly, A. 96, 119
Beeman, W.O. 73, 89
Bergh, G. 40, 50
Berman, R.A., & Slobin, D.I. 59, 60, 61, 68, 125, 130, 143
Berthele, R. 42, 50
Besson, M., Kutas, M. & van Petten, C. 89
Bialystok, E. 203, 205, 210
Bickerton, D. 149, 168
Bitchener, J. 167, 168
Block, D. 31, 35

Bloomfield, L. 10, 11, 12, 15, 16, 19, 21
Blumenthal, A., 10, 21
Bond, T. & Fox, C. 156, 168
Bono, M. 199, 200, 203, 206, 210
Boroditsky, L. 50, 68
Boroditsky, L., Schmidt, L.A. & Phillips, W. 173, 186, 188, 190
Bowerman, M. 60, 68, 69, 93, 94, 119, 218, 223
Bowerman, M. & Choi, S. 93, 96, 119
Boyd, J.K. & Goldberg, A.E. 127, 143
Boyd, J.K., Ackerman, F. & Kutas, M. 143
Brooks, P.J. & Tomasello, M. 127, 143
Bull, W.E. 111, 119
Burton, G. 202, 210
Butler, Y. 155, 166, 168
Bylund, E. & Athanasopoulos, P. 189, 190

Cabrelli Amaro, J., Flynn, S. & Rothman, J. 31, 35, 37
Cadierno, T. & Ruiz, L. 126, 143
Cadierno, T. 115, 119
Caplan-Carbin, E. 87, 89
Carroll, J. 14, 18, 20, 23, 224
Carroll, M. & Becker, A. 96, 115, 119
Carroll, M. & von Stutterheim, C. 125, 143
Carroll, S. 70, 71, 85, 89
Casasanto, D. 56, 68, 173, 190
Cenoz, J. 47, 50, 193, 194, 198, 199, 200, 202, 203
Cenoz, J. & Genesee, F. 196, 202, 211
Cenoz, U., Hufeisen, B. & Jessner, U. xv, 50, 210, 211, 212, 213, 214
Chandrasekhar, A. 199, 211
Chaudron, C. & Parker, K. 165, 168
Chen, L., & Guo, J. 132, 143
Chesterman, A. 7, 21, 149, 168
Choi, S. & Bowerman, M. 125, 143
Chomsky, C. viii, 11, 14, 18, 19, 21, 27, 31, 35, 36, 59
Christoffels, I., Firk, C. & Schiller, N. 76, 79, 89
Clark, E.C. & Hecht, B.F. 38, 50
Clark, E.C. 38, 50

Clyne, M. 199, 211
Cobb, T. 71, 74, 81, 89
Cook, V. 24, 26, 27, 28, 29, 31, 33, 35, 189, 190, 212, 215, 216, 217, 221, 222, 223
Cook, V.J.
Cook, V., Bassetti, B., Kasai, C., Sasaki, M. & Takahashi, J.A. 190
Cook, V.J. & Bassetti, B. 35, 53, 68, 69
Corbett, G.G. 175, 190
Corder, S.P. 19, 21, 46, 50
Costa, A., Caramazza, A. & Sebastián-Gallés, N. 72, 74, 76, 78, 88, 89
Costa, A., Santesteban, M. & Caño, A. 89
Coventry, K.R. & Guijarro-Fuentes, P. 95, 119
Coxhead, A. 82, 89
Cristoffanini, P.M., Kirsner, K. & Milech, D. 76, 77, 89
Croft, W., & Cruse, D.A. 217, 223
Croft, W., Barðdal, J., Hollmann, W., Sotirova, V. & Taoka, C. 125, 143
Cruttenden, A. 43, 50

Daller, M.H., Treffers-Daller, J. & Furman, R. 133, 144
Daulton, F. 85, 88, 89
Davis, C., Sánchez-Casas R., García-Albea J., Guasch M., Molero M. & Ferré P. 71, 76, 79, 89
De Angelis, G. & Dewaele, J.-M. xiii, xv, 196, 210
De Angelis, G. & Jessner, U. 206, 211
De Angelis, G. & Selinker, L. 199, 201, 211
De Angelis, G. 45, 47, 50, 194, 196, 197, 198, 199, 201, 206, 211
De Angelis, G., Jessner, U & Krésic, M. 211
De Bot, K. 28, 36, 202, 211
De Bot, K., W. Lowie & Verspoor, M. 211
De Groot, A. 26, 36
De Groot, A. & Keijzer, R. 76, 89
De Groot, A.M.B. & Nas, G.L.J. 76, 78, 84, 89
De Saussure, F. 31, 36
de Villiers, J. & de Villiers, P. 68
Dechert, H.W. 29, 36
Dechert, H. & Raupach, M. xiii, xv
DeKeyser, R. 147, 148, 168
Delsing, L.O. 48, 50
Dewaele, J.-M. 198, 199, 201, 202, 211
Dewaele, J.-M. & Véronique, D. 175, 190, 198

Dijkstra, A., Grainger, J. & van Heuven, W.J.B. 74, 76, 77, 78, 84, 89
Dijkstra, A., van Jaarsveld, H. & ten Brinke, S. 89
Dijkstra, T., Miwa, K., Brummelhuis, B., Sappelli, M. & Baayen, H. 89
Dimitropoulou, M., Duñabeitia, J.A. & Carreiras, M. 80, 89
Duke, J., Hufeisen, B. & Lutjeharms, M. 48, 50
Dulay, H., Burt, M. & Krashen, S. 1, 9, 10, 11, 13, 14, 21
Duyck, W., Warlop, N. 80, 89

Ecke, P. 198, 211
Ekiert, M. 154, 168
Elgort, I. 81, 90
Elliott, A.M. 4, 5, 6, 16, 21, 23
Ellis, N. & Robinson, P. 21
Ellis, N. 2, 4, 7, 10, 15, 21, 22, 31, 36, 119, 121, 122, 138, 144, 148, 168
Ellis, R. 9, 10, 21
Elston-Güttler, K. & Williams, J. 15, 21
Epstein, S.D., Flynn, S. & Martahardjono, G. 25, 36
Evans, V. & Green, M. xiv, xv
Eyckmans, J. 81, 90

Faerch, C. , Haastrup, K. & Phillipson, R. 38, 50
Falk, Y. & Bardel, C. 43, 50
Field, A. 134, 143, 144
Flaherty, M. 186, 188, 190
Flege, J.E. 26, 36
Flynn, S., Foley, C. & Vinnitskaya, I. 26, 36
Fodor, J. & Sag, I. 149, 168
Foley, C. & Flynn, S. 1, 2, 6, 9, 21
Forbes, J.N., Poulin-Dubois, D., Rivero, M.R. & Sera, M. 175, 186, 190
Foundalis, H. 175, 190
Fries, C. 8, 10, 17
Friesen, D.C. & Jared, D. 28, 36

Gabryś-Barker, D. xi, xiii, xv, 198, 212
Garcia Mayo, M. & Hawkins, R. 147, 168
García, G.E. 86, 90
Garrison, D. 86, 90
Gass, S. & Selinker, L. xiii, xv, 21, 35, 50, 89, 173
Gass, S.M. & Mackey, A. 121, 144, 168
Geeraerts, D. & Guyckens, H. xiii, xv, 217, 223

Gerard, L.D. & Scarborough, D.L. 77, 90
Gibson, M. & Hufeisen, B. 46, 50
Givon, T. 165, 168
Goldberg, A.E. 122, 144
Gollan, T.H. & Acenas, L.A.R. 77, 90
Gollan, T.H., Forster, K.I. & Frost, R. 80, 90
Gooskens, C. & van Bezooijen, R. 76, 90
Graham, G. 5, 10, 21
Graus, S. 207, 209, 212
Green, D.W. 28, 36, 196, 201, 202, 212
Greenhill, S.J., Blust. R. & Gray, R.D. 75, 90
Grosjean, F. 28, 30, 36
Gullberg, M. 21

Haastrup, K. 42, 50
Hall, C. 76, 83, 90
Halliday, M.A.K. & Mattheissen, C. 32, 36
Halliday, M.A.K. 32, 36
Hammarberg, B. xiii, xv, 22, 45, 50, 199, 212
Hammarberg, B. & Hammarberg, B. 15, 22, 198, 201, 212
Han, Z. 15, 22, 63, 64, 68, 148, 166, 168, 221, 223
Han, Z. & Cadierno, T. 22, 53, 68, 168
Han, Z-H. & Lew, W.M. 148
Hasher, L., Zacks, R.T., Rose, K.C. & Sanft, H. 121, 144
Haugen, E. 13, 14, 22
Hauser, M.D., Chomsky, N. & Fitch, T.M. 25, 36
Hawkins, J. 149, 150, 168, 169
Hawkins, R. & Chen, C. 25, 36
Helms-Park, R. & Perhan, Z. 87, 88, 90
Helms-Park, R. 198, 212
Helms-Park, R., Petrescu, M. & Dronjic, V. 81, 90, 222
Hendriks, H., Hickmann, H. & Demagny, A.C. 124, 125, 144
Hendriks, H., Ji, Y. & Hickmann, M. 144
Henriksen, B. & Haastrup, K. 44, 50
Henriksen, B. 44, 80
Herdina, P. & Jessner, U. 193, 194, 195, 196, 197, 203, 208
Hermans, D., Ormel, E., van Besselaar, R. & van Hell, J. 28, 36
Herskovits, A. 103, 119
Herwig, A. 205, 212
Hickmann, M. 61, 68, 145
Hirata-Edds, T. 26, 36
Ho, M.L. & Platt, J.T. 126, 144

Hoijer, H. 7, 22
Horst, M., White, L. & Bell, P. 85, 86, 88, 90
Hu, A. 27, 36
Huang, S.F. & Tanangkingsing, M. 125, 144
Huebner, T. 97, 119
Huerta, B. 111, 119

Ibarretxe-Antuñano, I. 119, 124, 144
Ijaz, I.H. 47, 51, 93, 119
Imai, M. & Gentner, D. 59, 68
Imai, M. 59, 68
Inagaki, S. 125, 144

Jakobson, R. 60, 68
James, C. 203, 206, 207, 208, 212
Janhunen, J. 72, 90
Jarvis, S. 47, 51, 99, 117, 119, 126, 144, 153, 154, 169, 218, 219, 223
Jarvis, S. & Odlin, T. 93, 97, 99, 119, 198, 212, 215, 222, 223
Jarvis, S. & Pavlenko , A. xiii, xv, 18, 20, 22, 25, 36, 45, 196, 198, 212, 215, 222, 223 Jessner, U. 193, 194, 196, 197, 199, 202, 203, 204, 205, 207, 209, 212, 213, 217, 222
Jessner, U. & Megens, M. 197, 208, 213
Jiang, N. 85, 90, 122, 138, 140, 144
Jiang, N. Larrañaga, P., Treffers-Daller, J., Tidball, F., & Ortega, M.-c. G. 166
Jiang, N., Novokshanova, E., Masuda, K. & Wang, X. 144, 166, 169
Jones, K. 81, 86, 88, 90

Kaivapalu, A. 49, 51
Karlsson, F. 48, 51
Karmiloff-Smith, A. 69
Katz, J.J. & Postal, P.M . 32, 36
Kecskes, I. 218, 224
Kellerman, E. 29, 37, 47, 51, 97, 119, 149, 169, 198, 213
Kellerman, E. & Bialystock, H. 205, 213
Kelley, A. & Kohnert, K. 86, 90
Kelly, L. 18, 22
Kirsner, K., Brown, H.L., Abrol, S., Chadha, A. & Sharma, N.K. 77, 90
Klein, E.C 198, 213
Kolers, P. 40, 51
Kondrak, G. 76, 90
Kopke, B. & Schmid, M. 30, 37
Krashen, S. 25, 37
Kroll, J. & de Groot, A. 37, 51, 91, 114, 210

Kroll, J.F. & Sunderman, G. 76, 77, 90
Kulundary, V. & Gabriele, A. 26, 37
Kupferberg, I. & Olshtain, E. 15, 22
Kurinski, E. & Sera, M.D. 173, 174, 176, 177, 178, 181, 185, 186, 187, 190

Labov, W. 32, 37
Lado, R. 1, 2, 3, 4, 7, 8, 9, 10, 13, 14, 16, 17, 19, 20, 22, 23, 215, 216, 224
Lakoff, G. & Johnson, M. 12, 22
Langacker, R. 12, 22, 94, 119, 217, 218, 224
Lantolf, J. 31, 37
Larsen-Freeman, D. & Long, M. 1, 9, 22, 218, 224
Larsen-Freeman, D. 10, 148, 169
Larsen-Freeman, D., & Long, M. 1, 9, 10, 22, 218, 224
Laufer, B. 40, 46, 51
Leacox, L. 86, 90
Leather, J. & James, A. 198, 213
Lee, D. 94, 116, 119, 217, 218, 224
Lehrer, A. 19, 22
Levelt, W. 5, 18, 22
Levinson, S.C. 56, 69, 93, 120
Li, P., Dunham, Y. & Carey, S. 59, 63, 89
Lindqvist, C. 41, 51, 1998, 213
Littlemore, J. 94, 120, 218, 224
Liu, D. & Gleason, J. 150, 154, 169
Lotto, L. & de Groot, A.M. B. 71, 76, 77, 84, 91
Lucy, J. 7, 22, 54, 55, 56, 58, 59, 63, 64, 68, 89
Lucy, J.A. & Gaskins, S. 57
Lyons, C. 149, 150, 151, 169
Lyons, J. 61, 69

MacWhinney, B. 131, 144
Marslen-Wilson, W. 75, 91
Mayer, M. 130, 144
McClellland, J.L. & Elman, J.L. 75, 96
McDonough, L., Choi, S. & Mandler, J.M. 96, 120
McNabb, R., Pal, S. & Sloane, P. 130, 144
McNamara, T. & Knoch, U. 155, 169
Meara, P. 47, 51
Megens, M. 205, 209, 213
Midgley, K., Holcomb P., & Grainger J. 76, 79, 91
Miles, L.K., Tan, L., Noble, G.D., Lumsden, J. & Macrae, C.N. 173
Misyak, J.B., Goldstein, M.H. & Christiansen, M.H. 122, 145

Morgan, C. & King, R. 11, 22
Mougeon, R., Nadasdi, T. & Rehner, K. 127, 145, 219, 224
Muikku-Werner, P. & Heinonen, M. 49, 51
Muikku-Werner, P. 49, 51
Müller-Lancé, J. 199, 213
Munnich, E., & Landau, B. 96, 98, 120
Murphy, R. 100, 120
Myford, C. & Wolfe, E. 158, 169

Nagy, W.E., García, G.E., Durgunoğlu, A. & Hancin-Bhatt, B. 86, 91
Nakayama, M., Sears, C.R., Hino, Y. & Lupker, S.J. 80, 91
Nation, P. 81, 91
Navarro, S. & Nicoladis, E. 126, 145
Newport, E.L. 63, 70
Nichols, J.D. & Nyholm, E. 73, 91
Niemeier, S. & Dirven, R. 56, 68, 69
Nippold, M.A. 59, 70
Nussbaum, E.M., Elsadat, S. & Khago, A. 134, 145

Odlin, T. & Yu, L. 4, 22
Odlin, T. xiii, xv, 3, 4, 13, 14, 15, 20, 22, 26, 27, 29, 37, 41, 44, 51, 149, 16
Onnis, L. 122, 145
Opitz, C. 31, 37
Osgood, C. 2, 22
Osgood, C. & Sebeok, T. 11, 22
Otwinowska-Kasztelanic, A. 15, 22, 87, 91
Özçalışkan, Ş. & Slobin, D.I. 143, 145

Paajanen, I. & Muikku-Werner, P. 49, 51
Park, H.I. & Ziegler, N. 98, 120
Paterson, N. & Goldrick, M. 86, 91
Pavlenko, A. 53, 68, 70, 173, 187, 188, 190, 198, 213
Pavlenko, A. & Jarvis, S. 198, 213
Peal, E. & Lambert, W.E. 203, 213
Pederson, E. Danzinger, E. Wilkins, D., Levinson, S. Kita, S. & Senft, G. 93, 120
Peeters, D., Dijkstra, T. & Grainger, J. 71, 76, 77, 79, 82, 84, 90
Perdue, C. & Klein, W. 66, 70
Perdue, C. 96, 119, 120
Petrescu, M. & Dronjic, V. 81
Petrescu, M. & Helms-Park, R. 82, 91
Peyraube, A. 123, 145
Piaget, J. & Inhelder, B. 62, 70
Pica, T. 155, 169

Plauen, E.O. 130, 145
Popper, K.R. 31, 37
Poulisse, N. & Bongaerts, T. 199, 202, 213
Prince, E. 149, 169

Radden, G. & Dirven, R. 150, 169
Ramat, P. 91
Rebuschat, P. & Williams, J.N. 121, 145
Reed, D., Lado, R. & Shen, Y. 14, 22
Regier, T. & Kay, P. 173, 190
Reves, T. & Levine, A. 42, 51
Ringbom, H. xiii, xv, xvi, 20, 23, 39, 47, 4, 50, 51, 52, 71, 91, 198, 202, 213, 215, 216, 219, 220, 222, 224
Ringe, D.A. 73, 91
Roberts, P.M. & Deslauriers, L. 76, 91
Robinson, P. & Ellis, N. xiii, xvi, 21, 22, 119, 169, 217, 224
Roemer, U. 138, 245
Romaine, S. 59, 70
Romberg, A.R. & Saffran, J.R. 127, 141, 145, 220, 224
Rosch, E.H. 221, 224

Saffran, J.R. 122, 145
Saffran, J.R., Aslin, R.N. & Newport, E.L. 121
Sajavaara, K. 39, 51, 52
Sanchez, L. 201, 213
Sánchez-Casas, R. & García-Albea, J.E. 76, 84, 91
Sánchez-Casas, R., Davis, C.W. & García-Albea, J.E. 78, 91
Sapir, E. 5, 6, 7, 12, 16, 22, 23
Scarborough, D.L., Gerard, L. & Cortese, C. 77, 84, 91
Schmitt, N. 81, 91
Schmitt, N. & Dunham, B. 121, 145
Schuhardt, H. 3, 5, 14, 19
Schumann, J. 97, 99, 120
Schwartz, B. & Sprouse, R. 25, 37
Sebastián-Gallés, N. & Bosch, L. 31, 37
Selinker, L. 7, 13, 14, 16, 19, 20, 21, 23, 27, 37, 148, 169
Selinker, L. & Baumgartner-Cohen, B. 50, 52, 201, 213
Sera, M.D., Berge, C. & del Castillo Pintado, J. 173, 174, 175, 176, 177, 185, 186, 188, 190
Sera, M.D., Elieff, C., Forbes, J., Burch, M.C. & Dubois, D. P 174, 175, 186, 188, 190
Seton. B. & Schmid, M. 30, 37

Sharwood Smith, M. xiii, 39, 52
Shirai, S. 72, 81, 92
Silva-Corvalán, C. 127, 145
Singleton, D. 44, 52, 204, 214
Singley, M. & Anderson, J. 5, 23
Sjöholm, K. 198, 214
Skinner, B. 11, 21, 23
Slobin, D.I. & Hoiting, N. 126, 146
Slobin, D.I. 12, 23, 56, 70, 121, 124, 125, 130, 142, 145, 168
Spada, N. & Tomita, Y. 147, 148, 169
Spivey, M.J. & Marian, V. 28, 37
Stockwell, R.P., J.D. Bowen & Martin, J.W. 19, 27, 114, 120, 218, 224
Su, I. 214
Swain, M. 43, 52
Szekely, A., Jacobsen, T., D'Amico, S., Devescovi, A., Andonova, E., Herron, D. 178, 190

Tabakowska, E. 151, 152, 169
Talmy, L. 123, 124, 125, 143, 144, 146, 219, 224
Tarone, E. & Parrish, B. 165, 169
Thomas, M. 1, 13, 18, 23
Thomason, S.G.& Kaufman, T. xiii, xvi, 6, 23
Todeva, E. & Cenoz, J. 193, 194, 214
Tokumaru, Y. 26, 27
Trask, R.L. 73, 92
Treffers-Daller, J. & Calude, A.S. 121, 122, 123, 128, 138, 140, 141
Treffers-Daller, J. & Tidball, F. 121, 125, 130
Trenkic, D. 151, 152, 165, 169
Tyler, A. 94, 116, 118, 119, 120, 218, 224
Tyler, A. & Evans, V. 95, 115, 118, 120

Ullman, M. 31, 37

Van Hell, J.G. & Dijkstra, T. 76, 80, 92
Vanhove, J. 42, 46, 52
Voga, M. & Grainger, J. 76, 84, 92
Von Humboldt, W. 4, 17, 149, 169
Von Stutterheim, C. & Nuse, R. 121, 146
Vulchanova, M. & Van der Zee, E. 134, 146
Vygotsky, L.S. 59, 62, 64, 70

Wardhaugh, R. 7, 8, 9, 10, 16, 17, 23, 216, 224
Warter, P. 75, 86, 92
Wei, L. 31, 35, 36, 37, 199, 214, 223

Weinreich, U. xiii, xvi, 2, 3, 4, 5, 6, 7, 8, 9, 10, 12, 13, 14, 16, 17, 18, 19, 23, 25, 26, 30, 37, 215, 216, 218, 224
Weiss, A. 11, 15, 23
Whitley, M.S. 111, 120
Whitney, W.D. 4, 5, 6, 16, 23
Whorf, B.L. 7, 12, 16, 19, 22, 23, 63, 68, 69, 70, 173, 190, 223, 224
Wilkins, M.S. & Hill, D.P. 93, 120
Williams, S. & B. Hammarberg 198, 199, 200, 201, 214
Winford, D. 6, 23
Wolff, P. & Holmes, K.J. 56, 70
Wrembel, M. 26, 37
Wunder, E-M. 198, 214

Yoo, I. 150, 169
Yu, L. 4, 126, 146

Zeevaert, L. 48, 52
Zipf, G. 195, 214
Zlatev, J. & Yangklang, P. 124, 146

For Product Safety Concerns and Information please contact our EU Authorised Representative:

Easy Access System Europe

Mustamäe tee 50

10621 Tallinn

Estonia

gpsr.requests@easproject.com